ASPECTS OF

The past decade has witnessed a dramatic increase of interest in the practical applications of memory research: large numbers of psychologists who study memory are now interested in applying their work to the real world. This second edition of *Aspects of Memory* brings together contributions by a team of internationally recognized experts, and reflects the considerable advances made in the past few years.

Beginning with a chapter on the methodological problems involved in applying memory research, *Aspects of Memory* goes on to deal with eyewitnessing and face recognition to show that psychology can make a valuable contribution to forensic problems of evidence. Other contributors describe work being done on amnesia and the problems of aging and memory, and show what psychologists can do to help ordinary people faced with major memory problems. The final chapters deal with topics which have only recently begun to be researched – prospective memory (remembering what to do in the future) and autobiographical memory (remembering your own past history). Both these are seen as vital in enabling individuals to function adequately as social animals.

Designed primarily with students in mind, *Aspects of Memory* provides an excellent up-to-date review of current approaches to applied memory research. A second volume will deal with the theoretical issues that underlie the practical applications.

Michael Gruneberg is Senior Lecturer in Psychology, University College, Swansea. **Peter Morris** is Professor of Psychology, University of Lancaster.

ASPECTS OF MEMORY

SECOND EDITION

Volume 1: The Practical Aspects

Edited by

Michael Gruneberg

and

Peter Morris

London and New York

First published in 1978 by Methuen & Co. Ltd.

This second edition published in 1992 by
by Routledge
11 New Fetter Lane, London EC4P 4EE

Simultaneously published in the USA and Canada
by Routledge
a division of Routledge, Chapman and Hall, Inc.
29 West 35th Street, New York, NY 10001

Typeset in 10 on 12 point Baskerville by
Falcon Typographic Art Ltd, Fife, Scotland
Printed and bound in Great Britain by
Biddles Ltd, Guildford and King's Lynn

British Library Cataloguing in Publication Data
Aspects of memory.
Vol. 1: The practical aspects. – 2nd ed
I. Gruneberg, Michael II. Morris, Peter, *1947–*
153.1
Library of Congress Cataloging in Publication Data
Aspects of memory / edited by Michael Gruneberg and Peter
Morris. –
2nd ed.
p. cm.
Includes bibliographical references and index.
Contents: v. 1. The practical aspects
1. Memory. I. Gruneberg, Michael M. II. Morris, P. E.
(Peter Edwin), 1947–
BF371.A7   1992
153.1′2 – dc20   91–39545

ISBN 0–415–06110–5
0–415–06111–3 (pbk)

CONTENTS

FIGURES AND TABLES

FIGURES

TABLES

CONTRIBUTORS

Deborah M. Burke   Pomona College, Claremont, USA.

Hadyn D. Ellis   University College of Cardiff, UK.

Alan E. Fruzzetti   University of Washington, Seattle, USA.

Michael M. Gruneberg   University College of Swansea, UK.

Douglas J. Herrmann   US Bureau of Labor Statistics, Washington, DC, USA.

Elizabeth F. Lotus   University of Washington, Seattle, USA.

A. Mayes   University of Liverpool, UK.

Peter E. Morris   University of Lancaster, UK.

Mark Palmisano   US Bureau of Labor Statistics, Washington, DC, USA.

John A. Robinson   University of Kentucky at Louisville, USA.

John W. Shepherd   University of Aberdeen, UK.

Stephen A. Teller   University of Washington, Seattle, USA.

Kelly Toland   University of Washington, Seattle, USA.

PREFACE

This volume represents an update of that part of the first edition of *Aspects of Memory* (Gruneberg and Morris 1978) devoted to practical applications. That the editors have found it necessary to devote a whole volume to this aspect of memory indicates vividly the dramatic growth of interest in this area of psychology since 1978. In that year the first International Conference on Practical Aspects of Memory was held in Cardiff, UK (Gruneberg, Morris and Sykes 1978). It showed conclusively that large numbers of psychologists who study memory were interested in applying their work to the real world. Since then, there has been a considerable growth in interest; books and articles on a wide range of topics now appear every year. Investigation of some of these topics, such as eyewitnessing, go back to well before the current interest in practical application, but others, such as autobiographical memory, can reasonably be said to have taken off as a result of the current interest in memory in the real world.

For this book the editors have selected a number of current topics, where it seems to us that considerable advance has been made over the last 15 or so years, as a result of the considerable increase in interest in practical application. The book starts with a chapter by the editors on applying memory research, in which the key methodological problems posed by investigation in the real world are addressed. Such a chapter is to some extent made necessary by the recent attacks on applied memory research by Banaji and Crowder (1989) who see application as both premature and theoretically arid.

The next two chapters, on eyewitnessing by Fruzzetti, Toland, Teller and Loftus and on face recognition by Ellis and Shepherd, show the contribution made by psychology to forensic problems involving the validity of court-room evidence. Whilst the findings are in many cases disturbing – eyewitness evidence is often suspect – there are major positive advances too, in, for example, the development of the Cognitive Interview as an aid to helping police elicit evidence.

The next two chapters, on brain damage by Andrew Mayes and on memory and aging by Debbie Burke, show the contribution made to clinical practice and clinical aspects of memory. Mayes' chapter outlines the possible causes of amnesia and discusses some possible remediation procedures. Similarly Burke examines the problems of aging and memory, distinguishing between 'normal' aging problems and pathological conditions such as Alzheimer's disease.

The educational – everyday-life contribution to many problems is discussed in the chapters by Herrmann and Palmisano and by Gruneberg. These chapters discuss ways in which normal memory can be facilitated by the use of strategies, covering a range of problems from overcoming memory blocks to studying for examinations. The chapter by Herrmann and Palmisano also highlights the degree to which memory must be considered as not a single 'thing', but as involving a multiplicity of factors if it is to be enhanced.

The final two chapters on prospective memory by Peter Morris and autobiographical memory by John Robinson address relatively new concerns amongst cognitive psychologists. Prospective memory refers to remembering what to do in the future, rather than what one has experienced in the past. The importance of understanding this process is self-evident when it is realized that, for example, lives are often dependent on taking medicines at particular points of time in the future. Autobiographical memory, i.e. memory for the individual's past history, is critical to the individual's self-concept. Without the ability to recall one's past history, one's place in the world is meaningless, actions have no context and personality ceases to exist. This is evident in cases where autobiographical memory collapses, as in Alzheimer's disease, for example.

No book such as this can cover all the current areas of interest, but we believe that the areas included give a coherent introduction to some of the major current approaches to applied memory research. The book is written at a level suitable for both undergraduates and postgraduates in the field of memory as a whole, not only for those interested in specifically applied memory research. It is our contention that the practical and the theoretical aspects of memory must be closely dependent on one another if significant advances in either are to be made.

Michael Gruneberg
Peter Morris

REFERENCES

Banaji, M.R. and Crowder, R.G. (1989) 'The bankruptcy of everyday memory', *American Psychologist* 44: 1185–93.

Gruneberg, M.M. and Morris, P.E. (eds) (1978) *Aspects of Memory*, London: Methuen.

Gruneberg, M.M., Morris, P.E. and Sykes, R.N. (eds) (1978) *Practical Aspects Of Memory*, London: Academic Press.

1

APPLYING
MEMORY RESEARCH

Michael M. Gruneberg and Peter E. Morris

The last fifteen years has seen an enormous increase in the interest taken by psychologists in the practical application of memory research. In 1978, for example, Neisser, in his address to the first International Conference on Practical Aspects of Memory, stated 'If X is an interesting or socially important memory phenomenon, then psychologists have hardly ever studied X'.

However, by the end of that conference Neisser admitted he was wrong. Some ninety papers, covering a range of topics including eyewitnessing, face recognition, mnemonic strategies, drugs, brain damage, etc., etc. clearly signalled that many eminent psychologists were concerned to extend the knowledge gained in the laboratory to matters of practical value. (Gruneberg, Morris and Sykes 1978).

Since the first conference a number of books on practical applications of memory research have appeared, including Loftus and Ketcham (1991) on eyewitnessing, Cohen (1989) on memory in the real world, Higbee (1988) on memory improvement. In 1987 the second International Conference on Practical Aspects of Memory (Gruneberg, Morris and Sykes 1988a, b) attracted more than twice the papers of the first conference and demonstrated beyond any doubt that practical aspects of memory research had moved centre stage in the field of memory. Indeed so dramatic has been the change of interest that at the second conference Neisser (1988) stated 'If X is an interesting or socially important memory problem, the chances are good – though not one-hundred per cent – . . ., that quite a few people are trying to study it'.

This interest almost certainly has a number of different strands. Psychologists such as Neisser see the experimental laboratory

1

approach to memory as limiting in terms of our understanding of memory phenomena *per se*, and see the need for an ecologically valid approach to memory in order to have a better understanding of memory *per se*. For the most part this involves observation and experimentation in real-life situations. A second strand in the increased interest in practical application is the belief that examining real-life memory problems will lead to the generation of further theoretical questions on the nature of memory, which can then be examined under controlled laboratory conditions. A third strand is the desire by some psychologists to solve real-life practical problems for their own sake, and thus to utilize the knowledge already gained in the laboratory or the field study to the advantage of the 'man or woman in the street'.

The implicit and explicit criticisms of the laboratory-based theoretical–experimental approach to memory have, however, recently led to a reaction by experimental psychologists. Banaji and Crowder (1989) attack the everyday memory approach with considerable vigour. Banaji and Crowder's basic concern is that psychologists who abandon the laboratory are likely to ignore the control of extraneous variables that affect experimental manipulations, so the results of such experiments are difficult, if not impossible, to interpret. Banaji and Crowder go on to equate ecologically valid studies with uncontrolled, non-laboratory studies, and equate practical application of memory research with a non-laboratory approach. Furthermore they denigrate the value of practical application as a valid and useful enterprise in its own right – 'the immediate gratification of technological applications is not obvious in our young field' (Banaji and Crowder 1989: 1191).

The first point to be made in response to Banaji and Crowder's attack on practical application of research is that the contrasts of laboratory-controlled versus observational studies, theoretical versus practical aims and artificially created versus naturally occurring phenomena for study are separate issues. Practical applications can be furthered either through laboratory examination or field study. Numerous studies of eyewitnessing, for example, have been carried out in the laboratory where the aim of such studies was to identify, under controlled conditions, some of the factors which are likely to affect accuracy (see Chapter 2). Yet it is inconceivable that a full understanding of eyewitnessing accuracy can be carried out exclusively in the laboratory. This is because emotional factors which attend real-life events such as a rape or a fatal accident, cannot easily be mimicked in the laboratory. Field studies such as that of Diges (1988), which examine real-life reaction to road accidents, of course have limited control, but are at least able to report real reactions to real events.

The question of control of extraneous variables is of course central to the argument. Yet even in the laboratory, such control is often lacking. Where the investigation of phenomena is new, for example, the important variables which require control are often unknown. Only after extensive investigation was it shown, for example, that in feeling of knowing (FOK) studies, the nature of materials affected the relationship between FOK and evidence of subsequent retention (Nelson, 1988).

Indeed, because, self-evidently, what is not known cannot be controlled within the laboratory, laboratory studies themselves suffer from uncertainty as to how widely any results can be generalized. In fact the problem for memory researchers is somewhat worse than this since it has been shown frequently that many findings in the laboratory do not readily generalize from one laboratory situation to another. Thus Underwood, Borsch and Malmi (1978), for example, found that even the traditional laboratory tasks of serial learning, paired associate learning and free recall correlate poorly and load on separate factors if performance of subjects is factor analysed. Memory is not one 'thing' or even a few 'things' but a large collection of different skills which interact with each other (see e.g. Herrmann and Palmisano, this volume). This means that laboratory-based experimentation, however well controlled, still has limitations as an approach to studying the underlying mechanisms of memory unless it can be demonstrated that such experiments lead to principles which are generalizable beyond the narrow experimental paradigm being studied. Banaji and Crowder (1989) emphasize the importance of the generalizability of research findings, but theoretically motivated and laboratory-based research has been at least as careless of demonstrating generalizability as has practical research. Those occasions where laboratory research is shown to generalize to real-world situations should be welcomed as strengthening the theories, not denigrated for failing to indicate the need for new conceptual frameworks.

However, the aim of this chapter is not to point out the inadequacies and limitations of a laboratory approach to memory. Few psychologists would doubt that the laboratory approach to memory has provided a large number of insights into how our memory system operates, from an examination of strategic behaviour (see e.g. Pressley and McDaniel 1988). Meta-memory (see e.g. Nelson 1988). Structural aspects of memory (see e.g. Baddeley 1986) and knowledge base (see e.g. Weinert 1988). It is the presumption that laboratory-based research is wholly good and non-laboratory-based research wholly bad which is open to challenge.

In the first place, it is sometimes possible to control real-life events in a way which is highly ecologically valid. Gruneberg, Morris and Sykes (1991) point to this in their defence of Banaji and Crowder's attack on practical application. They note, for example, the study of Morris, Tweedy and Gruneberg (1985) in demonstrating the difference between findings based on real-life and 'artificial' conditions. In the Morris et al. study, the retention of British soccer scores was examined under two conditions. In the first condition, the scores presented were the actual scores which had occurred and subjects knew they were the actual scores. In the second condition, subjects listened to plausible, but made-up scores, which they knew to be made-up. Prior to the experiment all subjects had filled in a questionnaire indicating their knowledge of football. For example, they were asked what was the name of the ground of particular teams, who played for whom and so on. At the end of the experiment, correlations were calculated between knowledge scores – which presumably reflect interest in soccer – and the extent of retention of the actual football scores they had heard. For the group given the made-up scores, the correlation was 0.36; for the group given the real scores the correlation was 0.82, confirming a previous experiment using real-life football scores, where the correlation between knowledge and retention was 0.81 (Morris, Gruneberg, Sykes and Merrick 1981). Quite clearly therefore, the real-life nature of the experience made a considerable difference to the results obtained. The danger, therefore, in generalizing from purely laboratory situations without examining what happens in real-life situations with the changed motivational factors involved is obvious.

Ceci and Bronfenbrenner (1991) have also carried out an experiment under carefully controlled conditions which is nevertheless highly ecologically valid and which shows major differences between performance inside and outside the laboratory. They had children monitor the passage of time so that they would take cup-cakes out of an oven before they burned. It was found that the pattern of monitoring the passage of time was completely different in a laboratory setting compared with a real-life home setting. Ceci and Bronfenbrenner conclude 'Had we studied them only in the laboratory we would have been led to an unjustifiably ungenerous estimation of their potential to deploy such complex cognitive strategies'. It is interesting that in both the Ceci and Bronfenbrenner study and the Morris *et al.* study, real-life settings led to considerably enhanced findings compared with non-real-life conditions.

Another example of the combination of memories occurring in the real world with close experimental control, comes from studies of memories of emotional events (Hayes, Conway and Morris 1991 (cited in Morris 1991)). In these studies autobiographical memories of emotional experiences were used to explore the similarities and differences between emotions such as happiness and anger and physical feelings such as warmth and wetness. Related studies tested the conditions that led to emotional memories for the information-processing stages predicted by Scherer (1984). For present purposes, there were several important features of this research. It was, admittedly, impossible to control the causes of the original emotions. That is, however, a normal problem for research on emotions. However, the recall of the emotions, and the information elicited from the participants about each memory was tightly controlled. In one study the ratings of the memory age, the event's pleasantness, expectation, causation, control, fairness, fit to plans, frequency, etc. were controlled by a microcomputer so that the response latencies could also be obtained. These detailed responses allowed a matching with the equally detailed predictions of Scherer which not only supported his model but also indicated where his predictions had been incorrect. For example, Scherer predicted that *shame* should be associated with an evaluation of having little control over an event or power to change its outcome. However, the results showed high ratings of control and power. This makes more sense than Scherer's original prediction, since there is little basis for shame if the action was not under the control of the person feeling the shame, or if they had no power to control the event. The use of autobiographical memories recalled under controlled conditions in which a rich amount of information can be elicited to test theories of emotions, demonstrates another area of research made possible only through using memories from everyday life.

It is clear, therefore, that laboratory studies can be ecologically valid and can control significant aspects of everyday memory, and it is clear also that in some situations laboratory studies can never

5

be ecologically valid, as in some aspects of eyewitness research. The former case presents no real problem to either the theoretical experimental psychologist or those interested in practical application. But what of the situation where for technical reasons, laboratory studies are not possible and control is less than adequate. The choice is stark – either such phenomena cannot be investigated or the investigation makes less than optimum solutions necessary. The case of eyewitnessing has been discussed above, but there are many others in the field of practical application, such as autobiographical and prospective memory, where laboratory investigation is at best of limited value.

One of the more interesting cases where a controlled laboratory investigation is not possible, is in very long-term retention. Bahrick (1984) for example reports a study of memory for Spanish for up to 40 years after acquisition. Understanding of how very long-term knowledge is stored and available, is of course not only of theoretical interest in coming to an understanding of the nature of memory, it is of critical importance in designing instruction programmes for materials which are intended to last a lifetime. To be fair to Banaji and Crowder (1991), they concede that such non-laboratory studies as that of Bahrick may be necessary where practical conditions make laboratory investigation impossible.

The concession by Banaji and Crowder (1991) is, however, a small one since they go on to argue that Bahrick's work, however interesting, adds nothing to what is already known about memory function. Indeed they concede nothing to their earlier argument that the pursuit of everyday memory research and its practical application has yielded nothing of theoretical value. There are nevertheless a number of arguments against concluding from this that the application of memory research is of no value.

In the first place, there are a number of examples which call into question this claim. Our understanding of metamemory – the knowledge that an individual has about his/her memory processes – and its significance for our understanding of memory processes, has clearly made considerable strides since the first studies by Hart (1965) on the feeling-of-knowing phenomenon and Brown and McNeill (1966) on the tip-of-the-tongue phenomenon. (See e.g. Nelson (1988) for a review.) Our understanding of the importance of knowledge base as influencing memory processing owes a considerable debt to studies of experts, e.g. Chase and Simon (1973). Again our understanding of memory strategies has been advanced by studying practical memory problems, e.g. Pressley and McDaniel (1988). As Weinert (1988) notes, one cannot understand memory without understanding the strategies that individuals adopt in experimental situations, and without understanding what subjects know about their memory systems (metamemory) and the effect of knowledge base on memory processing. More recently, Herrmann and Searlman's (1990) multimodal approach to memory improvement shows clearly that memory performance depends on a host of factors such as mood and depression and physical and mental context, all highlighted by examining practical problems of remembering. All of these areas owe a great debt to work on practical applications of memory research.

Even if this evidence were not accepted as showing the theoretical value of practical memory research, it can reasonably be taken as an act of faith that practical application will lead to theoretical insights. It has done so after all in other sciences, where applications of electricity, medicine and the search for the sources of disease such as cancer and AIDS have led to a much greater understanding of the underlying phenomena.

Even if Banaji and Crowder (1989) were correct, therefore, that little of theoretical interest has yet emerged from an orientation towards everyday memory and practical application, this would not be an argument against abandoning this approach in an effort to enhance theory. Unless psychology is truly different from other sciences, such theoretical advances will come.

Yet psychologists surely do not have to justify the study of practical applications of memory research in terms of its theoretical gains. The value of the discovery of penicillin does not conflict with an understanding of the nature of bacterial development for its own sake. Our view is therefore that practical application of memory research is of value in its own right, and that it is preferable to carry out research with technical limitations in terms of laboratory control, than to abandon application because control is less than perfect. That said, those interested in practical application have to ensure that if laboratory control is abandoned the results of intervention can be evaluated in a credible way. Two examples indicate some further problems in practical application that have to be faced in order to provide credible evaluation of procedures.

Cornoldi (1988) for example, argues that the use and value of mnemonic strategies in real life cannot be assessed by laboratory studies alone. Numerous experimental studies have found that mnemonic strategies which use visual imagery can materially enhance retention of, for example, word lists (Bugelski 1968), of face–name pairs (Morris, Jones and Hampson 1978), of foreign language vocabulary (Raugh and Atkinson 1975). Equally, however, a number of follow-up surveys of memory improvement courses which teach such methods of memory improvement have consistently failed to show that knowledge gained in such courses is applied in real life (Herrmann and Searlman 1990). As Gruneberg (this volume) notes, however, only an examination of real-life situations and problems of real-life application will show why such methods are not apparently used in real life, and indicate steps which may need to be taken in order to make their application possible. One possibility, for example, is that memory improvement courses instruct learners on how to use such techniques, but not on when and when not to use them in real-life situations.

Gruneberg and Jacobs (1991) note another example where technically it is difficult or impossible to carry out controlled laboratory experimentation. Linkword Language Courses (Gruneberg 1985, 1987) utilize the keyword technique of vocabulary acquisition to enhance foreign vocabulary learning within the context of a course which teaches grammar and sentence translation examples integrated with vocabulary learning. The amount of vocabulary taught in this manner varies between 350 and 800 words, depending on the format (text or auditory presentation) and the language concerned. The keyword technique has been shown in a large number of experimental studies to enhance foreign vocabulary acquisition (see e.g. Pressley and McDaniel 1988) so that at first sight the laboratory evaluation of integrated courses using this technique should present no technical problems. There are, however, two problems of evaluation which make any laboratory approach extremely difficult.

First, almost all laboratory studies examine relatively small amounts of vocabulary, 60–120 words, and use control groups instructed either in alternative strategies of vocabulary acquisition or given no instruction. Over small amounts of material this presents no real problem; over large amounts of vocabulary, the control group is liable to become bored and hence learn vocabulary less well than when presented with vocabulary in the context of courses which teach vocabulary integrated with grammar and sentence examples. However, a direct comparison between any two language courses is also problematic, since they deliver different amounts of vocabulary and grammar at different time points. Linkword courses, for example, deliver far more vocabulary at an early stage than do conventional courses.

These examples, then, present the psychologist interested in the practical application of memory research in order to solve practical problems, with a major problem. How can evaluations of procedures be made outside the laboratory, and in the absence of laboratory controls, yet at the same time be credible? In fact the area of memory research is by no means the first area within psychology to be faced with this dilemma. Organizational psychology has long had to balance the need for scientific evaluation against the technical limitations of the real world in respect of controls. The solution of organizational psychology has been to accept that in these situations less than optimal solutions are probably better than no solutions at all. Such an example from organisational psychology is the effect of job enrichment on productivity and job attitudes.

We quote Warr and Wall (1975):

> The modifications required by the different types of job design carry over across the conceptual boundaries between them and also spread into other areas of research. Whilst this might be unfortunate in preventing a tidy analysis of separate variables, it is inherent in the subject matter. Indeed it is debatable whether it is desirable to attempt to isolate the effects of any one component of change where changes themselves cannot be readily made in isolation.

A further major problem is that, in real life, adequate control groups are often not possible, that the numbers involved are necessarily small, on occasion precluding extensive statistical analysis. Clearly it would be foolish on the basis of any one or any few studies to conclude that a particular change was effective. What a number of eminent researchers in the field do do, however, is to look at patterns of results. Again we quote Warr and Wall:

> The vast majority of these experimentally orientated investi-gations point in the same direction: the introduction of greater variety and discretion into jobs is welcomed by employees. We must not, however, allow the relative consistency of these findings to mask some important limitations. In practice, the unsuccessful experiments are less likely to be reported than those with encouraging results. And amongst the latter the evaluation of the effects of job modification has not always

9

been entirely adequate. In relation to employee satisfaction, for instance, much of the evidence is based upon the subjective impressions of the investigators, selected verbatim reports or attitude measures which are only briefly described. Again for reasons of practicality few studies have used adequate control groups. Also, the changes introduced into jobs and the effects of these modifications on the larger organizational system, are often poorly described. This makes it difficult to identify possible causes of observed changes in employee attitudes and performance, as does the fact discussed earlier that redesigning jobs frequently involves simultaneous changes to many different aspects of the work situation.

In spite of these several limitations in the research evidence we are still left with the finding that most reported correlations and experimental studies in this area support the conclusion that jobs which offer variety and require the individual to exercise discretion over his work activities lead to enhanced well-being and mental health.

The thrust of our argument is that when it comes to applying memory research, and when it is not possible or practicable to carry out laboratory-based studies for the reasons described earlier, then the procedure we should adopt should be analogous to that adopted in organizational psychology. That is, evaluations should always be conservative, they should be based on patterns from a large or at least reasonable number of studies, and where possible should be related to established and laboratory-based studies. Of course mistakes might be made, but in certain cases the greater mistake may be in not accepting the probability that a manipulation works than in rejecting a manipulation as advantageous because no laboratory-based study can be performed.

The major problem with this approach in applied memory research is that, unlike organizational psychology, there are few publication outlets for 'imperfect' studies, so the possibility of building up a meta-analysis is likely to be severely limited in the immediate future. The present writers' view is that until such organs do appear, the possibility of significant applied advance is likely to be somewhat limited.

Let us again restate the main thrust of our argument. It is that in some situations, particularly where one is dealing with complex interactions in the real world, it is either difficult or impossible to carry out well-controlled, laboratory-based studies. In such cases the greater mistake might be in rejecting such evidence as there is, conservatively interpreted, than in accepting it. We are not arguing that we should not conduct controlled laboratory experiments where possible, as clearly they can and do add to our understanding of practical problems. Of course, in this chapter we have assumed what some may not accept – that the pursuit of practical solutions to real-world problems is a valid and desirable aim of cognitive psychologists – albeit not the only aim. For us the distinction between practical and theoretical is unimportant because of the way the two interact with each other.

How, then, would this approach affect the investigation of problems in applied memory for the three examples given above: eyewitness research, mnemonic strategy use in real life, and foreign language learning? Eyewitness research should examine eyewitnessing in real life in a case study approach as well as in laboratory investigation. The use of meta-analysis in the area of eyewitnessing research is not new. Bothwell, Brigham and Deffenbacher (1987) carried out a meta-analysis of studies which have investigated the confidence–accuracy relationship. This meta-analysis was for the most part based on controlled laboratory studies which nevertheless gave highly inconsistent and erratic results, suggesting more than anything else that laboratory studies were not controlling important variables affecting this relationship. Nevertheless the meta-analysis did at least draw together a range of different experiments and allow some sense to be made of the whole.

Clearly if such meta-analysis is of value in relation to laboratory studies, its use in detecting patterns of findings in less controlled real-life studies is also likely to be considerable. In the case of the use of mnemonic strategies, the difficulties in their actual use should be followed into real-life situations again with a case study approach. In the case of language learning, the effectiveness of any particular course should be investigated by field studies of actual use *in situ*, together with, where possible, independent evaluation and administration. In none of these examples is any one study likely to be definitive, but a meta-analysis of patterns of results from large numbers of studies are likely to give an indication of the real value of application outside the laboratory. The alternative is often to do nothing.

It has to be said that in our view, despite the considerably increased interest in practical application of memory research, relatively few psychologists have taken the step from the laboratory or occasional field study to the sustained effort needed to apply ideas in the outside world. Gruneberg (1988), for example, has argued that we have by and large failed to create the psychological equivalents of washing machines, electric lights, radios and telephones, which convince the public and politicians alike that the 'hard' sciences are good and the social sciences are bad. We have failed to create psychological engineering where the fruits of the laboratory are made tangible for those who need our help.

Part of this failure may be academic snobbery – Banaji and Crowder (1989) regard those who engage in practical application as 'rushing to answer Senator Proxmire'; part of the problem is that application takes considerable time and effort and often does not result in academically accepted productivity in the form of academic papers. Again, part of the problem has been discussed above – that evaluation of practical application is technically difficult because it may well mean abandoning the safety of the controlled laboratory for the real-world uncontrolled case study and field study.

Even for those interested in the implementation of practical aspects of memory, there are a number of nettles which need to be grasped. The first of these is making one's findings and knowledge available. Academics by-and-large don't like publicity, possibly because media approaches tend to trivialize what are often complex issues. Again as academic psychologists we are often interested in understanding the underlying mechanisms of memory and see a conceptual theoretical framework as necessary to guide future research. It is difficult to see how publicity can further this end. But many psychologists, we believe, are equally interested that ultimately such theoretical insights feed back into something that will benefit the man and woman in the street with his or her memory problems. One major way of doing this is through publicity and publication or both. It cannot be done by osmosis. Nor can it be done well by leaving it to others less expert than the developers, because they will often fail to understand what it is they are dealing with. It has to be stressed that in any case there is no army of technocrats out there waiting to take up our ideas. In order to let those outside psychology know of relevant and practical work, there is no choice but to publish or publicize memory research ourselves in a way that is intelligible to the non-psychologist. Elizabeth Loftus has done this with her court appearances on eyewitness evidence and a book of case studies written with the general public in mind (Loftus and

Ketcham 1991). Herrmann (1990) has done this in relation to new memory improvement methods, through the publication of a book written and promoted with the general public in mind. Geiselman and his colleagues (e.g. Fisher and Geiselman 1988) have done this in relation to police work and the cognitive interview. Ellis and his colleagues (Ellis and Shepherd, this volume) have done this in relation to identification of faces in forensic work, and Gruneberg has published foreign language courses which utilize mnemonic strategies (Gruneberg 1987). There are of course a number of other such attempts, but we think it fair to claim that such attempts by academic psychologists are few and far between. Of course not everyone, but in our view more academic psychologists, should involve themselves in publicizing their findings, and in presenting their work in such a way that others can readily find it and use it. For unless more academic psychologists interpret, as well as further, our current knowledge for the benefit of those outside psychology, are not we in danger of being regarded as self-indulgent?

Of course there are layers of interpretive levels, from the ultimate consumer at one level, to the professional educationalist or legal expert whose expertise is in an area one is trying to help – the linguist in foreign language teaching, the mathematician in mathematics teaching, the defence lawyer at another level. In our experience this is the layer where the greatest difficulty lies because to some extent suggesting ways of using a subject area more efficiently, for example, is a threat to professional competence by an 'interloper' who does not understand the subject. Furthermore one is in danger in attacking deep-seated philosophies of how a subject should be taught or approached, and 'memorizing' and, in education, memory strategies are often seen as low-level, indeed bizarre activities offering little in the way of achieving an 'understanding' of a topic. Some teachers may indeed genuinely believe that memory *per se* has no part to play in acquiring skill or a field of expertise. Indeed such a view of memory improvement strategies is not confined to non-psychologists. Howe (1970), for example, states 'If something is worth learning there is almost always a meaningful way of learning it'. Yet for many people, whether learning foreign language vocabulary, scientific formulae, or mathematical principles, such a view of the world is hopelessly idealistic. After all, that conventional approaches to language, mathematics and science teaching leave the great majority of our children lost and confused is hardly a matter of dispute. That alternative approaches which may help some of these people, some of the time, are treated with ridicule and contempt should, however, not be so surprising. Psychologists must be aware that in advocating any new approach, there is threat as well as promise. Yet, in the long run, psychologists have no choice. They have to grasp the second nettle. They must work with experts in other areas to appreciate memory problems in the context of a field as a whole, if we are going to break through. This doesn't mean trying to convince every expert or even the majority. It doesn't mean working with an expert from the beginning. One solution is to develop ideas independently of an expert, then consult. Experts in disciplines other than psychology often have preconceptions which need to be challenged. Nevertheless, consulting with experts in other disciplines is essential if some degree of professional and public credibility is to be achieved.

The problems outlined in this chapter should be seen in the context of a realization by many psychologists that problems of practical application of memory research need to be urgently addressed. It seems inconceivable that the 'hard' sciences should have made the advances they have if they had not been seen to be socially relevant in a myriad of different ways, from engineering to medicine to electronics and biotechnology. As Gruneberg, Morris and Sykes (1991) note, 'Compared to the successes of the other sciences, the successes of psychology in general, and memory research in particular, are pretty small beer'. The move towards practical application, as evidenced for example by the contents of this book, indicate the willingness of psychologists to face many of the problems we have outlined above, both in order to generate a better understanding of memory and to help those who might benefit from the application of our knowledge. Problems there are, but the advance in applied memory research since the first Conference on Practical Aspects of Memory has been little short of dramatic. As Gruneberg (1991) has noted elsewhere, our problems are more the problems of success than of failure.

In summary, this chapter has pointed to the different strands of interest in practical aspects of memory. These consist of those concerned with enhancing our theoretical understanding on the one hand, either by focusing on explanations of ecologically valid phenomena, or by having ecologically valid phenomena to generate further theoretical ideas, to those only concerned with solving practical problems on the other. We believe that both major strands are valid, and that both have shown some limited success. The attack by Banaji and Crowder (1989) on the everyday memory approach to understanding memory is of value in drawing attention to the desirability of using controls where possible, and forcing those who wish to apply memory research outside the laboratory to face up to the problems of carrying out work which, whilst lacking control, is credible. We believe that they have considerably overstated their case, however, since it can be demonstrated both that control of ecologically valid phenomena is sometimes possible, and that real-life and laboratory examination of the same phenomena can give completely different answers. The demonstration of this latter phenomenon questions the validity of a laboratory-only approach to understanding memory. We also believe that by adopting the model of organizational psychology in utilizing case studies and meta-analysis, some of the major problems of evaluation of memory phenomena in the real world can be overcome.

Finally, we would deny any major difference between experimental psychology and everyday memory approaches in their value in the furthering of our understanding of practical applications. Both have their part to play. It is clearly desirable to control extraneous variables where possible in the laboratory, and as studies reviewed in this chapter show, to use real life as a test-bed of theory as well as to further practical application in its own right. As the following chapters show, both approaches are commonly used by those interested in practical application.

REFERENCES

Baddeley, A.D. (1986) *Working Memory*, Oxford: Oxford University Press.

Bahrick, H.P. (1984) 'Semantic memory in permastore: 50 years of memory for Spanish learned in school', *Journal of Experimental Psychology: General*, 113: 1–29.

Banaji, M.R. and Crowder, R.G. (1989) 'The bankruptcy of everyday memory', *American Psychologist* 44: 1185–93.

Banaji, M.R. and Crowder, R.G. (1991) 'Some everyday thoughts on ecologically valid methods', *American Psychologist* 46 1: 78–9.

Bothwell, R.K., Brigham, J.C. and Deffenbacher, K. (1987) 'Correlation of eyewitness accuracy and confidence: Optimality hypothesis revisited', *Journal of Applied Psychology* 72: 691–5.

Brown, R. and McNeill, D. (1966) 'The "tip of the tongue" phenomenon', *Journal of Verbal Learning and Verbal Behavior* 5: 325–37.

Bugelski, B.R. (1968) 'Images as a mediator in one trial paired associate learning', *Journal of Experimental Psychology* 77: 328–34.

Ceci, S.J. and Bronfenbrenner, U. (1991) 'On the demise of everyday memory: The rumors of my death are much exaggerated (Mark Twain)', *American Psychologist* 46: 27–31.

Chase, W.G. and Simon, H.A. (1973) 'Perception in chess', *Cognitive Psychology* 4: 55–81.

Cohen, G. (1989) *Memory In The Real World*, London: Erlbaum.

Cornoldi, C. (1988) 'Why study mnemonics?', in M.M. Gruneberg, P.E. Morris and R.N. Sykes (eds) *Practical Aspects of Memory*, vol. 2, pp. 397–402, London: Wiley.

Diges, M. (1988) 'Stereotypes and memory of real traffic accidents', in M.M. Gruneberg, P.E. Morris and R.N. Sykes (eds) *Practical Aspects of Memory*, vol. 2, pp. 59–65, London: Wiley.

Fisher, R.P. and Geiselman, R.E. (1988) 'Enhancing eyewitness memory with the cognitive interview', in M.M. Gruneberg, P.E. Morris, and R.N. Sykes, (eds) *Practical Aspects of Memory: Current Research and Issues*, vol. I, pp. 34–9. Chichester: Wiley.

Gruneberg, M.M. (1985) *Computer Linkword French, German, Spanish, Italian, Greek, Russian, Dutch, Portuguese, Hebrew*, Penfield, New York: Artworx Software.

Gruneberg, M.M. (1987) *Linkword French, German, Spanish, Italian*, London: Corgi Books.

Gruneberg, M.M. (1988) 'Practical problems in the practical application of memory', in M.M. Gruneberg, P.E. Morris and R.N. Sykes (eds) *Practical Aspects of Memory*, vol. 1, pp. 555–557, New York: Wiley.

Gruneberg, M.M. (1991) 'The new approach to memory improvement: Problems and prospects', in D.J. Herrmann, A. Searlman, C. McAvoy and H. Weingartner (eds) *New Approaches To Memory Improvement*, New York: Springer.

Gruneberg, M.M. and Jacobs, G.C. (1991) 'In defence of Linkword', *Language Learning Journal* 3: 25–9.

Gruneberg, M.M., Morris, P.E. and Sykes, R.N. (1978) *Practical Aspects of Memory*, London: Academic Press.

Gruneberg, M.M., Morris, P.E. and Sykes, R.N. (1988a and b) *Practical Aspects Of Memory: Current Research And Issues*, London: Wiley.

Gruneberg, M.M., Morris, P.E. and Sykes, R.N. (1991) 'The obituary on everyday memory and its practical application is premature', *American Psychologist* 46 1: 76–8.

Hart, J. (1965) 'Memory and the feeling of knowing experience', *Journal of Educational Psychology* 56: 208–16.

Herrmann, D.J. (1990) *Super Memory*, Emmaus: Rodale.

Herrmann, D.J. and Searlman, A. (1990) 'The new multi-modal approach to memory impairment', in G. Bower (ed.) *Advances In Learning And Motivation*, New York: Academic Press.

Higbee, K. (1988) *Your Memory*, Englewood Cliffs, New Jersey: Prentice-Hall.

Howe, M.J. (1970) *Introduction to Human Memory*, New York: Harper & Row.

Loftus, E. and Ketcham, K. (1991) *Witness For The Defense*, New York: St. Martin's Press.

Morris, P.E. (1991) 'Cognition and consciousness', *The Psychologist* (in press).

16

Morris, P.E., Gruneberg, M.M., Sykes, R.N. and Merrick, A. (1981) 'Football knowledge and the acquisition of new results', *British Journal of Psychology* 72: 479–83.

Morris, P.E., Jones, S. and Hampson, P.J. (1978) 'An imagery mnemonic for the learning of peoples' names', *British Journal of Psychology* 69: 335–6.

Morris, P.E., Tweedy, M. and Gruneberg, M.M. (1985) 'Interest, knowledge and the memory of soccer scores', *British Journal of Psychology* 76: 417–25.

Neisser, U. (1978) 'Memory: What are the important questions?', in M.M. Gruneberg, P.E. Morris and R.N. Sykes (eds) (1978) *Practical Aspects of Memory*, pp. 3–24, London: Academic Press.

Neisser, U. (1988) 'Time present and time past', in M.M. Gruneberg, P.E. Morris and R.N. Sykes (eds) *Practical Aspects of Memory*, vol. 2, pp. 545–60.

Nelson, T.O. (1988) 'Predictive accuracy of the feeling of knowing across different criterion tasks and across different subject populations and individuals', in M.M. Gruneberg, P.E. Morris and R.N. Sykes (eds) *Practical Aspects Of Memory: Current Research And Issues*, London: Wiley.

Pressley, M. and McDaniel, M. (1988) 'Doing mnemonics research well. Some general guidelines and a study', in M.M Gruneberg, P.E. Morris and R.N. Sykes, (eds) *Practical Aspects of Memory*, vol. II, pp. 409–14, Chichester: Wiley.

Raugh, M.R. and Atkinson, R.C. (1975) 'A mnemonic method for learning a second language vocabulary', *Journal of Educational Psychology* 67: 1–16.

Scherer, K.R. (1984) 'Emotion as a multicomponential process: A model and some cross-cultural data', in P. Shaver and L. Wheeler (eds) *Review Of Personality And Social Psychology: vol. 5*, Beverly Hills: Sage.

Underwood, B.J., Borsch, R.F. and Malmi, R.A. (1978) 'Composition of episodic memory', *Journal of Experimental Psychology: General* 107: 393–419.

Warr, P. and Wall, T. (1975) *Work And Well Being*, Harmondsworth: Penguin.

Weinert, F.E. (1988) 'Epilogue', in F.E. Weinert and M. Perlmutter (eds) *Memory Development*, pp. 381–96, Hillsdale, New Jersey: Erlbaum.

2

MEMORY AND EYEWITNESS TESTIMONY

Alan E. Fruzzetti, Kelly Toland, Stephen A. Teller and Elizabeth F. Loftus

Few moments are more dramatic than when, prompted by the prosecutor, a courtroom witness outstretches an arm, finger extended, and declares with rock-solid certainty that the accused is the person she saw fleeing the scene of the crime. The jury, impressed with the witness' confidence in her identification, returns a verdict of guilty, transforming the accused into a convict. But how reliable are such identifications? Because the witness was certain, does that mean she was correct? The scientific evidence shows she will sometimes be wrong, and an innocent person will suffer while the real guilty person remains free to commit further crimes (Loftus and Ketcham 1991).

How many mistaken identifications have lead to wrongful convictions is difficult to estimate. Some analysts have suggested that in the USA the rate of false convictions may be as high as 5 per cent (Radin 1964). Even the more conservative estimates of misidentification are alarming. A rate of even 0.6 per cent wrongful identifications would mean that 10,000 or more people per year in the USA alone might be falsely convicted or convinced to plead guilty. Ten thousand people annually might be facing erroneous convictions in the USA, largely due to problems with eyewitness identification and testimony (Gross 1987).

In the past fifteen years, psychologists have learned a great deal about eyewitness memory. They have described some of the factors affecting eyewitness reliability, and have had impact upon the judicial systems' traditional reliance upon the eyewitness. This chapter discusses the role that memory-influencing factors play in the problem of mistaken eyewitness testimony, and explores some of their implications for the justice system.

In this chapter we focus on perception of events, retention of information, and later retrieval of memories. We demonstrate the malleability of memory and describe a theoretical controversy surrounding the topic of memory distortion. We detail the impact this distortion can have on the accuracy of eyewitness testimony, and discuss some implications of the research findings for legal systems' methods of data collection, including interview techniques and identity parades. Explorations of the reliability of memory and of the relationship between confidence and accuracy are also discussed. Finally, possible solutions to the problem are explored.

Determining what factors lead to inaccurate recall and identification, and what techniques facilitate accurate recall, will influence procedures that are used in criminal investigations and in the courts. Ultimately, this research should help to minimize misidentifications, and make more appropriate the tremendous impact that eyewitness testimony can have on a jury.

PERCEPTUAL FACTORS

A useful framework for thinking about eyewitness testimony involves three parts: perception, retention, and retrieval. The beginning of a memory involves, of course, perception. Many factors associated with the commission of a crime affect people's perceptions and thus affect the creation or acquisition of memory. Generally, they may be categorized broadly into two areas; witness factors and event factors. Witness factors include individual characteristics like age, gender, individual response to stressful situations, and also attitudinal factors, such as expectations and prejudices. Event factors, on the other hand, are part of the witnessed event itself. They include the duration of the event, how often it occurs, the level of violence, and the salience of the individual details that make up the event.

Witness factors

Age

Memory for witnessed events varies with age. For instance, in numerous tasks, children have been found to be generally less accurate and complete in their reports than adults. They typically provide fewer details when asked to recall events without prompting by questions (Dent 1988). They also often perform worse than adults when asked specific questions, although when the to-be-remembered details involve topics particularly of interest to the child, they can show adult levels of accuracy (King and Yuille 1987). Likewise, when the context of the original event is appropriately reinstated, children's performance can equal that of adults (Wilkinson 1988). Perhaps the most significant finding regarding children's testimony is that young children often tend to be more susceptible to suggestive or leading questions than adults (e.g. Goodman and Reed 1986; Ceci, Ross and Toglia 1987).

At the other end of the lifespan, a number of studies reveal that older people do not perform as well as younger or middle-aged adults on memory tasks (e.g. Farrimond 1968). They also perform worse at recognition of the faces of strangers seen only once. In some studies simulating eyewitnessing, the elderly have been shown to recall fewer details of the stimulus event (List 1986). The elderly, as were children, were also relatively susceptible to misleading postevent information, although this effect was mostly due to elderly males. Elderly females' mnemonic accuracy on this task was similar to that of the young adult (Loftus, Levidow and Duensing 1991).

Occupation

Few studies have compared mnemonic accuracy across various occupations, although some have compared the abilities of police and civilians. Ainsworth (1981) found that police performed similarly to non-police. Other studies have shown more errors by police, primarily because the police were too ready to see 'crimes' in a film of a street scene (Clifford 1976; Tickner and Poulton 1975). Tickner and Poulton found that the police reported more alleged thefts than the civilians, but that the civilians did just as well as police when it came to detecting actual crimes. On the other hand, Yuille (1984) showed that police give more detailed and accurate reports of events than people without police training. Moreover, Yuille also found police to be somewhat less influenced by misleading postevent suggestion than were non-police. This difference might have been due to either a selection effect, namely that a certain type of people decide to be police officers, or perhaps due to the training that officers receive. The latter suggestion is less plausible, given Yarmey's (1986) observation that 'very little training is given in police academies specifically on perceptual and memorial concerns' (p. 47).

Although no clear-cut advantages to police memory, as compared with civilian memory, emerge from the literature, people do tend to believe that police have special abilities as witnesses. For example, of 500 registered voters (i.e. potential jurors) in Dade County, Florida, nearly half believed that law enforcement agents have better memories than average citizens; only 38 per cent said no; the rest had no opinion (Loftus 1984; similarly, Yarmey and Jones 1983).

Stress

Although somewhat controversial in its application to the present topic (see Deffenbacher 1983), the well-known Yerkes–Dodson Law (the 'inverted U-shaped curve') describes the basic relationship between stress and a witness's ability to recall details of a crime accurately (Yerkes and Dodson 1908). The Yerkes–Dodson Law holds that performance is related to stress in a curvilinear fashion. Very low stress, that is, low arousal, begets poor performance, while a moderate amount of stress facilitates performance. Excessive stress drives performance back down (hence the inverted U, the peak of which is the optimal level of arousal). Individual differences in response to identical stressors can lead one person to have a somewhat different inverted U function from another.

This conclusion is supported by empirical studies, which suggest that the ability of witnesses to report crime details accurately is related to the level of stress they experience. Peters (1988) recruited subjects at a health clinic where they received inoculations. During their visit to the clinic, they met the nurse who injected them and another person (a researcher) for equal amounts of time. Subjects met the targets (the nurse and the researcher) only briefly, then attempted to identify them from a photo array one day or one week later. Peters found that subjects were able to describe and to identify the researcher much better than the nurse from an array of photographs. Peters concludes that as arousal increases much beyond the normal, accuracy of memory suffers.

However, the results of several laboratory studies (e.g. Heuer and Reisberg 1990; Christianson, Loftus, Hoffman and Loftus 1991; Christianson and Loftus 1991) and one naturalistic study show that high stress does not necessarily lead to poor memory. In the naturalistic study, 4 to 5 months after an actual shooting (in which one person was killed and another wounded), the researchers interviewed thirteen witnesses to the incident (Yuille and Cutshall 1986). Their reports were analysed for accuracy and also compared with earlier reports that the witnesses had given to the police. These investigations found that, although it was very stressful to them, the witnesses still had very accurate memories for the event. In addition, level of reported stress at the time of the crime was not significantly related to subsequent recall. However, one weakness in this study is that the higher-stress witnesses were closer and more involved in the crime. Thus, the close distance could have boosted memory for these individuals, and counteracted any detrimental effects of extreme stress.

Expectations

Several experimental studies support the notion that people's expectations influence their opinions and reports (e.g. Darley and Gross 1983; Snyder and Swann 1978; Snyder, Tanke and Bersheid 1977). This *confirmation bias* seems to apply to eyewitness testimony as well.

The confirmation bias is exemplified in the now-famous study by Hastorf and Cantril (1954) of highly partisan fans' perceptions and reports of the behaviour of two opposing football teams in a game between Dartmouth and Princeton. The authors showed game films to students from both universities, who were asked to count instances of inappropriate behaviour and fouls. In general, each group reported many more fouls from their rivals than they did from their own team. That is, their expectations influenced their perceptions.

In another study of expectations, Peterson (1976) showed subject-witnesses a 7 minute videotaped disturbance and fight occurring at a forum concerning Richard Nixon's proposed impeachment in 1974. Witnesses were given one of two sets of information prior to viewing the tape. This pre-event information was designed to bias or predispose their interpretations. They were informed that either (1) the main characters on the tape were disruptive radicals who intended to prevent a speaker from continuing, or (2) the main characters were free-speech advocates trying to ensure that both sides be heard. Witnesses who expected to see angry radicals remembered more details consistent with this view and fewer details in opposition to this view.

As had often been said, if five people view an event, there will be at least five different versions of the occurrence. Different people perceive and record information differently. Just how we differ, and how these differences affect our memories has been the topic of the last section. The next section focuses on factors that are inherent in the event itself.

Event factors

Exposure time

A typical eyewitness to a convenience store robbery might testify that during the 5 minutes' time that the robber was in the store, he (the witness) had a clear and unobstructed look at the criminal's face for at least 30 seconds. Other factors being equal, longer and more frequent exposure to a stimulus will facilitate accurate perception, and better recall or recognition (e.g. Laughery, Alexander and Lane 1971; Ebbinghaus 1885/1964). Thus, our witness may be viewed as more credible than if he had only got a few-second glimpse of the robber's face. The fact that longer exposure to a stimulus increases perceptive accuracy is well-known, practically a matter of common sense. What is not so well appreciated is that witnesses are not particularly accurate at estimating the *duration* of an event. This is an important factor in eyewitness testimony, since the duration of events, or segments of the events, can be crucial evidence in legal proceedings. Routinely, people overestimate these durations, and thus create the impression that they had longer to look at something than they really did.

For example, Loftus, Schooler, Boone, and Kline (1987) showed subjects a 30-second tape of a simulated bank robbery and asked subjects how long the robbery lasted. The average subject estimated the duration of the robbery at more than $2^1/2$ minutes, and very few correctly estimated or underestimated the event's duration. The overestimation found in this study is typical and suggests the existence of a pattern of overestimation of time sequences by eyewitnesses.

Detail salience

Another important event factor relating to eyewitness memory is detail salience. In stressful situations, such as during the commission of a crime, witness attention may be focused on, or distracted by, certain details of the situation. For example, the witness may be so distracted by a weapon pointed in his direction, that other details of the crime scene, such as the robber's face, size, or clothing, are not attended to during the crime. This phenomenon, called *weapon focus*, has been examined experimentally.

Loftus, Loftus and Messo (1987) monitored eye movements of subjects who were shown one of two filmed versions of an encounter in a restaurant. In one version the perpetrator pointed a gun at the cashier and she handed him money. In the other version, the perpetrator gave the cashier a cheque and she handed him money. The film versions were otherwise identical. Subjects in the 'weapon' version fixated on the weapon more that subjects in the 'non-weapon' version fixated on the cheque. Further, the subjects in the group that saw the weapon version of the crime showed poorer recall of other details and were less able to identify the robber from a photo array. See also Kramer, Buckhout and Eugenio (1990) and Maass and Kohnken (1989) for more recent explorations of the weapon focus phenomenon.

Thus, in a real crime, not only does the increased stress resulting from the presence of a weapon often diminish the perceptual abilities of witnesses, the heightened focus on the weapon will likely further reduce the range of perception and the opportunity for accurate acquisition of other details of the event.

Violence of the event

There is evidence that the violence associated with a crime may influence perception of details of the event. Clifford and Hollin (1981) investigated the impact of violence on memory with subject-witnesses to two different events. They showed subject-witnesses one of two films, either violent or non-violent, with the same two characters and of the same duration. In the violent episode, a woman is shown walking alone toward the camera when she is stopped by a man and forced backwards into a wall, at which point the man takes her handbag and runs away, leaving the woman crying. In the non-violent tape, the man approaches the woman, who stops. He asks for directions and then both continue on their ways. Subjects viewing the violent episode were consistently less accurate in their answers to questions about the event than subjects who had watched the non-violent event.

In another study, Loftus and Burns (1982) created two versions of a crime that differed only by the insertion of a shockingly violent scene in one version. In the violent version, a young boy was shot in the face near the end of the filmed event, as the robbers were making their getaway. The experimenters randomly assigned half of their subjects to see the violent version, and the other half saw the non-violent version. Subjects assigned to view the non-violent version were better able to recall and identify details of the crime portrayed. Subjects who witnessed the violent version, as in the Clifford and Hollin (1981) study, showed less accurate and less complete reporting of details from the event. In fact, memory was impaired not only for details immediately preceding the violent scene but also for details occurring up to 2 minutes earlier in the robbery. The authors suggested that the mental shock associated with the very violent scene might have disrupted essential memory processing necessary for information storage.

This and other perceptual factors form an important focus of the study of eyewitness memory. Holding sway as they do at the creation of a memory, they necessarily become an integral part of a person's conception of an event, and hence, part of the memory. Equally important, however, is the second part of the memory triad: Retention.

RETENTION: STORAGE OF MEMORIES

After an event has been perceived, and encoded into memory, it must be retained until the time comes to recall the event. However, the process of retention is not simply a passive storage of information, as if the information were a document in the filing cabinet of memory. Many factors can influence memory retention, enhancing or altering the information while it sits in storage. Detail information is especially susceptible to alteration during the retention interval.

It is well known that information is forgotten with the passage of time (Ebbinghaus 1885/1964; Wagenaar and Groeneweg 1990). In an unusual study of long-term forgetting, Wagenaar and Groeneweg compared testimonies and documentary evidence collected from seventy-eight concentration camp victims after the war with interviews conducted between 1984 and 1987. Although the most striking aspect of the comparison was the general agreement of the witnesses to basic facts, many details were forgotten. For example, out of thirty-eight witnesses who had been tortured by the camp 'Kapo',

Marinus De Rijke, all but three remembered his name after 40 years. On the other hand, most of the names of guards, which had been reported at the early interviews, were forgotten.

It should come as no surprise that people forget with the passage of time. What is less well-known is that information the witness learns of after the event can actually alter the witness's memory of how the event took place. Witnesses, without knowing that they are doing so, often incorporate postevent information into their recollections of what they saw and experienced. However, the mechanism by which witnesses are influenced by postevent information is one of the most controversial issues in the eyewitness domain. This section describes changes that may occur in memory during retention and outlines some of the controversy.

Postevent information and retention of details

Enhancing memory

Several studies have shown that mentioning details to witnesses after they watch a film of, say, an automobile accident raises the likelihood that witnesses will recall those details (Bekerian and Bowers 1983). Imagine that you are a witness to an auto accident. Before the police arrive, you overhear another witness discuss some detail. The very act of hearing this information will increase the likelihood that you recall that detail at a later date.

Compromise memories

Imagine now that instead of simply repeating known information, one of your fellow witnesses says something that you yourself did not notice, – for example, that one of the cars was going very fast. There is a reasonable chance that your recollection for the event may be altered by this other witness's statement. Research has shown that, after exposure to postevent information, memory of an event can become a *compromise* between actual events and postevent information. The mind incorporates, to varying degrees, the later information, partially altering the way the event is remembered.

For example, Loftus (1975) showed forty subject-witnesses a 3 minute videotape excerpted from a film (*Diary of a Student Revolution*) in which a lecture was disrupted by eight demonstrators. Subjects were later given one of two questionnaires each containing one experimental question and nineteen unimportant filler questions. Half of the subjects were asked, 'Was the leader of the twelve demonstrators who entered the classroom a male?' whereas the other half were asked, 'Was the leader of the four demonstrators who entered the classroom a male?'.

One week later, subjects given the question suggesting there had been twelve demonstrators reported an average of 8.9 demonstrators. Those given the question suggesting there had been four demonstrators reported having seen an average of 6.4. Most subjects seemed to compromise between the actual number and the misleading one, rather than choosing on or the other. This type of compromise seems to occur, not just with memory of numbers, but also of other factors that can be averaged (e.g. colour: Loftus 1977; Belli 1988).

Substitute memories

With the presence or absence of an object there is no opportunity for 'compromise' in memory, – either an object existed or it did not. And, just as the mention of true facts increases the likelihood that a witness will remember that fact, there is potential that introducing inaccurate details might affect a memory as well. Several studies spanning the last two decades have examined the consequences of introducing non-existent objects into the postevent experience of subjects (e.g. Lesgold and Petrush 1977; Ceci, Ross and Toglia 1987; Chandler 1989). The legal implications of including inaccurate details in memory are obvious: Consider the effects of an erroneous report of the existence of a weapon, or of the colour of a traffic light.

One early study showed subjects slides depicting a simulated accident involving a car and a pedestrian (Loftus, Miller and Burns 1978). In the critical slide, half the subjects saw a red car turn a corner near a stop sign, the other half of the subjects saw the car pass a yield sign instead. After turning the corner, the automobile struck a pedestrian. Immediately following the slides, subjects were asked several questions, included in one of which was the mention of either a stop sign or a yield sign. For half the subjects the question matched the actual scene presented, for the other half the question mentioned the existence of the sign they had not seen.

Later, subjects were asked to identify which slides they had seen from sequential pairs. Thus, subjects were presented either the yield or stop sign slide, which were otherwise identical. For those receiving consistent information, 75 per cent picked the slide with the sign they had actually seen, whereas only 41 per cent of those who had received inconsistent information chose correctly. Note that if they had simply guessed, subjects should have chosen correctly 50 per cent of the time.

These experiments provide evidence of the powerful influence of inaccurate or misleading postevent information on subsequent recall. Memory can be inaccurately supplemented (adding objects never actually seen) or transformed (substituting one type of object for another).

Researchers next undertook to discover what factors influence the degree to which accurate memories are compromised or replaced by misleading postevent information. Both the timing of the postevent information, and the role, whether central or peripheral, that the detail played in the original event have been shown to have important effects.

In exploring the effects of the temporal intervals between an event, postevent information, and subsequent recall, Loftus *et al.* (1978) gave subject-witnesses either consistent or inconsistent information (as described above) or no supplemental information, either immediately after viewing the slideshow, or just prior to a recall test. The recall test was administered after a retention interval of 20 minutes, 1 day, 2 days, or 1 week.

Results suggested that the amount of memory distortion was larger when more, rather than less, time had passed between the original event and the misleading information. Thus, the effectiveness of misleading information seems to be enhanced by fading of the original memory with time.

Critics of the application of memory research to legal settings have pointed to the fact that much of the experimental manipulation of memory is concerned with peripheral details of events, such as the number of demonstrators or type of sign on the corner. Central details of events, such as whether a perpetrator of a crime used a gun or a knife, are less malleable than peripheral details (Dritsas and Hamilton 1977).

Thus, it appears that the strength of a memory determines in part the extent to which it can be altered by postevent information. As memory fades, it is more liable to alteration. In addition, salient central details are less malleable than peripheral information in an event. There is, however, no way of knowing which remembered details were strong or salient enough to be less alterable, and which were not. Thus, the implication that memory can be altered in this way at all has important implications for legal systems' reliance on remembered events.

While the exact mechanisms involved when misleading postevent information alters memory are uncertain (e.g. Belli 1989), the erroneous reporting is unequivocal. Clearly, attempts to minimize the introduction and influence of postevent information should be made at every stage of legal proceedings. For example, in the retention stage, not allowing one witness to overhear an interview with another eyewitness would help to prevent an important source of bias from influencing reports of an event.

THEORETICAL ISSUES RELEVANT TO EYEWITNESS MEMORY

Underlying several findings and controversies reported here lies an ultimate question for memory research: What happens when we forget or misremember information? Scores of laboratory studies have demonstrated that misleading postevent information can alter an eyewitness's memory report (e.g. Belli 1989; Ceci *et al.* 1987; Chandler 1989).

In a typical study investigating this phenomenon, subjects witness a slide presentation of an event, such as an accident or a burglary. Half of the subjects later receive misleading information about specific 'critical' details from the slide presentation. At a later time, when subjects are tested on their memory for the critical details in the witnessed event, misled subjects do not report the original event as accurately as do the non-misled control subjects. This phenomenon has been called the 'Misinformation Effect' (Loftus and Hoffman 1989).

For example, in one misinformation study, subjects viewed a slide presentation depicting a young man shopping in a college bookstore and stealing a number of items in the process. While browsing, he meanders past a sweatshirt with Mickey Mouse on the front. Later, all subjects read a written narrative describing the same episode depicted in the slides, but for half of the subjects, the narrative inaccurately described the sweatshirt as having Daffy Duck on the front. When tested on their memory for the character on the sweatshirt, subjects who had received misleading information were significantly less accurate.

Although the altered memory reports have been demonstrated time and time again, the question of why they occur remains disputed. It is unclear whether the misinformation replaces the original memory or combines with it somehow (the *alteration hypothesis*), or whether they coexist in the mind of the subject, but the postevent information renders the event information inaccessible (the *coexistence hypothesis*). One critical difference between these competing hypotheses is the question of whether the original event information may ever be recovered.

Several empirical attempts have been made to induce accurate memory reports from misinformed subjects. The failure of those attempts has been characterized as being consistent with the alteration hypothesis. Attempts to recover the 'original memory' include giving subjects incentives for accurate reporting, 'second guess' techniques, and even hypnosis (Loftus 1979; Sheehan 1989).

On the other hand, coexistence theories derive support from fruitful attempts to recover details from the originally witnessed event after exposure to misleading postevent information. Such successful cases demonstrate that although not all original memories can be recovered, in some instances it is possible that misinformation affects memory reports without permanently destroying or altering the original memory trace. These fruitful attempts use techniques such as context reinstatement and the use of a warning before the misinformation phase of the study paradigm indicating that subjects should critically evaluate the misinformation for false statements (Bekerian and Bowers 1983; Christiaansen and Ochalek 1983).

Morton, Hammersley and Bekerian (1985) developed a specific coexistence theory of the misinformation effect, the *Headed Records theory*. According to this account, information is represented in memory units called Records. Each unit is headed by an access key, or Heading, that enables retrieval of memories by describing the information in the Record. When people search for a memory, an attempt is made to match a description of a Record (e.g. the location of one's sunglasses) to an appropriate Heading. The misinformation effect, according to Morton *et al.*, results when the Headed Record for the originally witnessed information is relatively less accessible than the Headed Record for the misleading information. When subjects report the misleading information, they do so because the Headed Records for the original and misleading information are not distinguishable, but the misinformation record is more recent and therefore recalled more easily.

Another, more recent explanation for the misinformation effect involves the notion of *source misattribution*. Source misattribution theory states that some inaccurate memories are the result of confusion between the sources of events. The misinformation effect comes from a confusion of the origin of the original event information and that of the misleading postevent information (Johnson and Lindsay 1986). Traces for the original and misleading information might both be represented in memory, but the source of the misleading information is mistakenly attributed to that of the originally witnessed event. As in Headed Records theory, source misattribution leads to inaccuracy because the postevent misinformation is more recent and therefore more salient in memory; thus, it is incorrectly assumed to be a memory of what was originally seen.

In contrast to the alteration and coexistence theories, McCloskey and Zaragoza (1985) suggest that the misinformation effect has little to do with memory impairment at all. They argue instead that it results from two biases inherent in the standard testing procedure, namely 'misinformation acceptance' and 'demand characteristics'.

If, as they argue, subjects typically fail to notice the 'critical' details, non-misinformed (control) subjects will simply guess when faced with a forced choice between the original detail and the misinformation of the standard post-manipulation test. On the other hand, misled subjects who never encoded the original detail, yet do remember the misleading suggestion and accept it as truth, would be biased toward choosing the misleading option on the standard test. Thus, the 'Misinformation Effect', they argue, does not reflect memory impairment because the original information was never stored in the first place.

A second criticism of the standard testing procedure is that subjects may respond based on a demand characteristic. Even if a subject remembers the original information as well as the postevent information, on the test that subject may still respond with the misleading option. In this case, the subject might assume that the misinformation must be correct because the experimenter provided it, or because he or she wants to 'do well' on the test. In neither case would the subject's response actually reflect a change in memory.

To prove their point, McCloskey and Zaragoza (1985) performed a series of six experiments using a clever test modification. The test did not allow the subject the option of choosing the misinformation. Now they found that misled and control subjects performed equally.

They concluded that misinformation had no effect on memory. Other researchers have criticized the conclusions reached by McCloskey and Zaragoza, however. The modified test, they argue, is insensitive to subtle impairments of original memories (Belli 1989).

As a result of the criticisms levelled against both the standard and modified testing procedures, recent misinformation research designs attempt to eliminate the possibility of response bias, but remain sensitive to possible memory impairment. For example, Tversky and Tuchin (1989) used the standard misinformation procedure, but substituted a 'yes/no' recognition test rather than the standard or modified test. In this procedure, all subjects answered 'yes' or 'no' to questions about whether they saw the original critical item, the misinformation item, or a novel item never presented.

Results revealed a typical misinformation effect: Relative to control, misled subjects were less accurate at recognizing the original event item and incorrectly accepted the misinformation item. However, both sets of subjects were equally adept at correctly rejecting the novel item. In addition, misled subjects often gave 'yes' responses to more than one version of the critical item. That subjects demonstrated memory for both items suggests that, at least for some subjects, the original item and the misinformation item coexist in memory. Tversky and Tuchin concluded that misinformation does interfere with the ability to accurately recognize originally-witnessed details.

Another researcher, Belli (1989), agreed with McCloskey and Zaragoza that some subjects might respond with the misinformation item, not because their original memory was impaired, but because the original item was never stored in memory in the first place. However, he also hypothesized that at least some proportion of the effect could be the result of memory impairment due to the misinformation. If, Belli argued, misinformation acceptance can single-handedly account for the misinformation effect, then depressed original item performance will be countered by equal and opposite enhanced performance on the novel item. In contrast, if reduced performance on the originally seen item is greater than enhanced performance on the novel item, this would constitute evidence for memory impairment contributing to the misinformation effect. Belli found that the performance decrement on the original item exceeded the performance increment on the novel item, and concluded that misinformation was causing some impairment of event memories.

Lindsay (1990), applying the logic of opposition (Jacoby, Woloshyn and Kelley 1989) to the misinformation paradigm, created another clever means of separating the Misinformation Effect from confounds. Under the logic of opposition, subjects are instructed before the memory test that the details they remember from the postevent narrative are in error, and were not shown in the original presentation.

To illustrate, assume again that subjects were shown slides depicting a burglar holding a hammer. Later, subjects in the misled condition received a misleading suggestion that the burglar was holding a screwdriver. For control subjects, on the other hand, the narrative referred to the critical detail neutrally, simply describing it as a tool. A subject who knows that she read about a screwdriver would know that the tool in the slides was not a screwdriver, and would then have to search her memory further to try to recall the original hammer. However, if she remembers the screwdriver, but not the source of that information, she might incorrectly attribute this memory to the slide presentation and report having seen it. Because control subjects have no details to recall from the postevent narrative, their performance depends solely on memories from the slides.

Lindsay reasoned that if subjects report misleading suggestions at test, those inaccurate responses must reflect true memory confusions. In addition, he predicted that under conditions that decrease the discriminability of the original and postevent information in memory, one might expect more source confusions, and therefore a greater misinformation effect. Lindsay manipulated this factor by systematically differing the encoding conditions surrounding the original event from those surrounding the postevent narrative in the high-discriminability condition, and by lengthening the time between the original event and the postevent information. In the low-discriminability condition, the encoding conditions surrounding the two phases of the experiment were very similar, and the event and postevent information were presented in the same session.

Using a cued recall test (i.e. 'The burglar was holding a tool. What type of tool was shown in the slides?'), subjects were less likely to accurately recall the original event item (hammer) in the misled condition than in the control condition. In addition, misled subjects were more likely than controls to report the postevent item in the low-discriminability condition but were no more likely to do so in the high-discriminability condition. Lindsay concluded that in the high-discriminability condition subjects were better able to identify the source of their postevent memory, and could thus avoid inaccurately-reporting the misinformation as the original.

However, source misattribution cannot explain why, in the high-discriminability condition, although subjects were able to accurately identify the source of their postevent memories and avoid reporting them, they were still unable to correctly recall the correct detail from the slides. Lindsay interpreted this finding as evidence that misleading suggestions, even when not reported at test, can impair subjects' ability to correctly recall originally-witnessed details.

In sum, the research addressing the permanence of memory traces has, over the past decade, yielded results to support multiple hypotheses. The question of whether or not the original trace of critical information is altered has not been unequivocally answered, and the debate rages on. Future research must further delineate the conditions that are conducive to such memory interference. However, the recent findings of Lindsay and others support the notion that eyewitness memory is malleable.

Memory reports for an event can be altered by later-acquired knowledge. The next section describes some ways psychology has contributed, and can contribute to use of the eyewitness by the legal finder of fact.

RETRIEVING MEMORIES – IMPLICATIONS FOR THE LEGAL SYSTEM

How players in the legal system gather information is likely to affect the accuracy of that information. Some methods of information gathering are conducive to full and accurate retrieval, whereas others may contribute to errors at the retrieval stage, including misidentifications, or they may allow witnesses to fail to remember details of the original event.

Interviews

Question type and wording

There is some truth to the maxim: 'The answer you get depends on the question you ask'. Different types of questioning lead to different kinds of retrieval. Interviewers may use fixed-answer or multiple-choice questions ('Was the light green or red?'), directed questions ('What colour jacket was he wearing?'), or more open-ended questions ('What did you see?'). Considerable information can be introduced into the memory of an eyewitness simply by limiting the answer options. Interviewers should take into account the specific way questions are worded. Care must be taken by police and other interviewers to avoid altering the memories of witnesses by asking loaded questions.

For example, in a highly controlled interrogatory format, where witnesses are asked specific questions, and must choose among listed answers (*multiple-choice* format), erroneous responses can be elicited. On the other hand, when open-ended, or *continuous-narrative* format is used, witnesses tend to be the most accurate, although also the least complete. That is, witnesses remember fewer details, but they also include fewer errors in their descriptions of events (Lipton 1977; Snee and Lush 1941). When specific questions are asked, but the field of possible answers is not limited (*controlled-narrative* format), witnesses can give short answers in narrative form and the interviewer can probe for information the witness might not otherwise recall. Here again, care must be taken that errors are not induced by the form.

Combining narratives and specific questions may yield an optimal mix of accuracy and completeness, while minimizing the potential for introducing biasing information. In such an interview, witnesses would first be asked to recall the event freely. Only then, in order to fill in gaps in the narrative, would questions be asked about specific details (Geiselman, Fisher, Firstenberg, Hutton, Sullivan, Avetissian and Prosket 1984; Hilgard and Loftus 1979; Timm 1983). Multiple choice questions should be asked with caution.

Given the potential biasing effects of postevent information, open-ended, non-leading questions would be least likely to introduce damaging postevent information. Thus, police should neither assume information from one informant is correct nor incorporate such information into subsequent interviews of any witnesses. Rather, police interviewers should avoid any reference to information collected from other witnesses, including descriptions of suspects, event details, and estimates of time intervals. Furthermore, interviewers should remain impassive, careful not to reinforce eyewitness testimony. Reinforcement (e.g. nodding the head, eager verbal replies, etc.) may reinforce any errors the witness makes, and may also encourage guessing (Hastie, Lansman and Loftus 1978).

Even small changes in the wording of questions can influence memory reports in substantial ways. For example, Harris (1973) showed that simply by asking subjects 'How tall was the basketball player?' as opposed to 'How short was the basketball player?' resulted in a 10 inch mean differential (79 v. 69 inches, respectively). Clearly, careful attention to non-biased wording of questions is essential to accurate memory retrieval.

The combination of type of interview and the wording of questions may profoundly influence the accuracy of an eyewitness's testimony. Interviewers should be careful not to inject any bias into questions, by keeping them relatively open-ended, non-assumptive, and allowing witnesses to give open narratives whenever possible. If necessary, these might be followed by more specific, but again carefully worded, questions about additional event details.

Improving retrieval

Hypnosis

Despite the fact that the use of hypnosis has found a niche in common lore and has been employed in many famous criminal cases, research about the efficacy of hypnosis has been much more sober. Although there has been occasional empirical support for the effectiveness of hypnosis in witness recall (e.g. Geiselman, Fisher, MacKinnon and Holland 1985), its use remains controversial. Myriad problems with the methods and interpretations have led many researchers to question its overall helpfulness in memory enhancement. After a comprehensive review of hypnosis research, Orne, Soskis, Dinges and Orne (1984) concluded that 'hypnotically induced testimony is not reliable' and that information recalled under hypnosis should not be considered accurate unless corroborated by independent physical evidence.

Courts in the USA worry that information retrieved via hypnosis may be especially susceptible to the types of interviewer biases described above. The outcome that the interviewer expects or wants may become the testimony of the witness after hypnosis. Thus, many jurisdictions in the USA now prohibit witnesses whose memories have been enhanced by hypnosis from testifying in court.

Context reinstatement

This method of facilitating, eyewitness memory does exactly what its name implies. It recreates, as closely as possible, the context of the event in question. Some research has shown that 'priming' subjects with some details of an event increases accurate recall of other aspects of the event (e.g. Krafka and Penrod 1985). Thus, reinstating as many factors as possible, such as the exact location, time of day, lighting, noise level, etc., has been hypothesized to help witnesses retrieve memories more accurately and more fully.

Malpass and Devine (1981) began to explore this hypothesis with subject-witnesses who were exposed to a staged (but surprise) act of vandalism. Several months later the same subjects were asked to identify the perpetrator from a photographic lineup in one of two conditions. One group was asked to identify the suspect 'cold', and only 40 per cent of subjects did so correctly. The other group was guided through sequential recall and reconstruction of the event and objects associated with the original 'crime'. In contrast to the first group, 60 per cent of this group correctly identified the suspect.

However, the efficacy of context reinstatement as a memory enhancement technique has been questioned by other researchers. McCloskey and Zaragoza (1985) found no effect of context reinstatement, and Loftus, Manber and Keating (1983) found a small negative effect. Thus, although somewhat promising, context reinstatement remains a somewhat hit and miss procedure for memory enhancement. For a recent volume on context effects see Davies and Thomson (1988).

Cognitive interview

In contrast to hypnosis, the use of a 'cognitive interview' seems quite promising as a method for enhancing memory (Fisher, Geiselman and Raymond 1987; Geiselman, Fisher, MacKinnon and Holland 1985, 1986). Building upon elements of context reinstatement, the cognitive interview adds other mnemonic techniques in a specific methodological format. Witnesses are asked to systematically mentally reinstate the various situational and personal details of the event. The following is taken from Geiselman *et al.* (1985), which compared the cognitive interview with hypnosis and the standard police interview:

A four-item list of the techniques was placed in full view of the witness during the entire interview as a reference guide.

The following descriptions of the techniques were read by the interviewer to the subject verbatim at the beginning of the interview:

(a) Reinstate the Context: Try to reinstate in your mind the context surrounding the incident. Think about what the surrounding environment looked like at the scene, such as rooms, the weather, any nearby people or objects. Also think about how you were feeling at the time and think about your reactions to the incident.

(b) Report Everything: People hold back information because they are not quite sure that the information is important. Please do not edit anything out of your report, even things you think may not be important.

(c) Recall the Events in Different Orders: It is natural to go through the incident from beginning to end. However, you also should try to go through the events in reverse order. Or, try starting with the thing that impressed you the most in the incident and then go from there, working both forward in time and backward.

(d) Change Perspectives: Try to recall the incident from different perspectives that you may have had, or adopt the perspectives of others that were present during the incident. For example, try to place yourself in the role of a prominent character in the incident and think about what he or she must have seen.

These techniques are designed to create as many recall cues as possible, in hopes that some of them will trigger otherwise unrecalled details of the event.

Several studies have found the use of the cognitive interview to result in significantly greater accuracy compared with hypnosis, and with standard police interviewing techniques. Further, it does not generally lead to the generation of more incorrect information or increased eyewitness confidence in the incorrect information, as does hypnosis. For these reasons, the cognitive interview technique may be a highly significant contribution of cognitive psychology to the legal system.

Photo spreads and lineups (identity parades)

One important state in the eyewitness process occurs when the eyewitness makes an identification. In one real-world interview study of lineup practice in Northern England, researchers found that a significantly larger percentage of witnesses who failed to identify a suspect reported feelings of nervousness, as compared with witnesses who did identify the suspect (Ainsworth and King 1988). The authors point out that while the psychological research which addresses the effects of stress on memory is plentiful, 'surprisingly, very few practical steps are taken in an attempt to make the witness's task easier', or to improve witness accuracy (Ainsworth and King 1988: 68). They suggest that the use of one-way mirrors to restrict suspects' vision of the witness, and 'notes of guidance', intended to familiarize witnesses with the lineup procedure, might improve witnesses' ability to pick out perpetrators, by reducing stress levels during the memory retrieval task involved in the lineup test.

Other researchers have pointed out that at times the witness's job is too easy. For example, after pointing out that a lineup is essentially a multiple-choice recognition test, Loftus (1979) states:

> Although in theory witnesses know that the culprit may not be [present], in practice many witnesses believe that the police would not be conducting the test unless they had a good suspect. Thus, they try hard to identify the true criminal, but failing that, they often indicate the person who best matches their recollection of the criminal.
>
> The composition of the lineup is [therefore] a matter of great importance; how many people are in it, what the people look like, what they are wearing – all these are crucial issues that can influence the degree to which the lineup is free from suggestive influences and thus determine its value. [I]t is important that the persons, other than the suspect, be similar to the suspect in appearance. Otherwise the 'distractors' can be immediately rejected as implausible and the true suspect picked by default.

In attempting to quantify the fairness of a lineup to the suspected perpetrator, Wells *et al.* (1977) created a procedure for calculating the 'functional size' of a lineup. A random sample of non-witnesses is provided with a general description of the suspect, and shown photographs of the members of the lineup. If the lineup is fair, the non-witnesses should pick out the suspect with no more than chance levels of accuracy. If the lineup is biased, the suspect will be chosen more often that the other lineup members (called 'foils'). The functional size is the number of non-witness participants divided by the number of them who pick the suspect. Thus if half of the participants, who never saw the criminal, pick out the suspect, the functional size of the lineup is two, regardless of the number of foils present.

In such a situation, the fact that a witness picked the suspect is much weaker evidence than if the functional size of the lineup is large. Defence attorneys would therefore be well advised to photograph the lineups in which their clients stand, and then perform this test. If the lineup is unfair, the test results can be used to lessen the impact of a witness's recognition of the client.

Photographs of suspects are often used by the police as well. When a crime has been committed, witnesses will frequently be presented with photographs of potential suspects and asked if they recognize anyone. Sometimes, only one photograph is shown. If a witness picks out one of the suspects from the photograph, a common next step is to form a lineup with the suspect and a number of foils. Even if the functional size of a lineup is fair, the fact that the witness has already seen the suspect's photo may cause a bias.

Brown, Deffenbacher, and Sturgill (1977) showed dramatic evidence of this bias in a laboratory study. Subject-witnesses viewed two groups of five 'criminals' (total strangers) for 25 seconds each. The subjects were told to scrutinize the criminals carefully since they might have to pick them out from mugshots later that evening and from a lineup the following week. About an hour and a half later the subjects viewed fifteen 'mugshots', or photographs of 'suspects', including some people who were the 'criminals' seen earlier, and some who were not. One week later several lineups were staged and the subject-witnesses were asked to indicate whether each person had been seen at the original 'crime' scene.

Of the people in the lineup who had never been seen before, 8 per cent were mistakenly identified as 'criminals'. However, if a person's 'mugshot' had been seen, his chances of being falsely identified as one of the 'criminals', rose to 20 per cent. None of these people had been among the 'criminals', nor had they ever been seen in person before, but they were now 'recognized' in the lineup because their photograph had been seen earlier.

Confidence and accuracy in memory

Every trial attorney knows that a confident witness is much more believable that one who is hesitant or unsure. Jurors and judges simply lend more credence to testimony given with solid certainty; a fact amply supported by empirical research (Wells, Ferguson and Lindsay 1981; Lindsay, Wells and O'Connor 1989; Fox and Walters 1986: Whitley and Greenberg 1986, among others). In fact, in a laboratory study of juror decision making, Cutler, Penrod and Stuve (1988) found witness confidence to be the *only* significant predictor of jurors' judgements of the probability that the accused was guilty. Out of ten manipulated witness and situational variables (e.g. apparent confidence of witness, retention interval, stressfulness of event), only witness confidence reliably affected jury verdicts. In the USA, witness confidence even has the backing of the Supreme Court. In Neil v. Biggers (1972) the US Supreme Court codified witness certainty as one of the five criteria for evaluating the reliability of eyewitness identification, making it legally relevant to the conviction or acquittal of an accused person.

Unfortunately, this great reliance on eyewitness self-reported certainty is largely undeserved. Research suggests that the degree to which a witness's confidence actually relates to accurate identifications is quite low, or at most only moderate (Clifford and Scott 1978; Wells 1978; Wells, Lindsay and Ferguson 1979; Bothwell, Deffenbacher and Brigham 1987). Estimates of the strength of the correlation between confidence and accuracy range from a correlation coefficient of 0.08 to one of 0.42 (Bothwell *et al.*, 1987). Thus, in general, witnesses who express solid certainty in their testimony are not necessarily more accurate than those who allow for the possibility that they could be mistaken.

However, this statement does not describe the whole picture. While the relationship between confidence and accuracy does not, in the general case, deserve the reliance it receives from systems of justice, situational factors do appear to influence the relationship. An explanation offered by Deffenbacher (1980), the 'optimality hypothesis', predicts that any improvement in witnessing conditions will result in a stronger relationship between confidence and accuracy. As yet, the hypothesis appears to be holding up to empirical scrutiny.

For example, the length of time the witness has to observe the target person's face appears to increase the correlation between confidence and accuracy in memory (Deffenbacher 1980; Bothwell *et al.* 1987). Additionally, the distinctiveness and attractiveness of the target person's face, both of which are predictors of the level of accuracy a typical subject will show in identifying a target, appear to be related to the correlation between confidence and accuracy.

41

Brigham (1990) showed that less distinctive-looking targets yielded lower correlations than did targets who were average or above average in distinctiveness, and that lessening the attractiveness of the target also strengthened the correlation.

Finally, Clifford and Hollin (1981), and Brigham, Maass, Martinez and Whittenberger (1983) have found that increased arousal reduced the confidence accuracy correlation. In both studies, while the confidence accuracy relationship was significant under moderate arousal conditions, higher arousal either reduced the correlation to non-significant levels, or reduced the number of subjects whose correlations were significant. Thus, when accuracy is likely to be higher because of either witness or event factors contributing to the optimality of the viewing conditions, the confidence expressed by the witness should be given some credence.

What if a witness is tested on lots of details. Will she be more confident on correct details than on incorrect details? Smith, Kassin and Ellsworth (1989), using a within-subjects approach, addressed this issue, they compared confidence and accuracy of particular subjects on large numbers of memory reports. They, too, conclude that witness confidence is not a useful predictor of the accuracy of memory.

These results point towards cautious use of witness confidence by the courts. In some situations witness confidence may relate to identification accuracy, but knowing when this relationship is likely to exist is expertise rarely possessed by psychological laypeople. Given this situation, one solution to courtroom overreliance on witness confidence may be to inform judges and jurors about the lack of consistent relationship between confidence and accuracy.

EDUCATING THE LEGAL SYSTEM

We have suggested that eyewitness testimony is not always as reliable as both jurors and courts believe: Eyewitnesses are susceptible to incorrect postevent information, often incorporating it into their memories of events. Even a confident eyewitness is not necessarily a more accurate eyewitness, although courts and jurors may tend to think so. But juries are impressed with confident testimony and, as a result, accused defendants are sometimes convicted despite their innocence, and the guilty party goes free.

Various solutions have been proposed to reduce and make more appropriate the credence lent to eyewitnesses (e.g. Woocher 1978).

Eyewitness testimony might never be allowed, if it is the sole evidence supporting a conviction; other corroborating evidence could be required. In actuality, courts and attorneys are very much wedded to the use of eyewitnesses. They cannot be excluded, nor can corroborating evidence be required in every case, because of the great increase in the likelihood that guilty people would go free. Exclusion of eyewitness testimony, or creating the necessity of corroborating evidence, would take too much away from prosecutors. Instead, what can be done is to try to make judges and jurors aware of the psychological facts; to educate them. Two methods are available to this end, special jury instructions and the testimony of experts.

Jury instructions are intended to inform the jury about how they should apply the law to the facts presented. They would therefore appear to be the ideal method for informing the jury how to evaluate eyewitness testimony. They could include information about the effects of various perceptual factors, such as the duration of the observation, the distances involved, the light or lack of light, and the witness's state of mind at the time. They could also include descriptions of the possibilities of postevent misinformation and biased lineups, and of the effects of the length of time between observation and identification.

The judicial systems of both the USA and Great Britain have considered the use of jury instructions (see United States v. Telfaire 1972; Devlin 1976). In many jurisdictions in the USA, the judge is not allowed to comment on the evidence, and therefore cannot help the jury apply the various memory factors listed. In addition, jury instructions are often long and tedious, and are often not well understood, or well considered by the jury (Charrow and Charrow 1979; Sales, Elwork and Alfini 1978). In Great Britain, where judges have much greater powers to comment upon the evidence, a report by Lord Devlin to the Home Secretary in 1976 recommended that judges inform juries of the appropriateness of convictions based upon eyewitness testimony. If no corroborating evidence exists and there are no exceptional circumstances surrounding the identification, the report recommends that the judge direct the jury to return a verdict of guilty.

However, even in Great Britain, where juries may be more likely to follow their instructions, the judge giving the instructions is not an expert in the psychological issues surrounding eyewitness memory. Instead, an expert in the field could be brought in. This expert could tell the jury how to apply the scientific research to the particular case at hand (see, e.g., Loftus and Ketcham 1991). In this way, the jury would have more information with which to evaluate the eyewitness evidence fully and properly.

And, in fact, the presence of expert testimony regarding the quality of eyewitness testimony has been shown to affect the impact of the eyewitness on the jury. Cutler, Penrod and Dexter (1989) asked subjects to view a realistic mock-trial on videotape. In the trial, several aspects of the evidence were varied, including the presence or absence of expert testimony. Subjects who heard the expert testimony gave more weight to witnessing and identification conditions, and less weight to witness confidence when evaluating the accuracy of the identification.

Fox and Walters (1986) also studied expert testimony. In their research, both general and specific expert testimony were compared with no testimony on the reliability of eyewitnesses, and witness confidence was manipulated to two levels: high and low confidence conditions. Expert testimony lowered subjects' estimates of the accuracy of the eyewitness and increased their knowledge of the eyewitness behaviour. However, subjects were still impressed with witness confidence. Mock-jurors viewing high-confidence witnesses believed that the defendant was more guilty than did those viewing low-confidence witnesses. The researchers suggest that the effect of witness confidence may have endured, despite expert testimony about its unreliability, because the witness appeared *before* the expert in the course of the trial.

Nevertheless, experts can apparently have a partially desired effect. The ideal education method would present the facts of the eyewitness research simply and clearly, in such a way that the decision maker could adequately understand and apply the information to the case. Although criticisms have been raised that the use of experts can be confusing, especially when each side brings expert testimony to bear, no one has yet proposed a better solution to the problem of wrongful convictions and verdicts based on faulty eyewitness testimony.

Few moments are more dramatic than a courtroom identification, this is clear. But how reliable is that identification? We have tried in this chapter to provide some insight into the complexity of this question and its answers. The memory triad, (perception, retention, and retrieval) is a malleable structure, susceptible to distortion under certain circumstances. It is our goal to educate potential jurors, as well as whole legal systems, about the specifics of those questionable circumstances in order to improve the likelihood that justice is done.

ACKNOWLEDGEMENT

The writing of this chapter was supported in part by grants from the National Institute of Mental Health and the National Science Foundation.

REFERENCES

Ainsworth, P.B. (1981) 'Incident perception by British police officers', *Law and Human Behavior* 5: 231–6.

Ainsworth, P.B. and King, E. (1988) 'Witnesses' perceptions of identification parades, in M.M. Gruneberg, P.E. Morris and R.N. Sykes (eds.) *Practical Aspects of Memory: Current Research and Issues*, vol. 1, London: Wiley.

Bekerian, D.A., and Bowers, J.M. (1983) 'Eyewitness testimony: Were we misled?', *Journal of Experimental Psychology: Learning, Memory and Cognition* 9: 139–45.

Belli, R.F. (1988) 'Color blend retrievals: Compromise memories or deliberate compromise responses', *Memory and Cognition* 16: 314–26.

Belli, R.F. (1989) 'Influences of misleading post-event information: Misinformation interference and acceptance', *Journal of Experimental Psychology: General* 118: 72–85.

Bothwell, R.K., Deffenbacher, K.A. and Brigham, J.C. (1987) 'Correlation of eyewitness accuracy and confidence: Optimality hypothesis revisited', *Journal of Applied Psychology* 72: 691–5.

Brigham, J.C. (1990) 'Target person distinctiveness and attractiveness and moderator variables in the confidence accuracy relationship in eyewitness identifications', *Basic and Applied Social Psychology* 11: 101–15.

Brigham, J.C., Maass, A., Martinez, D. and Whittenberger, G. (1983) 'The effect of arousal on facial recognition', *Basic and Applied Social Psychology* 4: 279–93.

Brown, E., Deffenbacher, K., and Sturgill, W. (1977) 'Memory for faces and the circumstances of encounter', *Journal of Applied Psychology* 62: 311–18.

Ceci, S.J., Ross, D.F. and Toglia, M.P. (1987) 'Suggestibility of children's memory: Psycholegal implications', *Journal of Experimental Psychology: General* 116: 38–49.

Ceci, S.J., Toglia, M.P. and Ross, D.F. (1988) 'On remembering . . . more or less: A trace strength interpretation of developmental differences in suggestibility', *Journal of Experimental Psychology: General* 11: 201–3.

Chandler, C.C. (1989) 'Specific retroactive interference in modified recognition tests: Evidence for an unknown cause of interference', *Journal of Experimental Psychology: Learning, Memory and Cognition* 15: 256–65.

Charrow, R.P. and Charrow, V.R. (1979) 'Making legal language understandable', *Columbia Law Review* 79: 1306–74.

Christiaansen, R.E. and Ochalek, K. (1983) 'Editing misleading information from memory: Evidence for the coexistence of original and post-event information', *Memory and Cognition* 11: 467–75.

Christianson, S.A. and Loftus, E.F. (1991) 'Remembering emotional events: The fate of detailed information', *Cognition and Emotion* 5: 81–108.

Christianson, S.A., Loftus, E.F., Hoffman, H. and Loftus, G.R. (1991) 'Eye fixations and accuracy in detail memory of emotional neutral events', *Journal of Experimental Psychology: Learning, Memory and Cognition*, 17: 693–701.

Clifford, B.R. (1976) 'Police as eyewitnesses', *New Society* 36: 176–7.

Clifford, B.R. and Hollin, C. (1981) 'Effects of type of incident and the number of perpetrators on eyewitness memory', *Journal of Applied Psychology* 66: 364–70.

Clifford, B.R. and Scott, J. (1978) 'Individual and situational factors in eyewitness testimony', *Journal of Applied Psychology* 63: 352–9.

Cutler, B.L., Penrod, S.D. and Stuve, T.E. (1988) 'Juror decision making in eyewitness identification cases', *Law and Human Behavior* 12: 41–55.

Cutler, B.L., Penrod, S.D. and Dexter, H.R. (1989) 'The eyewitness, the expert psychologist, and the jury', *Law and Human Behavior* 13: 311–32.

Darley, J.M. and Gross, P.H. (1983) 'A hypothesis-confirming bias in labelling effects', *Journal of Personality and Social Psychology* 44: 20–33.

Davies, G. and Thomson, D. (eds) (1988) *Memory in Context: Context in Memory*, New York: Wiley.

Deffenbacher, K.A. (1980) 'Eyewitness accuracy and confidence: Can we infer anything about their relationship?', *Law and Human Behavior* 4: 243–60.

Deffenbacher, K.A. (1983) 'The influence of arousal on reliability of testimony', in S.M.A. Lloyd-Bostock and B.R. Clifford (eds) *Evaluating Witness Evidence*, pp. 235–51, Chichester: Wiley.

Dent, H.R. (1988) 'Children's eyewitness evidence: A brief review', in M.M. Gruneberg, P.E. Morris and R.N. Sykes (eds) *Practical Aspects of Memory: current research and issues*, vol. 1, pp. 101–6, Chichester: Wiley.

Devlin, Honourable Lord Patrick (chair) (1976) *Report to the Secretary of State for the Home Department of the Departmental Committee on Evidence of Identification in Criminal Cases*, London: Her Majesty's Stationery Office.

Dritsas, W.J. and Hamilton, V.L. (1977) 'Evidence about evidence: Effects of presuppositions, item salience, stress, and perceiver set on accident recall', unpublished manuscript, University of Michigan.

Ebbinghaus, H.E. (1885/1964) *Memory: A Contribution to Experimental Psychology*, New York: Dover.

Farrimond, T. (1968) 'Retention and recall: Incidental learning of visual and auditory material', *Journal of Genetic Psychology* 113: 155–65.

Fisher, R.P., Geiselman, R.E. and Raymond, D.S. (1987) 'Critical analysis of police interview techniques', *Journal of Police Science and Administration* 15: 177–85.

Fox, S.G. and Walters, H.A. (1986) 'The impact of general versus specific expert testimony and eyewitness confidence upon mock juror judgment', *Law and Human Behavior* 10: 215–28.

Geiselman, R.E., Fisher, R.P., Firstenberg, I., Hutton, L.A., Sullivan

S., Avetissian, I. and Prosket, A. (1984) 'Enhancement of eyewitness memory: An empirical evaluation of the cognitive interview', *Journal of Police Science and Administration* 12: 74–80.

Geiselman, R.E., Fisher, R.P., MacKinnon, D.P. and Holland, H.L. (1985) 'Eyewitness memory enhancement in the police interview: Cognitive retrieval mnemonics versus hypnosis', *Journal of Applied Psychology* 70: 401–12.

Geiselman, R.E., Fisher, R.P., MacKinnon, D.P. and Holland, H.L. (1986) 'Enhancement of eyewitness memory with the cognitive interview', *American Journal of Psychology* 99: 385–401.

Goodman, G.S. and Reed, R.S. (1986) 'Age differences in eyewitness testimony', *Law and Human Behavior* 10: 317–32.

Gross, S.R. (1987) 'Loss of innocence: Eyewitness identification and proof of guilt', *Journal of Legal Studies* XVI: 396–453.

Harris, R.J. (1973) 'Answering questions containing marked and unmarked adjectives and adverbs', *Journal of Experimental Psychology* 97: 399–401.

Hastie, R., Lansman, R. and Loftus, E.F. (1978) 'Eyewitness testimony: The dangers of guessing', *Jurimetrics Journal* 19: 1–8.

Hastorf, A.H. and Cantril, H. (1954) 'They saw the game: A case study', *Journal of Abnormal and Social Psychology* 49: 129–34.

Heuer, F. and Reisberg, D. (1990) 'Vivid memories of emotional events: The accuracy of remembered minutiae', *Memory and Cognition* 18: 496–506.

Hilgard, E.R. and Loftus, E.F. (1979) 'Effective interrogation of the eyewitness', *International Journal of Clinical and Experimental Hypnosis* 27: 342–57.

Jacoby, L.L., Woloshyn, V. and Kelley, C.M. (1989) 'Becoming famous without being recognized: Unconscious influences of memory produced by dividing attention', *Journal of Experimental Psychology: General* 118: 115–25.

Johnson, M.K. and Lindsay, D.S. (1986) 'Despite McCloskey and Zaragoza, suggestibility effects may reflect memory impairment', unpublished manuscript, Department of Psychology, Princeton University.

King, M.S. and Yuille, J.C. (1987) 'Suggestibility and the child witness', in S.J. Ceci, M.P. Toglia and D.F. Ross (eds) *Children's Eyewitness Memory*, pp. 24–35, New York: Springer.

Krafka, C. and Penrod, S. (1985) 'Reinstatement of context in a field experiment on eyewitness identification', *Journal of Personality and Social Psychology* 49: 58–69.

Kramer, T.H., Buckhout, R. and Eugenio, P. (1990) 'Weapon focus, arousal, and eyewitness memory: attention must be paid', *Law and Human Behavior* 14: 167–84.

Laughery, K.R., Alexander, J.E. and Lane, A.B. (1971) 'Recognition of human faces: Effects of target exposure time, target position, pose position, and type of photograph', *Journal of Applied Psychology* 55: 477–83.

Lesgold, A.M. and Petrush, A.R. (1977) 'Do leading questions alter memories?', unpublished manuscript, University of Pittsburgh.

Lindsay, D.S. (1990) 'Misleading suggestions can impair eyewitness's ability to remember event details', *Journal of Experimental Psychology: Learning, Memory and Cognition*, 16: 1077–83.

Lindsay, R.C., Wells, G.L. and O'Connor, F.J. (1989) 'Mock-juror belief of accurate and inaccurate eyewitnesses: A replication and extension', *Law and Human Behavior* 13: 333–9.

Lipton, J.P. (1977) 'On the psychology of eyewitness testimony', *Journal of Applied Psychology* 62: 90–3.

List, J. (1986) 'Age and schematic differences in the reliability of eyewitness testimony', *Developmental Psychology* 22: 50–7.

Loftus, E.F. (1975) 'Leading questions and the eyewitness report', *Cognitive Psychology* 7: 560–72.

Loftus, E.F. (1977) 'Shifting human color memory', *Memory and Cognition* 5: 696–9.

Loftus, E.F. (1979) *Eyewitness Testimony*, Cambridge, Massachusetts: Harvard University Press.

Loftus, E.F. (1984) 'Eyewitnesses: Essential but unreliable', *Psychology Today* Feb: 22–6.

Loftus, E.F. and Burns (1982) 'Mental shock can produce retrograde amnesia', *Memory and Cognition* 10: 318–23.

Loftus, E.F. and Hoffman, H.G. (1989) 'Misinformation and memory: The creation of memory', *Journal of Experimental Psychology: General* 118: 100–4.

Loftus, E.F. and Ketcham, K. (1991) *Witness for the Defense*, New York: St. Martin's Press.

Loftus, E.F., Levidow, B. and Duensing, S. (1991) 'Who remembers best?: Individual differences in memory for events that occurred in a science museum', *Applied Cognitive Psychology* (in press).

Loftus, E.F., Loftus, G.R. and Messo, J. (1987) 'Some facts about weapon focus', *Law and Human Behavior* 11: 55–62.

Loftus, E.F., Manber, M. and Keating, J.P. (1983) 'Recollection of naturalistic events: Context enhancement versus negative cueing', *Human Learning* 2: 83–92.

Loftus, E.F., Miller, D.G. and Burns, H.J. (1978) 'Semantic integration of verbal information into visual memory', *Journal of Experimental Psychology: Human Learning and Memory* 4: 19–31.

Loftus, E.F., Schooler, J.W., Boone, S.M. and Kline, D. (1987) 'Time went by so slowly: Overestimation of event duration by males and females', *Applied Cognitive Psychology* 1: 3–13.

Maass, A. and Kohnken, G. (1989) 'Eyewitness identification: Simulating the "weapon effect"', *Law and Human Behavior* 13: 397–408.

McCloskey, M. and Zaragoza, M. (1985) 'Misleading post-event information and memory for events: Arguments and evidence against memory impairment hypotheses', *Journal of Experimental Psychology* 114: 1–16.

Malpass, R.S. and Devine, P.G. (1981) 'Guided memory in eyewitness identification', *Journal of Applied Psychology* 66: 343–50.

Morton, J., Hammersley, R.H. and Bekerian, D.A. (1985) 'Headed records: A model for memory and its failures', *Cognition* 20: 1–23.

Neil v. Biggers (1972) 409 US 188, 93 S.Ct. 575, 34 L.Ed.2d 401.

Orne, M.T., Soskis, D.A., Dinges, D.F. and Orne, E.C. (1984) 'Hypnotically induced testimony', in G. Wells and E. Loftus (eds), *Eyewitness Testimony: Psychological Perspectives*, Cambridge: Cambridge University Press.

Peters, D.P. (1988) 'Eyewitness memory and arousal in a natural setting', in M.M. Gruneberg, P.E. Morris and R.N. Sykes (eds), *Practical Aspects of Memory: Current Research and Issues*, Vol. 1, pp. 89–94, Chichester: Wiley.

Peterson, M.A. (1976) *Witnesses: Memory of Social Events*, unpublished doctoral dissertation, University of California at Los Angeles.

Radin, E.D. (1964) *The Innocents*, New York: William Morrow.

Rubenstein, C. (1982) 'Psychology's fruit flies', *Psychology Today*, July: 83–4.

Sales, B.D., Elwork, A. and Alfini, J.J. (1978) 'Improving comprehension for jury instructions', in B.D. Sales (ed.)*Perspectives in Law and Psychology*, New York: Plenum.

Sheehan, P.W. (1989) 'Response to suggestions of memory distortions in hypnosis: Sampling cognitive and social factors', in V.A. Gheorghiu, P. Netter, H.J. Eysenck and R. Rosenthal (eds) *Suggestion and Suggestibility: Theory and Research*, pp. 295–303, Berlin: Springer.

Smith, V.L., Kassin, S.M. and Ellsworth, P.C. (1989) 'Eyewitness accuracy and confidence: Within versus between-subjects correlations', *Journal of Applied Psychology*, 74: 356–9.

Snee, T.J. and Lush, D.E. (1941) 'Interaction of the narrative and interrogatory methods of obtaining testimony', *Journal of Psychology* 11: 229–36.

Snyder, M. and Swann, W.B., Jr (1978) 'Behavioral confirmation in social interaction: From social perception to social reality', *Journal of Experimental Social Psychology*, 14: 148–62.

Snyder, M., Tanke, E. D. and Bersheid, E. (1977) 'Social perception and interpersonal behavior: On the self-fulfilling nature of social stereotypes', *Journal of Personality and Social Psychology* 35: 656–66.

Tickner, A.H. and Poulton, E.C. (1975) 'Watching for people and actions', *Ergonomics* 18: 35–51.

Timm, H.W. (1983) 'The factors theoretically affecting the impact of forensic hypnosis techniques on eyewitness recall', *Journal of Police Science and Administration* 11: 442–50.

Tversky, B. and Tuchin, M. (1989) 'A reconciliation of the evidence on eyewitness testimony: Comments on McCloskey and Zaragoza', *Journal of Experimental Psychology: General* 118: 86–91.

United States v. Telfaire (1972) 469 F.2d 552; 152 U.S. App D.C. 146.

Wagenaar, W.A., and Groeneweg, J. (1990) 'The memory of concentration camp survivors', *Applied Cognitive Psychology* 4: 77–87.

Wells, G.L. (1978) 'Applied eyewitness-testimony research: system variables and estimator variables', *Journal of Personality and Social Psychology* 12: 1546–57.

Wells, G.L., Ferguson, T.J. and Lindsay, C.L. (1981) 'The tractability of eyewitness confidence and its implications for triers of fact', *Journal of Applied Psychology* 66: 688–96.

Wells, G.L., Leippe, M.R., Baumgartner, M.H., Simpson, D.D., Lingle, J.,

Geva, N., Petty, R.E., Bassett, R.L. and Ostrom, T.M. (1977) 'Guidelines for empirically assessing the fairness of a lineup', unpublished manuscript, Ohio State University.

Wells, G.L., Lindsay, C.L. and Ferguson, T.J. (1979) 'Accuracy, confidence, and juror perception in eyewitness identification', *Journal of Applied Psychology* 64: 440–8.

Whitley, B.E. and Greenberg, M.S. (1986) 'The role of eyewitness confidence in juror perceptions of credibility', *Journal of Applied Social Psychology* 16: 387–409.

Wilkinson, J. (1988) 'Context effects in children's event memory', in M.M. Gruneberg, P.E. Morris and R.N. Sykes (eds) *Practical Aspects of Memory: Current Research and Issues*, vol. 1, pp. 107–11, Chichester: Wiley.

Woocher, F.D. (1977) 'Did your eyes deceive you? Expert psychological testimony on the unreliability of eyewitness identification', *Stanford Law Review* 29: 969–1030.

Yarmey, A.D. (1986) 'Perceived expertness and credibility of police officers as eyewitnesses', *Canadian Police College Journal* 10: 31–52.

Yarmey, A.D. and Jones, H.P.T. (1983) 'Is the psychology of eyewitness identification a matter of common sense?', in S.M.A. Lloyd-Bostock and B.R. Clifford (eds) *Evaluating Witness Evidence*, pp. 13–40, Chichester: Wiley.

Yerkes, R.M. and Dodson, J.D. (1908) 'The relation of strength of stimulus to rapidity of habit-formation', *Journal of Comparative and Neurological Psychology* 18: 459–82.

Yuille, J.C. (1984) 'Research and teaching with police: A Canadian example', *International Review of Applied Psychology* 33: 5–24.

Yuille, J.C. and Cutshall, J.L. (1986) 'A case study of eyewitness memory of a crime', *Journal of Applied Psychology* 71: 291–301.

3

FACE MEMORY –
THEORY AND PRACTICE

Hadyn D. Ellis and John W. Shepherd

When we began our research into memory for faces some twenty
years ago, there was only a small literature on the topic and no
theory at all (see Ellis 1975). We have been, in turn, surprised and
pleased at the rapid developments in both data collection and model
building that have taken place in the last two decades. By 1985 some
six hundred publications in psychological sources had been accumu-
lated (Ellis 1986a); and, since the rate of progress was exponential,
the number by now must be in excess of a thousand. Included among
this body of literature are at least seven books devoted entirely to
face memory (Davies, Ellis and Shepherd 1981; Shepherd, Ellis
and Davies 1982; Bruyer 1987; Ellis, Jeeves, Newcombe and Young
1986; Bruyer 1986; Bruce 1988; Young and Ellis 1989a). Each of
these contains comprehensive reviews of the major topics related
to face memory so we shall not attempt here to do any more than
cover a few selected topics that have both theoretical and practical
significance. Even the issues that we have selected for description
and comment will not be treated exhaustively: there are enough
alternative sources for the interested reader easily to follow up in
more detail any specific topic.

   In this review we shall first indicate how present models of
recognition of a familiar face have evolved and then indicate how
such modelling has been useful, *inter alia*, for our understanding of
neurological and psychiatric disorders in face recognition. Second,
we shall discuss the way newly encountered faces are learned (here
the issue of certain stimulus factors will be highlighted). Third, we
shall turn to the forensically important problems of recalling faces
using composite techniques such as Photofit. Finally, we shall outline

some of our own work on a computerized mug-shot retrieval system that combines both the recall and recognition skills of witnesses to a crime.

We shall not explore the relationships between face processing and recognition of other objects. Much has been written concerning the specialness of faces (Ellis 1975; Davidoff 1986; Ellis and Young 1989). The possible requirement to posit different mechanisms for faces and objects need not imply that the underlying processes are fundamentally different – a point most cogently made by A. Ellis, Young and Hay (1987), who argue for a basic pattern of processing underlying face, object and word recognition. It is the fact that, however special, faces provide a useful test bed for general pattern recognition processes that has attracted the attention of computer scientists, who still strive to produce automatic recognition systems that can match the human brain (Stonham 1986; Bruce and Burton 1989).

MODELLING FACE RECOGNITION

Prior to 1980 there were no comprehensive models of face recognition, though Ellis (1975) and Bruce (1979) made tentative attempts to make some theoretical sense of the existing data. The first substantial model was put forward by Hay and Young (1982). They developed the parallel drawn by Ellis (1981) between face processing and word processing, in particular his suggestion that Morton's (1969) logogen model of word recognition seemed to offer some scope for analysing the way familiar faces are processed. According to Morton the logogen system is a store of known words: it contains no semantic information but provides a link between patterns of letters and an ultimate identification of their meaning. Logogens are a means for initially establishing that the word string is legitimate and familiar. Hay and Young suggested that, following early perceptual processing, faces are first examined for their familiarity by a system of Face Recognition Units (FRUs) that are comparable to logogens, i.e. for every known face a FRU exists – not unlike the concept of 'pictogens' suggested for object recognition by Seymour (1979). Only after familiarity has been established are faces categorized along semantic dimensions, including occupation and other biographical knowledge. This level of analysis is achieved by Person Identity Nodes (PINs).

The Hay and Young model was refined and elaborated by Ellis

(1983) and Rhodes (1985) to include considerations of cerebral laterality; but it was most comprehensively rounded off by Bruce and Young (1986), who offered the model which is still the best heuristic we have for understanding the literature on face recognition at least up until 1990.

Bruce and Young's (1986) model

Bruce and Young (1986) were able to make more substantial suggestions than had Hay and Young (1982) for the early perceptual or structural encoding stage. More importantly, they argued for the existence of a set of satellite face-processing modules not directly involved in establishing a person's identity. As Figure 3.1 shows, Bruce and Young's model posits, in addition to FRU and PIN systems, three independent parallel modules; these deal with, respectively, facial expression; lip reading and visually derived semantic information (e.g. sex, age and race). The evidence for supposing that these non-identity face-processing modules are separated from each other and from the set of sub-modules dealing with identity comes from a variety of sources that include latency data (see Bruce, 1988) and double dissociations between patients with different types of dysfunction for facial analysis described within the neurological literature (e.g. Campbell, Landis and Regard 1986; Malone, Morris, Kay and Levin 1982; Warrington and James 1967). We shall not detail these here; instead we wish to concentrate on the sub-modules shown in Figure 3.2, which illustrates the proposed sequential nature of information flow from structural encoding, through FRUs and PINs until, finally, the person's name is accessed. Evidence for the serial and independent nature of this cognitive architecture also comes from latency studies, i.e. with normal subjects and observations on neurological patients. In addition, the results found by Young, Hay and A. Ellis (1985) on everyday errors made by students, who kept diaries of misidentifications over a 7 week period, confirmed the notion that blocking can occur at different points in the chain, which results in limited or incorrect information being signalled. However, when a block occurred at one point, subjects never reported being able to analyse subsequent information. For example, the commonly reported experience of knowing that a face is familiar but not being able to access stored semantic details about the person is never accompanied by knowledge of the person's name. Following A. Ellis (1990), we have produced in Table 3.1 a list of observed patterns of report, together with patterns that were never reported by the subjects in the diary study of Young *et al.* (1985).

We shall shortly return to Table 3.1 because the proposed sequential architecture for identification, shown in Figure 3.2, is most strongly supported by the diary study data. Latency data are more problematic. Studies showing that reaction times (RTs) are longer for deeper levels of processing *may* reveal an underlying set

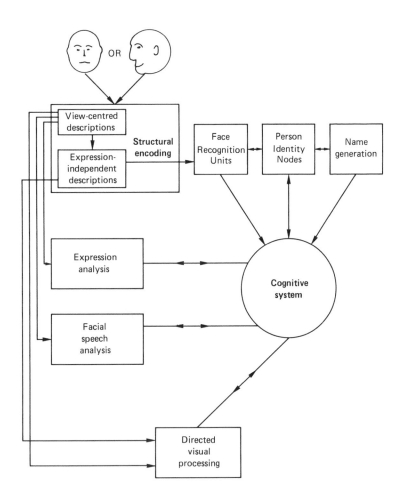

Figure 3.1 The Bruce and Young (1986) model of face recognition (redrawn from the original).

of sequential stages. (Is it a face? Is it familiar? Is it a politician? Is it George Bush?) But as Townsend (1990) has cogently argued, RT data that offer *prima facie* evidence for serial models can usually also be made to fit models that posit parallel processing of sub-stages: it takes quite sophisticated methodology to separate them. Equally, although there is some neurological evidence to show that prosopagnosia, the profound inability to recognize people by face (following, usually, bilateral occipito-temporal lesions), may manifest itself as either a perceptual or an associative disorder (Hecaen 1981; Ellis 1986b) which supports the schema shown in Figure 3.2, the data are not clear-cut. Still, the primary support for the sequential model remains the diary study and the resulting patterns of breakdown in facial identification shown in Table 3.1.

Table 3.1 According to the Bruce and Young (1986) model of face recognition, certain patterns of deficit and ability are possible and some are not. Most data from normal Ss and neurological patients with prosopagnosia fit the predictions

	Structural encoding	Face recognition units	Person identity nodes	Names
Possible patterns	x	x	x	x
	√	x	x	x
	√	√	x	x
	√	√	√	x
Impossible patterns	x	√	√	√
	√	x	√	√
	√	x	√	√

After A. Ellis (1990)

Imagine, however, a face recognition system behaving more like that shown in Figure 3.3. This arrangement is not unlike a general model of object recognition recently described by McCarthy and Warrington (1990). It suggests that familiarity and identification systems exist in parallel rather than in sequence. Of course it is easy to hypothesize such an architecture but rather more difficult to prove it. Let us admit at the outset that, at this stage, we can do no more than raise some suspicions. Mandler (1980) proposed the independence of familiarity and identity analyses and argued that for recognition to occur the output of each of these parallel systems has to be combined or fused in some way to produce recognition. Should the familiarity-checking process be impaired, or its output disconnected, one would expect some sort of phenomenological difficulty – despite the fact that the identity system may give sufficient information for recognition to occur.

There are tantalizing pieces of evidence in the neurological literature to give at least some support for this view, and in the field of psychiatry there are even more cases that can be interpreted (though admittedly not necessarily so) as evidence for identification without a prior sense of familiarity. First the neurological evidence: Pick (1903) described cases of what he termed 'reduplicative paramnesia'. Following, usually, right cerebral hemisphere lesions patients may sometimes report that places or objects do not seem right. The strangeness may then be attributed to the fact that the place or object is a duplicate of the real one (Alexander, Stuss and Benson 1979; Kapur, Turner and King 1988). There are other categories

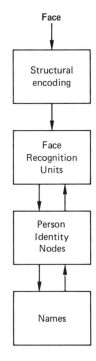

Figure 3.2   A simplified version of the Bruce and Young (1986) model of face recognition showing only the 'identification' elements.

56

of reduplicative disorder but for our present purposes these are the symptoms of interest for they could imply identification without an accompanying sense of familiarity – a clinical variety, perhaps, of the phenomenon known as 'jamais vu'.

The psychiatric literature on delusions also contains some potential sources of evidence. Capgras and Reboul-Lachaux (1923) reported the case of a woman who believed that members of her family had been replaced by doubles. Since then many more cases of the delusional misidentification syndrome, now named after Capgras, have been reported. All are characterized by the belief that people, usually, but not exclusively, close to the patient have been replaced by imposters, robots or are identical twins. Ellis and Young (1990) have recently offered a theoretical interpretation of the disorder that assumes that there are at least two routes to recognition. Bauer (1984) found that a prosopagnosic patient could reveal some covert ability to discriminate famous name/face combinations when skin conductance responses were measured, even though the patient was unable consciously to make any such discrimination. He argued for a primary (ventral) route to recognition, which is damaged in prosopagnosic patients, and a secondary (dorsal) route which

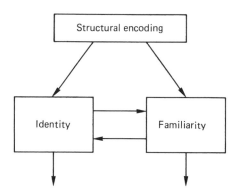

Figure 3.3 Illustration of a system in which familiarity and identity are processed in parallel.

signals something of the face's emotional significance. Ellis and Young (1990) suggested that the symptoms of Capgras' Syndrome may be the mirror reversal of covert recognition in prosopagnosics, i.e. the primary route is intact but the secondary one is not functioning properly. If, for argument's sake, one further assumes that the secondary route corresponds in some way to the familiarity system we outlined earlier, then it is possible to see in patients with Capgras' Syndrome the consequences of identification without an accompanying sense of familiarity. Returning to Table 3.1 we see that the 'inadmissible' pattern of errors where identification can happen without any accompanying sense of familiarity may indeed occur.

As we as much admitted earlier, our proposals lack the cogency we should wish but they do have the merit of widening up debate on how faces are recognized. Moreover, they may invite further discussion as to the biological significance of any scheme such as that depicted so comprehensively in the model of Bruce and Young (1986). What purpose, for example, is served by separating FRUs from PINs? If no distinction is logically necessary, it possibly arises from a separation between a phylogenetically older form of identification (familiarity) shown by many species, including primates and other social animals (Perret *et al.* 1986; Kendrick and Baldwin 1987), and a newer, conceptually-driven system that evolved to cope with ever-increasing demands of human social intercourse. This system would necessarily be involved in complex categorical processes placing known people into a myriad of relationships, combining both episodic and semantic information. Such a system, we argue, is likely to coexist with, rather than replace, any simpler one with more limited aims.

The Interactive Activation (IAC) Model

Burton, Bruce and Johnston (1990) have implemented the Bruce and Young model on a general connectionist model published by McClelland, Rumelhart and the PDP Research Group (1986). The IAC architecture contains active units that are connected by modifiable links. The units themselves are collected in pools where they are interconnected with inhibitory links in contrast to the excitatory links between associated units in different pools. The pools map on to the FRU and PIN and name stages of Bruce and Young's model, together with a third pool, concerned with semantic information (Figure 3.4). The main advantage of the Burton *et al.* (1990) approach is that it not only allows a simulation test of Bruce and Young's model, but it also has enabled a clearer understanding of what may occur under various novel situations. The IAC model has been particularly useful in helping us to understand the processes that may underly face priming effects.

Face priming has been extensively studied by Vicki Bruce and her colleagues as well as Andrew Ellis and Andrew Young. Without digressing too much, it is essential for us to mention two principal priming phenomena: identity priming, where a repetition of the same face facilitates making certain judgements of the face, and semantic priming where the previous occurrence of an associate of the person facilitates processing (e.g. seeing Prince Charles after Princess Diana enables a faster response to be made to decide that Prince Charles' face is familiar). Identity priming is a within-modality effect but semantic priming (sometimes called associative priming) may occur across modalities.

According to the IAC model of Burton *et al.* the activation of any unit persists after the face has disappeared. If there is a repeat of the face the fact that the unit is at a level of activity higher than its resting state means that it more quickly surpasses any detection threshold. For associative or semantic priming, Burton *et al.* suggest that the linkage between individual PINs is achieved via common semantic information. For example, Figure 3.4 shows that Prince Charles' PIN and Princess Diana's PIN are connected indirectly by the 'royals' category held in the semantic information store. Since such connections are facilitating, it follows that if Prince Charles' PIN is activated so too will be Princess Diana's but to a level below the threshold for identification. This activation level is soon reduced by the arrival of another face which forces down other activation levels. Thus semantic priming usually operates over short stimulus onset asynchronies.

Neurological applications

Whether or not the model architecture as shown in Figures 3.1 and 3.2 will ultimately prove to be correct, it has already proved not only to be important theoretically, but it has provided limited, practically useful means of diagnosing neurological damage (Ellis 1986b, in press). Even the simple distinction between unfamiliar and familiar faces is of clinical importance (Warrington and James 1967). Moreover, other forms of delusional misidentification than Capgras' Syndrome may be interpreted within that theoretical framework

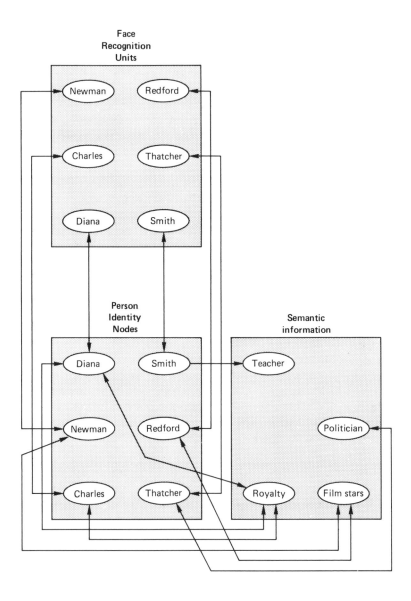

Figure 3.4   The Interactive Activation Model of face recognition
(redrawn from Burton *et al.* 1990).

(Ellis and Young 1990). While proving useful for diagnosis, however, models of face recognition have not yet been particularly applicable for designing remedial programmes for brain-damaged patients. It may be, of course, that prosopagnosia cannot be ameliorated by training. Ellis and Young (1988) were unsuccessful with any of their attempts to teach a prosopagnosic child, KD, how to discriminate among photographs of faces; and even simple schematic faces proved too difficult for her to learn. The model of Bruce and Young, though, did prompt a test of KD's ability to interpret emotional expressions and recognize voices, each of which she was able to do (Young and Ellis 1989b).

A more hopeful approach to remediation may be offered by some recent observations of covert recognition by prosopagnosics that, at first glance, may seem to have enormous theoretical potential but little practical relevance. As mentioned earlier, Bauer (1984) and Tranel and Damasio (1985) showed that prosopagnosic patients may reveal autonomic discrimination of familiar from unfamiliar faces. In each study it was observed that electro-dermal activity was higher when patients were shown previously familiar faces than when shown unfamiliar faces. Young and his associates have further shown that a patient, PH, e.g. learns correct name/face associations faster than incorrect ones; discriminates famous faces better using internal (i.e. eyes, nose, mouth) compared with external facial features (e.g. hair and chin line) and shows normal priming of famous face to associated famous name (say Princess Diana's face and Prince Charles' name) (Young, 1988; De Haan, Young and Newcombe 1987).

The covert recognition findings could be explored as a basis for teaching prosopagnosics to discriminate faces – rather in the manner suggested by Schacter (1987) for aiding amnesics to improve their retrieval of information by capitalizing upon implicit knowledge. The precise methods for assisting prosopagnosics to become aware of processes that seem to have become disconnected from consciousness (Young, De Haan and Newcombe 1990) have yet to be established but the possibilities for successfully doing so are rather better than they were – at least for those prosopagnosics who show covert recognition.

LEARNING NEW FACES

Another face recognition model, this one proposed by Ellis (1986c), specifically attended to the process of how a new face becomes a familiar face. In a series of studies we attempted systematically to examine this problem empirically (Ellis and Shepherd 1987). Until then much was known about memory for faces seen just once and for highly familiar faces but the processes by which new data may be added to the corpus of familiar faces were a mystery. At the same time as examining the way faces in general are acquired, Ellis and Shepherd (1987) took the opportunity to analyse the role of stimulus factors. Not all faces are equally memorable (Peters 1917; Shepherd and Ellis 1973; Light, Kayra-Stuart and Hollander 1979). Faces that are easily learned are also less likely to be falsely recognized as being familiar (Bartlett, Hurry and Thorley 1984).

Ellis and Shepherd (1987) first showed a large pool of male faces to 394 subjects and 2 hours later tested their ability to recognize them. For every face we established a wide range of measurements (physiognomic, anthropometric as well as semantic) and so the resulting memorability scores were easily related to any or all of these attributes. One analysis involved absolute z scores for 17 anthropometric measures being computed and correlated with memorability. The resulting coefficient ($r = 0.14$) was significant, though accounting for only a tiny portion of the variance. Two other correlations were significant: hair length ($r = 0.21$) and face width ($r = 0.16$). Each of these dimensions had proved important in multidimensional scaling (MDS) analyses of facial similarity (Shepherd, Davies and Ellis 1981) and, as we shall show later, are salient facial characteristics when people try to recall faces.

Rated semantic or personality characteristics associated with memorability were: ambition ($r = 0.26$), determination ($r = -0.20$), and intelligence ($r = 0.22$). Surprisingly, none of these traits occurred in the first two factors when factor analysis was carried out. Also surprising, given earlier work by Shepherd and Ellis (1973) and Peters (1917), was the fact that attractiveness and pleasantness did not correlate significantly with memorability.

The correlation data, though revealing some consistent but weak relationships, were disappointing. Others had chosen a more global approach to memorability. Light *et al.* (1979), for example, distinguished 'typical' from 'distinctive' faces and so we selected the ten most memorable and ten least memorable faces and asked subjects to select from an array of twenty faces first the most distinctive face, then the next most distinctive, etc. until all faces were ranked. The mean distinctiveness ranks of the ten most- and 10 least-memorable were 5.4 and 15.6, respectively, indicating almost perfect agreement between the two measures. Thus people appear easily to compute from faces those attributes that render them distinctive (and, in turn, memorable). Our attempts to capture this process, using a large set of different types of facial measurements, however, were distinctly less successful.

In the next experiment we repeatedly presented subjects fifteen times over with a random sequence of the ten most- and ten least-memorable faces. On each repetition the twenty faces were mixed with a fresh set of unknown faces and subjects' accuracy and latency for judging familiarity were recorded. As Figure 3.5 clearly shows, the RTs to decide that faces were familiar become monotonically faster with repetition. The improvement in performance was approximately constant for both memorable and non-memorable faces (i.e. no interaction between memorability and trials). The memorable or distinctive faces were always responded to more quickly and also produced fewer errors (3 per cent v. 17.2 per cent) (Ellis, Shepherd, Gibling and Shepherd 1988).

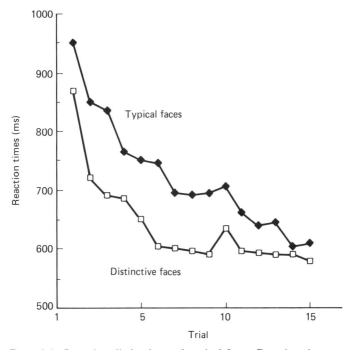

Figure 3.5 Learning distinctive and typical faces. Reaction times over one to fifteen repetitions.

A replication of the last experiment was carried out with repetitions extended to twenty. Again, the distinctive/memorable faces were consistently recognized faster than the non-memorable faces. The learning seemed to reach asymptote after about ten repetitions but the differential mean RTs between memorable and non-memorable faces still remained constant. This is not so surprising, perhaps, given the findings presented by Valentine and Bruce (1986). They observed distinctive famous faces to be processed more quickly than typical-looking faces of celebrities equally well known – so it would seem that, whatever the processing disadvantages offered by having typical facial features, they are never reduced by familiarity.

Shepherd, Gibling and Ellis (1991) further examined the role of distinctiveness in face learning by varying the temporal parameters of exposure time and interval before testing. Subjects were given fifteen distinctive and fifteen typical faces each for either 1s or 5s. Memory was tested after an interval of a day or a month. Figure 3.6 illustrates the results. As expected, distinctive faces were better recognized, and 5s presentation was superior to 1s presentation. But there was no interaction between these two factors. Nor was there any main effect or interaction involving delay interval. The absence of a main effect was to be expected as memory for faces seen even just once is known to be robust over time (Goldstein and Chance 1971; Deffenbacher, Carr and Leu 1981; Shepherd, Ellis and Davies 1982). The absence of an interaction with distinctiveness, however, was not anticipated. It was expected that memory for typical faces might be particularly adversely affected by the larger delay interval.

Repetition of encounter with slides of faces, as one would expect, produces learning. But how? Ellis, Shepherd and Davies (1979) found that familiar faces were better recognized from inner features (i.e. eyes, nose and mouth) compared with outer features (i.e. hair and jaw shape). Faces seen just once, however, are equally well identified from inner and outer features. Therefore one may suppose that, at some point in the learning process, there is a shift in the cognitive representation of a face, favouring internal features.

Ellis *et al.* (1979) speculated that repeated encounter with a person may cause us to concentrate more and more on expressive features (eyes and mouth), which, in turn, would cause these inner features to become better represented. So far in this chapter we have discussed research that has exclusively used photographs or slides of faces. Shepherd *et al.* (1982) showed that the mode at presentation and at test of recognition were important but virtually no other research on face memory has used live, filmed or videoed faces. Admittedly much research on eyewitness identification has employed live incidents – see Shepherd *et al.* (1982) for reviews – but little or no face memory work has employed moving faces as stimuli. This omission is understandable given the need often to measure RTs from stimulus onset, but the use of static views of faces does mean that the data may lack ecological relevance.

Ellis and Shepherd (1987) adopted the following method, combining still photographs and video sequences, to investigate the shift towards a more robust internal representation of inner compared with outer facial features. Subjects were first shown twenty slides of faces. Then over a 4 week period they observed short video sequences of each face moving and revealing different emotional expressions. Tests of recognition of the full faces, internal features alone and external features alone, mixed with equal numbers of distractor

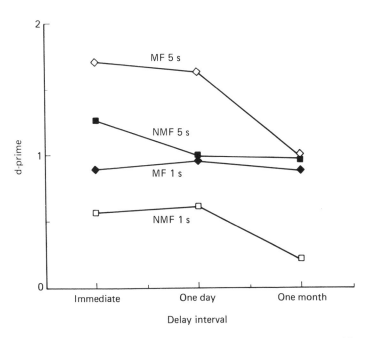

Figure 3.6 Mean *d*-prime values for memorable and non-memorable faces as a function of delay and presentation time (from Shepherd *et al.* 1991).

faces, masked in comparable ways, were made at the beginning, at the mid-point and at the end of the overall training period. As Figure 3.7 indicates there was a shift in accuracy as measured by the Statistical Decision Theory parameter, d, from there being no difference between internal and external features at the first two tests to a significant difference in favour of internal features by the final test. Unfortunately, a possible artefact in our experimental design means that some caution must be urged in interpreting these data. Half-way through the training period subjects were invited to make personality trait judgements of the stimulus people. Conceivably this may have contributed to the shift from no preference to an internal features advantage. Nevertheless, Ellis and Shepherd (1987) concluded that they had demonstrated a qualitative change in the way faces are processed as they become more familiar. The point at which the qualitative shift in stimulus processing needs to be charted more finely and any accompanying change in other

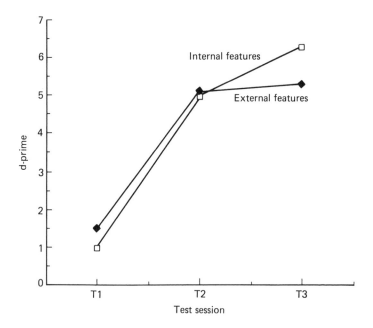

Figure 3.7 Mean d-prime values to faces masked to reveal inner or outer features as a function of learning. By the third test there is a clear advantage to inner features.

processing strategies needs to be fully investigated, especially the way knowledge of the physical/structural attributes of new faces becomes linked with cognitive and other information.

FACIAL PROTOTYPES

One approach to learning faces is to assume that each one is encoded in relation to one or more typical or canonical representations (Perrett *et al.* 1986). Dukes and Bevan (1967) showed that varying views of a face was a particularly effective way of improving its acquisition compared with repetition of the same views. The role of variety of encounter for the way we learn faces had not been systematically explored, however.

We examined this ourselves by presenting to subjects in the experimental groups either four repetitions of the same facial pose (left three-quarter, right three-quarter, left profile or right profile), compared with showing subjects four different views. Recognition was tested by presenting full-face poses of the target faces (i.e. a pose not previously encountered by any but control subjects who saw the full-face pose four times).

The mixed-pose experience led to a mean hit rate that was significantly (almost 30 per cent) higher than those produced by subjects in the single pose conditions. Indeed, it led to a slightly, but not significantly, higher hit rate than the control condition. Similar results were found when expression rather than pose was used as facial variant (Ellis and Shepherd 1987).

General prototype

Valentine (in press) has constructed a theoretical framework for analysing face recognition data, particularly relating to distinctiveness, based upon the assumption that there is an average or prototypical face in some sort of multi-dimensional representation of faces. Typical faces cluster around the prototype and are therefore more difficult to discriminate than are distinctive faces which occupy points far removed from the centre in areas less densely populated.

This idea is not too different from that suggested by Light *et al.* (1979). They argued that typical faces never previously encountered arouse greater feelings of familiarity than do distinctive faces, by virtue of their greater proximity to the average face. Distinctive faces, in contrast, tend to be more uniquely encoded.

A similar reasoning may be applied to the finding reported by Valentine and Bruce (1986) that in an experiment where faces had to be distinguished from jumbled faces, typical physiognomies are more quickly identified as being faces. Distinctive faces require a longer processing time – perhaps because they are more distant from the average or prototypical face.

Race

Valentine (in press) tries to deal with the awkward fact that faces of people from another race are both distinctive (by definition) and yet are not easily recognized (Malpass and Kravitz 1969; Shepherd, Deregowski and Ellis 1974). Valentine suggests that what happens when we encounter an other-race face is that it is encoded according to features general to that race rather than by reference to specific, individually based information. In other words, the internal representations of, say, black faces for white observers are closely packed around a point which is distant from their prototypical region for white faces.

Ellis and Deregowski (1981) found that cross-racial difficulties in face recognition are increased when different photographs are used at study and test. In other words, when learning about own-race faces, even after a single, short exposure, we are able to recognize them following transformation of pose etc. For other-race faces, however, this cognitive flexibility is less evident. Indeed, Ayuk (1990) has recently shown that when white and black faces are presented in a mixed sequence the cross-racial effect is modified so that the interaction between race and pose found by Ellis and Deregowski (1981) disappears, implying that encoding strategy may be altered when the own-race/other-race input is random rather than blocked.

Caricature

Perkins (1975) argued that we internally represent faces in some sort of 'super fidelity' fashion. By this he meant that we store them as caricatures, accentuating deviations from the norm. This view was later supported by Rhodes, Brennan and Carey (1987), who made automatic line-drawn caricatures of faces using a computer algorithm which exaggerated features that deviated from average in increasing steps up to a 50 per cent increase. They found that caricatures were processed more quickly and were preferred to the originals.

It could be argued that the results of Rhodes *et al.* (1987) are attributable to the use of line drawn stimuli. Benson and Perrett (1991), however, have devised a program that makes caricatures and anti-caricatures of facial photographs. Their stimuli produced data consistent with those of Rhodes *et al.* (1987). Processing time and preference favoured caricatures over faces that were untransformed or made less distinctive (anti-caricaturing). The caricature process makes a face more distinctive and, conceivably, parallels what happens when we ourselves process facial images.

Attractiveness

To date, research on the relationship between facial attractiveness and recognition has produced a set of contradictory findings. Light, Hollander and Kayra-Stuart (1981) reported a negative correlation between attractiveness and recognition: attractive faces were less well recognized than unattractive faces. Cross, Cross and Daly (1971) reported the opposite effect: faces previously identified as attractive were recognized more easily than unattractive faces. Shepherd and Ellis (1973) and Fleishman, Buckley, Klosinsky, Smith and Tuck (1976) reported a curvilinear relationship between attractiveness and memorability: high and low attractive faces were recognized more accurately than medium attractive faces. The fact that high attractive faces are more easily recognized than moderately attractive faces is difficult to reconcile with the work of Langlois and Roggman (1990), who propose that attractive faces are those which represent the average or prototypical region of faces encountered, i.e. the region which, according to Valentine (in press), is densely packed with typical faces that are difficult to discriminate. Langlois and Roggman (1990) made their assertion on the basis of experiments in which they averaged or superimposed digitized faces on a computer and found that the resulting composite face was judged to be more attractive than the individual faces from which it was made. Langlois and Roggman also reported a strong similar trend between rated attractiveness and the number of faces comprising the composite. They argued that the more 'average' the composite was, the more highly rated it became along a dimension of beauty. Moreover, they speculated as to the evolutionary pressures that favour attraction to the norm rather than to deviations from it.

At this stage it is not possible to reconcile the data of Langlois and Roggman (1990) with the studies of Shepherd and Ellis (1973) and the theories of Valentine (in press). Clearly, however, at some stage these strands must be brought together.

RECALLING FACES

So far we have addressed ourselves only to the situation where people are asked to say whether the face before them is known or not. On other occasions they may need to convey to someone else what another person looks like. The most obvious example is when a witness to an incident provides a description of a suspect to the police, but there are times in everyday intercourse where communication about the facial appearance of another is required. In these instances the person's task is to recall an impression of the face in question.

Robertson and Ellis (1987) described a study of people's ability to recall the names of thirty-six famous faces shown a day earlier. The celebrities had been drawn from six occupational classes (politicians, pop-stars, film stars, TV personalities, comedians and sports person-alities) but were shown in a different random sequence for each of twenty-four subjects.

When asked to recall the names of those presented, subjects revealed two interesting clustering trends. They tended to produce together names of people from the same occupation but, within these clusters, to recall names of people who looked similar. The physical similarity parameters did not yield anywhere near such strong effects as the semantic ones: nonetheless they imply that the organization of face/name recall may be governed by both and that they interact in a way that can be modelled mathematically (Robertson and Ellis 1987).

Ellis (1986d) approached the issue of face recall in a number of more direct ways. His basic approach was to ask people for recollections of the appearance of famous faces or faces seen just once. In each case he concentrated on the occasions when subjects could remember only partial information. When they were in this 'edge of image' state, subjects most commonly recalled face shapes and details of hair, including colour – even when nothing else could be reported, these two features remained.

Interestingly, knowledge of the details concerning face shape and hair, together with age – which Ellis (1986b) termed 'cardinal features' – corresponds with the findings described by Shepherd, Davies and Ellis (1981) from multidimensional scaling (MDS) analyses following paired comparisons of large numbers of faces on the basis of their similarity. They observed face shape, hair and age to be the principal dimensions along which faces could be arranged in a three-dimensional solution.

Facial composites

For more than thirty years police forces throughout the world have been using aids to enable witnesses to crimes to recall the faces of wanted persons. Davies (1981) reviewed the principal first-generation composite systems, including Identikit, PhotoFIT and the Minolta Montage System. All of these systems are limited in the degrees of freedom offered witnesses both in selection of features and in how they allow configural variations among the features selected. From what is known about the efficiency of these composite systems it could be inferred that face recall is rather poor (Ellis, Shepherd and Davies 1975; Laughery and Fowler 1980). In order to illustrate the kinds of research done with these first-generation facial composite systems we shall describe some of the work we conducted with Graham Davies using the PhotoFIT system.

PhotoFIT

PhotoFIT was developed by Penry (1971), who first introduced it to the UK. It comprises sets of photographed features (hair, eyes, nose, mouth, chin) from which witnesses to a crime may choose. The elements are fitted together rather like a jigsaw and some vertical adjustment is possible. There are kits for male caucasians, female caucasians and male Afro-Asians. PhotoFIT has been subjected to extensive experimental analysis (e.g. Ellis, Shepherd and Davies 1975; Ellis, Davies and Shepherd 1978; Davies and Milne 1985). Results generally favour the conclusion that PhotoFIT is not particularly good for achieving a close likeness to a target face: instead it seems quite good at producing a type likeness, i.e. the composites bear a general resemblance to whomever is being recalled. Whether these likenesses are of much value to the police is questionable. Indeed any advantage of PhotoFIT over asking the witness to draw the face is difficult to find (Ellis *et al.* 1978). Moreover, Christie and Ellis (1981) found that the verbal descriptions given by witnesses were a more efficient means of conveying the impression of the target person than were the subsequent PhotoFIT composites. The level of expertise in the PhotoFIT operator, however, is quite important (Davies, Milne and Shepherd 1983): an experienced operator helps witnesses to produce much more accurate likenesses than does an inexperienced operator. Regrettably in most police forces the level of expertise among its PhotoFIT operators is not high (Kitson, Darnborogh and Shields 1978), though in recent years intensive training schemes have been introduced to improve these skills.

All that we have said of PhotoFIT is probably true of the other first-generation composite systems. They are limited in their usefulness. We shall now turn to an alternative approach.

E-FIT

In a recent review (Shepherd and Ellis 1990) we have examined second-generation face composite systems that depend on computer graphical techniques to achieve greater flexibility. Commercial systems include Compusketch, Mac-a-Mug, and E-FIT. The first two involve line drawn elements, while the last uses photographic quality elements. None, however, has yet been tested with the rigour applied to Identikit and PhotoFIT, so it is not yet possible to ascertain just what advantage, if any, is conferred by modern computer technology.

An example of some of the psychological benefits to be gained from computer-based composite recall systems is provided by E-FIT. This system was developed jointly, under Home Office auspices, by Aberdeen University and IO Research Ltd.

E-FIT is an acronym for Electronic Facial Identification Technique. It comprises two screens, one of which is used to enter descriptions and menu-driven instructions from a keyboard to manipulate the image, while the other displays the facial image with 128 grey levels giving a photographic quality composite. In addition, there is a tablet which drives a graphics paint program for artistic enhancement of the image at the operator's discretion.

Composites are constructed from a library of features. These have been specially cut from photographs of volunteers, to provide over 1000 exemplars of general face shape, hair, eyebrows, eyes, nose, mouth and ears, plus additional facial hair, glasses and other accessories in each of two databases, one for caucasian faces, and one for Afro-Caribbean faces. Each feature has been coded using a set of descriptors based upon those developed in the work of the Aberdeen group on facial databases (Shepherd 1986), and has been treated to ensure a 'seamless' blend with any other features.

Features are accessed by the verbal description of a witness which is entered via menus displayed on screen. The description may be as detailed or as sparse as the witness can achieve. For example, the hair may be described in terms of its length, texture (straight, curly, etc.), density (how much of the head it covers), colour, style, and how it is brushed or where the parting occurs. The more of these descriptors which are entered, the smaller the set of features the subject will have to inspect. Should the witness be able to give only one descriptor, say 'short hair', a large set of features can be inspected. Where no information about a feature is provided a 'default' exemplar is selected to maintain the integrity of the composite. When all of the witness's description has been entered a complete composite is assembled and displayed on the second screen. If the witness is not satisfied with any feature, alternative features can be displayed *in situ* by pressing a single key. The witness can thus 'flick through' features which satisfy the initial description.

A variety of amendments can be carried out on any feature. The position can be changed in any direction, the feature can be made taller or shorter, fatter or thinner, or darkened or lightened. Some of the range of facilities are illustrated in Figure 3.8. At any stage a composite may be saved to a file and retrieved for further work. A complete log of all operations carried out in producing the composite is retained so that precise replication on another machine is possible.

There are a number of reasons to expect a computer-based composite system such as E-FIT to be superior to the earlier manual systems. When confronted with a face recall task, a witness must first try to form an image of the target face, and then attempt to describe the component elements, features as well as configuration, from the image. It is probable that different strategies are required for this than for recognizing faces. For example, Wells and Hryciw (1984) found that a holistic strategy (making a character attribution) was a more effective mode of encoding faces than a 'partist' strategy of describing each feature when recognition was subsequently tested, but the reverse was true when recall was tested.

Most of the earlier systems required witnesses to select the features of the face they were recalling from a printed array of isolated features. However, since viewing features in isolation is a more error

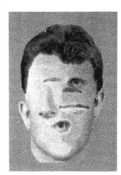

Figure 3.8 Illustrations of facilities available on E-FIT: (a) composite compiled by entering a description via menus; (b) original composite in (a) modified; all the original features have been manipulated by resizing them (face has been shortened, eyes enlarged, nose made narrower, and mouth made narrower with thicker lips); (c) composite from (b) with moustache added; (d) composite from (a) but with 'ageing' treatment (age lines, receding hairline, and greying hair); (e) rearranged composite (a) demonstrating *ad absurdum* the facility to manipulate configuration of features.

prone procedure than viewing features in the context of a face (Davies and Christie 1981), E-FIT always presents features in the context of a complete face. Furthermore, the use of the verbal description given by the witness to select a small range of appropriate features reduces the search task which confronts the witness in comparison with using a purely visual index.

Configural information is important in the representation of faces in memory (Sergent 1984; Rhodes 1985; Hosie 1991), and the inability to make adjustments to the configuration of the features once selected was one of the principal handicaps of the PhotoFIT and Identikit systems. The facility in E-FIT to move any feature independently of any other feature overcomes this problem, and permits radical as well as subtle adjustments to the configuration of features. Note, in Figure 3.8, that the background face automatically fills in the gap created by moving the feature.

Whether all these advantages will result in the production of superior composites has yet to be tested systematically. An earlier study by Christie, Davies, Shepherd and Ellis (1981) which compared a computer-based version of PhotoFIT with its manual equivalent found no difference in accuracy of identification from composites produced by the two systems. In evaluating this result it should be borne in mind that the computer version was a prototype, that the computer operator was much less experienced than the PhotoFIT operator, and that the photographic quality of the computer image used for the recognition and rating measures was poorer than that for the PhotoFIT composites. Furthermore, the computer system in that study used digitized PhotoFIT features. In contrast to this, E-FIT has a larger selection of features as well as greater flexibility than the earlier computer prototype.

The success of a composite system such as E-FIT depends on how it performs 'in the field'. This is surprisingly difficult to ascertain. For example, the quality of the composite can only be determined if the suspect is arrested. The arrest of the suspect may depend on the quality of the composite, but also on the efficiency of the police, or the priority the police may be prepared to give the particular case. The number of arrests which occur when composites are used may reflect the quality of the witnesses, the competence of the operator, the effectiveness of the composite system, the efficiency of the police, or all of these.

In any case, E-FIT is such a new tool that it is probably too early to attempt any comprehensive assessment of its value. However, one documented instance of the successful use of E-FIT was in a case of sexual assault. A victim in a spate of such assaults which had been going on for six months, produced an E-FIT composite of her assailant which was circulated to the local police. A custody officer who had been issued with a copy of the E-FIT composite recognized the likeness to a man being questioned for a similar offence, who was arrested, charged and later convicted of the offence. The E-FIT composite, together with a photograph of the convicted man, can be seen in Figure 3.9.

The primary reason for developing E-FIT was to provide the police with a more effective device for producing facial composites. There may, however, be theoretical opportunities opened by the new technique. For example, it was mentioned above that people's recall of faces was not very good. The evidence for this was based mostly on work using PhotoFIT as the means of producing the recalled face. Since PhotoFIT is quite crude compared with computer-based systems, the quality of the composite may have been affected as much by the technical limitations of the equipment as by the psychological

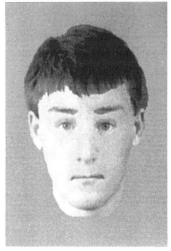

Figure 3.9 Photograph of a man convicted of assault, together with E-FIT composite constructed by a victim of his attack.

limitations of the witness. With improved methods of assessing recall, we may achieve a more realistic indication of the ability of people to recall faces, and more refined measures of the nature of errors or biases which may occur in the process of recall.

Mug-shot retrieval

Given that, however sophisticated the device for enabling witnesses to recall a face, people's ability to report an image of a face in a way that can be used to convey an accurate impression may be limited, what can be offered as an alternative?

Shepherd (1986) described a system for enabling semi-automatic retrieval of information from a database of mugshots that provides a partial solution. This computer system, originally known as the Facial Retrieval And Matching Equipment (FRAME), uses the broadly accurate verbal descriptions that witnesses might provide prior to attempting to reconstruct the face with a composite system and codes this information in a manner which allows an automatic search of its stored database to select the faces that best match the description. These faces may be inspected by the witness who, if the target face is not there, also may volunteer that one is most like it, and a new search is done using its facial parameters; or s/he may indicate, say, that one's hair, another's nose and another's eyes look approximately correct, and these may be 'combined' to form the basis of another search for faces similar to that blend.

The advantage of FRAME is that it uses what limited information witnesses can recall and capitalizes on his or her better developed face recognition capacity. It avoids the problems of interference etc. that arise when witnesses have to search through mug-shot albums containing hundreds of faces. Davies, Shepherd and Ellis (1979) showed that the experience of looking at just a hundred faces produced a change in recognition, principally by altering subjects' criteria in a more conservative direction.

Ellis, Shepherd, Shepherd, Flin and Davies (1989) made a direct comparison between FRAME and a traditional mug-shot album search. For this work (and other experiments described by Shepherd (1986) a database of 1000 male faces was established. From these, four typical and four distinctive faces were chosen as targets (mean ratings 3.7 and 5.4 on a seven point scale of distinctiveness given by twenty subjects).

One hundred and twenty eight subjects served in one of two

conditions: retrieval using FRAME, or mug-shot album search. Each subject saw one three-quarter view target face for 10 seconds and was informed that memory for the face would subsequently be tested. Then the subject either gave a description from memory and then looked through mug-shot albums containing a total of 1000 faces, or gave a description for encoding into the FRAME system.

Table 3.2 Results of subjects' searches in FRAME and Album conditions

Face type	Score	Search condition FRAME	Album
Distinctive		n = 32	n = 32
	Hits (%)	75	78
	Confidence rating	4.4	4.4
	Time (min)	13.2	14.6
	False alarms (%)	9	12
	Misses (%)	6	9
	Non-retrieval* (%)	9	
Typical		n = 32	n = 32
	Hits (%)	69	44
	Confidence rating	4.4	4.6
	Time (min)	15.2	14.5
	False alarms (%)	9	47
	Misses (%)	0	9
	Non-retrievals* (%)	22	

After Ellis *et al.* (1989)
*Not applicable for Album search trials

The results of this experiment are summarized in Tables 3.2 and 3.3. Three findings are most interesting: one refers to the fact that for distinctive faces there was no difference between album search and FRAME; the second is that, for typical faces, there was a substantial advantage for the FRAME system; and, as Table 3.3 indicates, there was a clearly progressive impairment in ability to recognize typical faces when they occurred later and later in the albums. Ellis *et al.* (1989) also present some interesting details of the frequency with which different facial features were recalled by their subjects but these will not be considered here. FRAME, then, seems to provide many useful advantages for detective work; any limitations are likely to be practical but these are not insurmountable.

Table 3.3 Results of Album search trials showing position effects

Face type		Position in Album			
		97	353	649	898
Typical					
	Hits	6	4	3	1
	(Time)*	11.3	12	21.7	20
	(Confidence)	4.4	5	4.7	4
	False alarms	2	2	5	6
	Misses	0	2	0	1
Distinctive					
	Hits	7	4	8	6
	(Time)	8.3	17.5	16.7	18
	(Confidence)	4	4.7	4.9	4.2
	False alarms	0	3	0	1
	Misses	1	1	0	1
Fisher's exact test (Hits v. rest)		>0.40	>0.38	= 0.0203	= 0.0128

After Ellis *et al.* (1989)
The value of each cell (except Time and Confidence) represents the total number of subjects
*Average time in minutes

SUMMARY

In this review we have tried to indicate the present state of theory and practice in face-processing research. Although we have endeavoured to make connections between them – particularly relating to stimulus characteristics and training – it will have been obvious to the reader that, at present, these are limited and tenuous. The major theoretical advances over the last 10 years have concerned the way people recognize familiar faces. The principal forensic problem is, and always will be, how witnesses to a crime can later recall the face of an unfamiliar culprit and identify it at an identity parade or photo line-up. The lot of some of us has been to try to integrate findings from these disparate types of study and to point out the issues that cut across them. In applications to the neurological and neuropsychiatric fields, though, face recognition theory has been more successful.

ACKNOWLEDGEMENTS

Some of the work reported in this chapter was supported by an ESRC grant (C00232260) and a contract from the Home Office Scientific

Research Branch. We should also like to thank Dr Judith Hosie for her helpful comments. For permission to reproduce Figures 3.1, 3.4 and 3.9 we thank, respectively, Professor Vicki Bruce, Professor Andy Young and Dr Mike Burton, and Grampian Police Force.

REFERENCES

Alexander, M.P., Stuss, D.T. and Benson, D.F. (1979) 'Temporal gradients in the retrograde amnesia of patients with Korsakoff's disease', *Archives of Neurology* 36: 211–16.

Ayuk, R.E. (1990) 'Cross-racial identification of transformed, untransformed, and mixed-race faces', *International Journal of Psychology* 25: 509–27.

Barlett, J.C., Hurry, S. and Thorley, W. (1984) 'Typicality and familiarity of faces', *Memory and Cognition* 12: 219–28.

Bauer, R.M. (1984) 'Autonomic recognition of names and faces: A neuropsychological application of the Guilty Knowledge Test', *Neuropsychologia* 22: 457–69.

Benson, P.J. and Perrett, D.I. (1991) 'Perception and recognition of photographic quality facial caricatures: Implications for the recognition of natural images', *European Journal of Cognitive Psychology* 3: 105–35.

Bruce, V. (1979) 'Searching for politicians: An information-processing approach to face recognition', *Quarterly Journal of Experimental Psychology* 31: 373–95.

Bruce, V. (1988) *Recognising Faces*, Hillsdale, New Jersey: Erlbaum.

Bruce, V. and Burton, M. (1989) 'Computer recognition of faces', in A.W. Young and H.D. Ellis (eds) *Handbook of Research on Face Processing*, Amsterdam: North Holland.

Bruce, V. and Young, A. (1986) 'Understanding face recognition', *British Journal of Psychology* 77: 305–27.

Bruyer, R. (1986) *The Neuropsychology of Face Recognition and Emotional Expression*, Hillsdale, New Jersey: Erlblaum.

Bruyer, R. (1987) *Les Mecanismes de Reconnaissance des Visages* Grenoble: Universitaires de Grenoble.

Burton, A.M., Bruce, V. and Johnston, R.A. (1990) 'Understanding face recognition with an interactive activation model', *British Journal of Psychology* 81: 361–80.

Campbell, R., Landis, T. and Regard, M. (1986) 'Face recognition and lip reading: A neurological dissociation', *Brain* 109: 509–21.

Capgras, J. and Reboul-Lachaux, J. (1923) 'Illusion des sosies dans un delire systématisé chronique', *Bulletin de la Société Clinique de Medecine Mentale* 2: 6–16.

Christie, D.F.M. and Ellis, H.D. (1981) 'Photofit constructions versus verbal descriptions of faces', *Journal of Applied Psychology* 66: 358–63.

Christie, D.F.M., Davies, G.M., Shepherd, J.W. and Ellis, H.D. (1981) 'Evaluating a new computer-based system for face recall', *Law and Human Behavior* 5: 209–18.

Cross, J.F., Cross, J. and Daly, J. (1971) 'Sex, race, age, and beauty as factors in recognition of faces', *Perception and Psychophysics* 10: 393–6.

Davidoff, J. (1986) 'The specificity of face perception: Evidence from psychological investigations', *The Neuropsychology of Face Perception and Expression*, Hillsdale, New Jersey: Erlbaum.

Davies, G.M. (1981) 'Face recall systems', in G. Davies, H. Ellis and J. Shepherd (eds) *Perceiving and Remembering Faces*, London: Academic Press.

Davies, G. and Christie, D. (1981) 'Face recall: An examination of some factors limiting composite production accuracy', *Journal of Applied Psychology* 67: 103–9.

Davies, G.M. and Milne, A. (1985) 'Eyewitness composite production as a function of mental or physical reinstatement of context', *Criminal Justice and Behaviour* 12: 209–20.

Davies, G.M., Ellis, H.D. and Shepherd, J.W. (1981) *Perceiving and Remembering Faces*, London: Academic Press.

Davies, G.M., Milne, A. and Shepherd, J. (1983) 'Searching for operator skills for face composite production', *Journal of Police Science and Administration*, 11: 405–9.

Davies. G., Shepherd, J. and Ellis, H. (1979) 'Effects of interpolated mugshot exposure on accuracy of eyewitness identification', *Journal of Applied Psychology* 64: 232–7.

Deffenbacher, K.A., Carr, T.H. and Leu, J.R. (1981) 'Memory for words, pictures and faces: Retroactive interference, forgetting, and reminiscence', *Journal of Experimental Psychology: Human Learning and Memory* 7: 299–305.

De Haan, E., Young, A. and Newcombe, F. (1987) 'Faces interfere with name classification in a prosopagnosic patient', *Cortex* 23: 309–16.

Dukes, W.F. and Bevan, W. (1967) 'Stimulus variation and repetition in acquisition of naming responses', *Journal of Experimental Psychology* 74: 178–81.

Ellis, A.W. (1990) Paper given at ESRC Face Recognition Meeting, Grange-over-Sands.

Ellis, H.D. (1975) 'Recognising faces', *British Journal of Psychology* 66: 409–26.

Ellis, H.D. (1981) 'Theoretical aspects of face recognition', in G. Davies, H. Ellis and J. Shepherd (eds) *Perceiving and Remembering Faces*, London: Academic Press.

Ellis, H.D. (1983) 'The role of the right hemisphere in face perception', in A.W. Young (ed.) *Functions of the Right Cerebral Hemisphere*, London: Academic Press.

Ellis, H.D. (1986a) 'Introduction to aspects of face processing: Ten questions in need of answers', in H.D. Ellis, M.A. Jeeves, F. Newcombe, and A.W. Young (eds) *Aspects of Face Processing*, Dordrecht: Nijhoff.

Ellis, H.D. (1986b) *Disorders of Face Recognition*, in K. Poeck, H.-J. Freund and H. Ganshirt (eds) *Neurology*, Berlin: Springer.

Ellis, H.D. (1986c) 'Processes underlying face recognition', in R. Bruyer (ed.) *The Neuropsychology of Face Perception and Facial Expression*, Hillsdale,

New Jersey: Erlbaum.

Ellis, H.D. (1986d) 'Face recall: A psychological perspective', *Human Learning* 5: 189–96.

Ellis, H.D. (in press) 'Assessment of deficits in facial processing', in J. Crawford, D. Parker and W. McKinlay (eds) *Principles and Practice of Neuropsychological Assessment*, Hillsdale, New Jersey: Erlbaum.

Ellis, H.D. and Deregowski, J.B. (1981) 'Within-race and between-race recognition of transformed and untransformed faces', *American Journal of Psychology* 94: 27–35.

Ellis, H.D. and Shepherd, J.W. (1987) 'Analysis of the mechanisms by which human observers acquire knowledge of faces', Final Report to Economic and Social Research Council (Award No. C00232260).

Ellis, H.D. and Young, A.W. (1988) 'Training in face-processing skills for a child with acquired prosopagnosia', *Developmental Neuropsychology* 4(4): 283–94.

Ellis, H.D. and Young, A.W. (1989) 'Are faces special?' in A. Young and H. Ellis (eds) *Handbook of Research on Face Processing*, Amsterdam: North-Holland.

Ellis, H.D. and Young, A.W. (1990) 'Accounting for delusional misidentifications', *British Journal of Psychiatry* 157: 239–48.

Ellis, H.D., Davies, G.M. and Shepherd, J.W. (1978) 'A critical examination of the Photofit system for recalling faces', *Ergonomics* 21: 297–307.

Ellis, H.D., Shepherd, J.W. and Davies, G.M. (1975) 'An investigation of the use of the Photofit technique for recalling faces', *British Journal of Psychology* 66: 29–37.

Ellis, H.D., Shepherd, J.W. and Davies, G.M. (1979) 'Identification of familiar and unfamiliar faces from internal and external features: Some implications for theories of face recognition', *Perception* 8: 431–9.

Ellis H.D., Jeeves, M.A., Newcombe, F. and Young, A.W. (1986) *Aspects of Face Processing*, Dordrecht: Nijhoff.

Ellis, H.D., Shepherd, J.W., Gibling, F. and Shepherd, J. (1988) 'Stimulus factors in face learning', in M.M. Gruneberg, P.E. Morris and R.N. Sykes (eds) *Practical Aspects of Memory: Current Research and Issues*, vol. 1, Chichester: Wiley.

Ellis, H.D., Shepherd, J.W., Shepherd, J., Flin, R.H. and Davies, G.M. (1989) 'Identification from a computer-driven retrieval system compared with a traditional mug-shot album search: a new tool for police investigations', *Ergonomics* 32: 167–77.

Ellis, A., Young, A. and Hay, D. (1987) 'Modelling the recognition of faces and words', in P. Morris (ed.) *Modelling Cognition*, Chicester: Wiley.

Ellis, A.W., Young, A.W., Flude, B.M. and Hay, D.C. (1987) 'Repetition priming of face recognition', *Quarterly Journal of Psychology* 93A: 193–210.

Fleishman, J.J., Buckley, M.L., Klosinsky, M.J., Smith, N. and Tuck, B. (1976) 'Judged attractiveness in recognition memory of women's faces', *Perceptual and Motor Skills* 43: 709–10.

Goldstein, A.G. and Chance, J.E. (1971) 'Visual recognition memory for complex configurations', *Perception and Psychophysics* 9: 237–41.

Hay, D.C. and Young, A.W. (1982) 'The human face', in A. Ellis (ed.) *Normality and Pathology in Cognitive Functions*, New York: Academic Press.

Hecaen, H. (1981) 'The neuropsychology of face recognition', in G. Davies, H. Ellis and J. Shepherd (eds) *Perceiving and Remembering Faces*, London: Academic Press.

Hosie, J. (1991) 'Feature and configural factors in face processing', Thesis submitted for PhD degree to University of Wales.

Kapur, N., Turner, A. and King, C. (1988) 'Reduplicative paramnesia: possible anatomical and neuropsychological mechanisms', *Journal of Neurology, Neurosurgery and Psychiatry* 51: 579–81.

Kendrick, K.M. and Baldwin, B.A. (1987) 'Cells in the temporal cortex of conscious sleep can respond preferentially to the sight of faces', *Science* 236: 448–50.

Kitson, S., Darnborogh, M. and Shields, E. (1978) 'Lets face it', *Police Research Bulletin*, No. 30: 7–13.

Langlois, J.H. and Roggman, L.A. (1990) 'Attractive faces are only average', *Psychological Science* 1: 115–21.

Laughery, K.R. and Fowler, R.H. (1980) 'Sketch artist and Identikit procedures for recalling faces', *Journal of Applied Psychology* 65: 307–16.

Light, L.L., Hollander, S. and Kayra-Stuart, F. (1981) 'Why attractive faces are harder to remember', *Personality and Social Psychology Bulletin* 7: 269–76.

Light, L.L., Kayra-Stuart, F. and Hollander, S. (1979) 'Recognition memory for typical and unusual faces', *Journal of Experimental Psychology: Human Learning and Memory* 5: 212–28.

McCarthy, R.A. and Warrington, E.K. (1990) *Cognitive Neuropsychology*, Academic Press.

McClelland, J.L., Rumelhart, D.E. and the PDP Research Group (1986) *Parallel Distributed Processing: Explorations in the Microstructure of Cognition*, vol. 2, *Psychological and Biological Models*, Cambridge, Massachusetts: MIT Press.

Malone, D.R., Morris, H.H., Kay, M.C. and Levin, S. (1982) 'Prosopagnosia: a double dissociation between the recognition of familiar and unfamiliar faces', *Journal of Neurology, Neurosurgery and Psychiatry* 45: 820–2.

Malpass, R.S. and Kravitz, J. (1969) 'Recognition for faces of own- and other-race', *Journal of Personality and Social Psychology* 13: 330–4.

Mandler, G. (1980) 'Recognizing: The judgment of previous occurrence', *Psychological Review* 87: 252–71.

Morton, J. (1969) 'Interaction of information in word recognition', *Psychological Review* 76: 165–78.

Penry, Jacques (1971) *Looking at Faces and Remembering Them: A Guide to Facial Identification*, London: Elek Books.

Perkins, D. (1975) 'A definition of caricature, and caricature and recognition', *Studies in the Anthropology of Visual Communication* 2: 1–24.

Perrett, D.K., Mistlin, A.J., Potter, D.D., Smith, P.A.J., Head, A., Chitty, A.J., Broenimann, A.J., Milner, R. and Jeeves, M.A. (1986) 'Function organization of visual neurones processing facial identity', in H. Ellis, M. Jeeves, F. Newcombe and A. Young (eds) *Aspects of Face Processing*, Dordrecht: Martinus Nijhoff.

Peters, A. (1917) 'Gefulh and Wiederkennen', *Fortschritte der Psychologie und ihrer Anwendungen* 4: 120–33.

Pick, A. (1903) 'On reduplicative paramnesia', *Brain* 26: 260–7.

Rhodes, G. (1985) 'Lateralized processes in face recognition', *British Journal of Psychology* 76: 249–71.

Rhodes, G., Brennan, S. and Carey, S. (1987) 'Recognition and ratings of caricatures: Implications for mental representations of faces', *Cognitive Psychology* 19: 473–97.

Robertson, C. and Ellis, H.E. (1987) 'Estimating the effects of various clustering schemes on recall order', *British Journal of Mathematical and Statistical Psychology* 40: 1–19.

Schacter, D.L. (1987) 'Implicit memory: History and current status', *Journal of Experimental Psychology; Learning, Memory and Cognition* 13: 501–18.

Sergent, J. (1984) 'Configural processing of faces in the left and the right cerebral hemispheres', *Journal of Experimental Psychology: Human Perception and Performance* 10: 554–72.

Seymour, P.H.K. (1979) *Human Visual Cognition*, London: Collier MacMillan.

Shepherd, J.W. (1986) 'An interactive computer system for retrieving faces', in H. Ellis, M. Jeeves, F. Newcombe and A. Young (eds) *Aspects of Face Processing*, Dordrecht: Nijhoff.

Shepherd, J.W. and Ellis, H.D. (1973) 'The effect of attractiveness on recognition memory for faces', *American Journal of Psychology* 96: 627–33.

Shepherd, J.W. and Ellis, H.D. (1990) 'Systeme zum abruf von gesichts-informationen', in G. Kohnken und S.L. Sporer (eds) *Identifizierung von Tatverdachtigen durch Augenzeugen. Verlag fur Angewandte Psychologie*, Stuttgart.

Shepherd, J.W., Davies, G.M. and Ellis, H.D. (1981) 'Studies of saliency', in G.M. Davies, H.D. Ellis and J.W. Shepherd (eds) *Perceiving and Remembering Faces*, London: Academic Press.

Shepherd, J.W., Deregowski, J.B. and Ellis, H.D. (1974) 'A cross-cultural study of recognition memory for faces', *International Journal of Psychology* 9: 205–12.

Shepherd, J.W., Ellis, H.D. and Davies, G.M. (1982) *Identification Evidence: A Psychological Evaluation*, Aberdeen: Aberdeen University Press.

Shepherd, J.W., Gibling, F. and Ellis, H.D. (1991) 'The effects of distinctiveness, presentation time and delay on face recognition', *European Journal of Cognitive Psychology* 3: 137–45.

Stonham, J. (1986) 'Automatic face recognition – science fiction or commercial fact?', Paper presented at ESRC Faces Workshop V, Grange-over-Sands.

Townsend, J.T. (1990) 'Serial v Parallel Processing: Sometimes they look like Tweedledum and Tweedledee but they can (and should) be distinguished', *Psychological Science* 1: 46–54.

Tranel, D. and Damasio, A.R. (1985) 'Knowledge without awareness: An autonomic index of facial recognition by prosopagnosics', *Science* 228: 1453–4.

Valentine, T. (1991) 'A unified account of the effect of distinctiveness, inversion and race in face recognition'. *Quarterly Journal of Psychology* 43A: 161–204.

Valentine, T. and Bruce, V. (1986) 'The effects of distinctiveness in recognising and classifying faces', *Perception* 15: 525–35.

Warrington, E.K. and James, M. (1967) 'An experimental investigation of facial recognition in patients with unilateral cerebral lesions', *Cortex* 3: 317–26.

Wells, G.L. and Hryciw, B. (1984) 'Memory for faces: encoding and retrieval operations', *Memory and Cognition* 4: 338–44.

Young, A.W. (1988) 'Functional organization of visual recognition', in L. Weiskrantz (ed.) *Thought Without Language*, Oxford: Oxford University Press.

Young, A.W. and Ellis, H.D. (1989a) 'Semantic processing', in A. Young and H. Ellis (eds) *Handbook of Research on Face Processing*, Amsterdam: North Holland.

Young, A.W. and Ellis, H.D. (1989b) 'Childhood prosopagnosia', *Brain and Cognition* 9: 16–47.

Young, A.W., Hay, D.C. and Ellis, A.W. (1985) 'The faces that launched a thousand slips: Everyday difficulties and errors in recognizing people', *British Journal of Psychology* 76: 495–523.

Young, A.W., Hay, D.C. and Ellis, A.W. (1986) 'Getting semantic information from familiar faces', in H.D. Ellis, M.A. Jeeves, F. Newcombe and A. Young (eds) *Aspects of Face Processing*, Dordrecht: Nijhoff.

Young, A.W., De Haan, E.H.F. and Newcombe, F. (1990) 'Unawareness of impaired face recognition', *Brain and Cognition* 14: 1–18.

Young, A.W., De Haan, E.H.F., Newcombe, F. and Hay, D.C. (1990) 'Facial neglect', *Neuropsychologia* 28: 391–415.

Young, A.W., Hay, D.C., McWeeny, K.H., Flude, B.M. and Ellis, A.W. (1985) 'Matching familiar and unfamiliar faces on internal and external features', *Perception* 14: 737–46.

4

BRAIN DAMAGE AND MEMORY DISORDERS

A. Mayes

INTRODUCTION

Memory disorders are among the commonest results of brain damage. They often occur with other cognitive deficits also caused by the brain damage, but even by themselves may make it impossible for the victim to continue a normal life. Indeed, people with severe, but selective impairments of memory require constant attention and supervision, so that they either have to be maintained in institutions or cause a drastic emotional drain on their families. It is, therefore, important to discover more about the nature of these disorders in order to help devise better means to enable the victims and their families to cope, and, ultimately, to devise means of rehabilitation.

Although current knowledge is insufficient to offer a final classification scheme for memory disorders, it is reasonable to divide observed disorders into five different kinds. First, damage to various posterior association neocortex regions (and possibly also frontal association cortex) causes impairments of immediate memory for various specific sorts of information. The best studied such disorder is of phonological short-term memory (for example, see Shallice and Warrington 1979 and Vallar and Baddeley 1984). These disorders seem to involve only very specific kinds of information and disrupt not only immediate memory, but also long-term memory for *the same specific kinds of information.* Thus, although patients with impairments of phonological short-term memory can learn new stories or word lists normally when these are spoken, they cannot learn to remember spoken non-words or words in an unknown foreign language where they have to rely solely on phonological representations. The patients' memory for spoken stories and word lists in their own language is preserved because they can access meaning very rapidly and their memory for meaning is entirely normal.

Second, damage to posterior association neocortex can cause severe impairments in the ability to remember previously very well-established memories that are usually for semantic information, which comprises those kinds of information that constitute our mental dictionaries and encyclopaedias. Unlike specific deficits in immediate and long-term memory, this kind of disorder greatly disrupts the capacity to cope with daily life. It is particularly associated with progressive dementias such as Alzheimer's disease, but is also found in more specific forms following vascular accidents and viral encephalitis. Indeed, one of the most interesting things that has emerged in the past decade is that the loss of semantic memories can affect highly specific categories of knowledge, such as that concerning animate objects, inanimate objects or even narrower categories such as fruits and vegetables (see Hart, Berndt and Caramazza 1985). It has even been argued that the pattern of semantic memory disorders that are found supports the view that there are different semantic memory systems that must be organized somehow on category-specific lines, which are approximately duplicated in different modalities (for example, Warrington and Shallice (1984) have argued for verbal and visual semantic memory systems organized along category-specific lines). The issue is polemical and revolves in part on being able to distinguish storage from access failures, which depends on the acceptability of criteria, such as those of Shallice (1989), for distinguishing between the two kinds of failure.

The third group of memory disorders are those caused by frontal lobe lesions. This is a large brain region and therefore lesions to different parts of it are likely to have different effects. It is widely believed that the frontal association cortex is associated with planning, so that frontal lobe damage is particularly likely to disrupt kinds of memory that are heavily dependent on mental operations that are non-routine and require the initiation and maintenance of appropriate strategies. Thus, frontal lobe lesions have been reported to cause problems with free recall rather than recognition, perhaps because free recall involves more elaborative encoding and retrieval operations (see Mayes 1988). For similar reasons, patients with frontal lobe lesions may tend to show extravagant confabulations (i.e. spontaneous, sustained, wide-ranging falsifications of memory evident in a subject's everyday conversation) (Stuss and Benson

1984), impaired ability to judge how effective their memory is and how it works, which is often referred to as metamemory (Hirst 1985), and increased susceptibility to interference even over short time periods (for example, Moscovitch 1982). Some memory deficits that are caused by frontal lobe lesions are harder to explain as secondary to failures of planning, and the pattern of results outlined here has not always been reported. Most notably, Corsi (see Milner, Petrides and Smith 1985) found that frontal lobe lesions disrupted memory for the temporal order in which list items had been presented, and it has been argued by Hasher and Zacks (1979) that this kind of information is encoded automatically so that disruption of elaborative and planned kinds of processing should not affect memory for it. This issue remains unresolved, although some believe that, contrary to Hasher and Zacks' view, temporal order memory does depend on effortful processing. With respect to anomalous findings, Delbecq-Derouesne, Beauvois and Shallice (1990) have described a patient with normal free recall and impaired *recognition*, which is the reverse of the pattern usually reported in patients with frontal lobe damage. It remains unproved that the deficit was caused by frontal lobe damage, and, even if it was, it may have involved damage to a different region to the one where lesions are responsible for free recall deficits. The patient's poor recognition seems to have arisen because of his confident tendency to pick foil items as familiar. It is possible, therefore, that the deficit is a kind of judgemental failure reflecting a particular kind of problem with planning, whereas deficient free recall following frontal lobe lesions is caused by a different sort of planning problem.

The fourth group of memory disorders is a hotchpotch comprising deficits of classical conditioning and various sorts of skill learning. There is evidence that the classical conditioning of certain kinds of motor response, such as the eye blink reflex, is impaired by cerebellar lesions not only in animals like rabbits, but also in human beings (Lye, O'Boyle, Ramsden and Schady 1988; Solomon, Stowe and Pendlbeury 1989). The lesions that impair the learning and retention of motor and perceptual skills have also begun to be explored, and there is some evidence that damage to the basal ganglia is involved. Thus, patients with Huntington's chorea, who have atrophy of the caudate nucleus, have been found to be impaired at learning the skill of reading mirror-reversed words (Martone *et al.* 1984) and at learning a pursuit rotor task even when matched to controls on pretraining levels of performance (Heindel, Butters and Salmon 1987). There is even evidence that Parkinson patients, who have atrophy of the substantia nigra and a secondary disruption of other basal ganglia structures, are impaired at learning cognitive skills such as the Tower of Hanoi task, which involves moving five blocks one at a time from one of three pegs to another, never placing a larger block on a smaller one. Subjects can learn to solve this task in an optimum of thirty-one moves, but are unable to articulate what strategy they are following.

The fifth kind of memory disorder comprises what is referred to as organic amnesia. This is the classic memory disorder and corresponds to most lay people's perception of what a memory disorder should be: namely, a difficulty remembering everything that has recently been experienced, together with a problem remembering things that happened before the relevant brain damage occurred, in the face of relatively preserved intelligence and general cognitive functioning. It is important to stress that amnesia is the name of this specific memory impairment and is not a vague term that refers to organic memory impairments of any kind. The rest of this chapter will focus on this disorder because it is the one about which we know most, because it can have the most devastating effect on normal life, and because it is relatively common. The chapter will sketch amnesia's aetiologies, the brain damage that underlies it, its possible heterogeneity, the precise kinds of memory deficit associated with the syndrome, kinds of memory that are preserved in it, theories of the functional deficit that underlies it and what this may reveal about normal memory, and, finally, what, if anything, can be done to help victims cope with the condition or to rehabilitate them.

Before starting this brief sketch of organic amnesia one point is worth stressing. Most patients do not show completely pure deficits. Their memory deficit is often compounded with non-memory cognitive impairments that may make it harder to help them cope with their memory difficulties. Several memory deficits may also be found together in one patient. For example, patients with Alzheimer's dementia may show an amnesia, problems with short-term memory and failures in memory for previously well-established semantic information as well as non-mnemonic cognitive impairments even in the relatively early stages of the disease.

THE AETIOLOGY OF ORGANIC AMNESIA

Patients with selective amnesia have preserved intelligence and short-term memory as assessed by tests such as digit span or

Corsi blocks (which taps spatial short-term memory) in the face of impaired recall and recognition for facts and events experienced premorbidly, i.e. before the occurrence of the critical brain damage (retrograde amnesia), and post-morbidly (anterograde amnesia). But, much more commonly, the disorder is accompanied by other cognitive deficits. If one includes both 'pure' and 'impure' cases of amnesia, and mild as well as severe cases, then the condition is one that will eventually affect a substantial portion of the population. It is well known that normal ageing is associated with a deterioration in memory, and part of this deterioration may be caused by a mild amnesic condition. This suggestion gains some plausibility from evidence which indicates that the hippocampus, one of the structures known to be damaged in some amnesics, is particularly likely to show age-related neuronal losses and that neurofibrillary tangles appear there in healthy aged subjects even before they appear in the neocortex (see Squire 1987). The point is, however, hard to prove conclusively because the atrophic changes are slight compared with the damage found in severely amnesic patients, and the elderly also show atrophic changes in brain systems, such as the frontal lobes, that are not obviously implicated in amnesia, and kinds of memory deficit, such as difficulty in finding the names of well-known people or objects, that are forms of semantic memory impairment rather than features of amnesia.

Alzheimer's disease is a primary degenerative dementia that affects people under 65, but becomes increasingly common with age. Its precise prevalence is still unknown partly because it is hard to discriminate from other progressive dementias, but estimates have gone as high as 20 per cent for individuals over 80 (see Roth and Iversen 1986). The early stages of the dementia are often marked by a severe and relatively selective amnesic deficit. It is unresolved to what extent a common process underlies both presenile and senile forms of the disease. It is also unresolved whether there is a continuum between 'healthy' aging and Alzheimer's and possibly other dementias. If there were a continuum, then individuals would differ with respect to genetic and environmental factors that determine the degree to which the destructive processes of Alzheimer's and other dementias operate. The early stages of Alzheimer's disease have been associated with atrophic changes in the medial temporal lobes that particularly disrupt the hippocampus and its cortical links. These atrophic changes certainly contribute to the amnesia so characteristic of the early stages of the disease. Their origin is still a matter for speculation, but it has been suggested that dysfunction and loss of cortical pyramidal neurons occurs early in the disease, is responsible for its major psychological symptoms, and is particularly severe in medial temporal lobe structures (Bowen 1990). This loss of cortical pyramidal cells is likely to cause the loss of cholinergic and serotonergic subcortical neurons that also occurs early in the disease, although this is hard to prove (Bowen 1990). Others have speculated that glutamate, the excitatory neurotransmitter of many cortical pyramidal cells, can act as an excitotoxin at relatively low concentrations if neurons have a metabolic abnormality as is found in Alzheimer's disease. The progress of the disease may depend on other factors. For example, recent work has suggested that the amyloid protein found in the neuronal plaques of pyramidal neurons in dementing patients is neurotoxic and so itself may contribute to the disease (Yankner et al. 1990). To what extent genetic and environmental factors lead to the hypothesized operation of these atrophic processes is uncertain.

The other causes of amnesic states are diverse. The major causes are closed head injuries produced by falls or car accidents, and both haemorrhagic and ischaemic vascular accidents. Head injuries commonly cause focal cerebral contusions in the temporal and basal frontal lobes and these lesions may be mainly responsible for the memory problems that such patients often suffer (see Levin 1990 for a review of these problems). But closed head injury is variable in its effects, and deficits such as prosopagnosia (i.e. an inability to recognize familiar faces, not explained by defective visual acuity or reduced alertness, and caused by brain damage) may also be found. Patients with this aetiology rarely have selective amnesias. Although much the same can be said of the association between vascular accidents and selective amnesias, anoxic incidents (where the brain's oxygen supply is cut off as may occur, for example, in cases of near drowning or attempted suicide by hanging) or ischaemic incidents (where the blood supply is cut off as, for example, may occur transiently during cardiac bypass surgery) have been reported to cause very selective impairments. For example, an ischaemic incident caused bilateral damage to the CA1 field of the hippocampus of the patient R.B. and very little other damage, so that he showed a very selective amnesia (Zola-Morgan, Squire and Amaral 1986). Subarachnoid haemorrhages caused by ruptured aneurysms and the operations that follow often cause mild, and sometimes severe memory deficits, but the effects are very variable and there is no evidence that amnesia is more likely to occur when the aneurysm is at one arterial site rather than at another (Richardson 1989). In general, although closed head injury and vascular accidents often cause some degree of amnesia, the memory disorder is usually part of a larger picture of cognitive impairment.

One commonly studied form of amnesia is Korsakoff's syndrome, which develops after nutritional deficiency (particularly for thiamine) that is usually associated with years of alcoholic abuse. Many, but not all, patients undergo an acute phase, known as Wernicke's encephalopathy, in which motor, cognitive and affective functions are impaired. This is typically followed by a chronic phase in which amnesia is the major, but not the only symptom because the syndrome is usually associated with widespread brain damage in regions such as the frontal association cortex, cerebellum, and locus coeruleus as well as to the diencephalic structures around the third ventricle (Victor, Adams and Collins 1989: Shimamura, Jernigan and Squire 1988). It remains unclear to what extent the syndrome is caused directly by chronic excessive intake of alcohol and to what extent by an accompanying deficiency in thiamine intake. But cases of the disorder have apparently been found that were probably secondary to thiamine deficiency, because it seems unlikely that alcohol intake was particularly excessive. For example, Becker, Furman, Panisset and Smith (1990) have described a case with the syndrome, who showed a history of small bowel maladsorption and obstruction of the colonic interpositus, but no history of prolonged alcoholism.

Very severe amnesia also results from Herpes simplex encephalitis, which usually causes widespread damage to the medial temporal lobes, orbitofrontal and cingulate cortex, and the basal forebrain. Other brain infections such as meningitis may cause amnesia, although the location of the damage responsible for the problem is more variable. Antiviral drugs such as Acyclovir are now used to treat Herpes simplex encephalitis, so that the survival rate is now much higher, but a sad consequence has been that the survivors are frequently crippled with severe memory deficits.

Tumours around the third ventricle or in the region of the medial temporal lobes have been associated with amnesia, but patients with this aetiology have not been much studied. The most studied patients have been the rare ones in whom the critical damage was either inflicted surgically, as was the case with the bilateral temporal lobectomy used to treat the famous patient H.M.'s epilepsy, or was

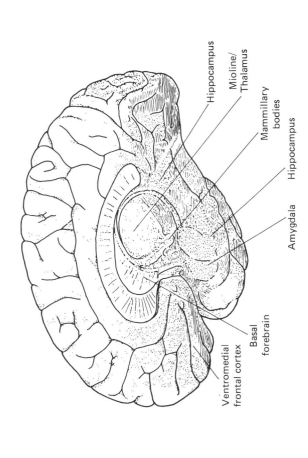

Figure 4.1 A medial view of the human brain with lines indicating structures in the basal forebrain, the medial temporal lobe and the midline diencephalon – the three main regions implicated in amnesia. The ventromedial frontal cortex is also indicated because Mishkin has argued that damage to this region causes amnesia as well.

inflicted accidentally by a penetrating injury as was the case with N.A., who had a miniature fencing sword thrust through his right nostril into his left diencephalon (see Shimamura 1989).

All the causes of amnesia that have been described usually lead to a permanent amnesia although there may be partial or even complete recovery, particularly with some aetiologies such as that associated with Korsakoff's syndrome (Victor *et al.* 1989). Amnesia may, however, be a transient condition as it is after a course of electroconvulsive therapy (Squire, Slater and Chace 1981). There is also a condition known as transient global amnesia (TGA) in which anterograde and retrograde amnesia have a rapid onset and commonly last for several hours. The condition usually ends with complete or nearly complete recovery and is often devoid of notable cognitive impairments of other kinds. Its origins are unknown although they may be heterogeneous since evidence in different cases points to migraine, epilepsy and transient ischaemic incidents (see Kritchevsky 1989). Attacks associated with epilepsy are more likely to recur and typically have shorter duration, whereas the majority of cases of classical TGA do not appear to be associated with transient ischaemia although there is a significant association with migraine (Hodges and Warlow 1990). The disorder could be caused by a process such as spreading depression that triggers both TGA and migraine. This would cause reduced metabolic activity in the medial temporal lobes, and several studies using SPECT and PET have shown reduced blood flow in this brain region (for example, see Stillhard *et al.* 1990). During an attack the victim is often confused and may repeatedly ask certain questions such as 'What's wrong? Have I had a stroke?' and, following recovery, there will be little or no memory for the events that occurred during the attack although usually premorbid memories return for events up to a short period before the attack.

THE NEUROANATOMY OF AMNESIA

Amnesia can be caused by damage to structures in the medial temporal lobes, the midline diencephalon, or the basal forebrain (Figure 4.1). All these structures lie close to the midline of the brain, which may explain why damage is often bilateral. Although there is controversy about which structures within these regions need to be damaged to produce amnesia, the regions are quite strongly interconnected, so that the amnesias resulting from lesions

94

to each of the three regions may be functionally indistinguishable. For example, the hippocampus in the medial temporal lobes receives a projection from the underlying entorhinal cortex and itself projects directly to the anterior thalamus via the fornix and also indirectly via the forniceal projection to the mammillary bodies. The anterior thalamic nucleus projects to the cingulate cortex, which projects in turn back to the hippocampus via the entorhinal cortex. Similarly, there are projections from several cortical regions, including the orbitofrontal, insular and anterior temporal cortices, to the amygdala

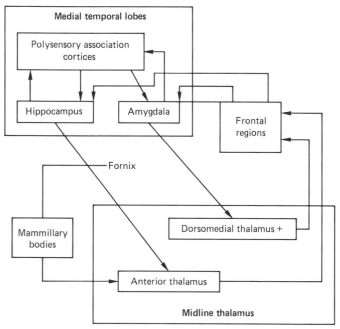

Figure 4.2 The hippocampal and amygdalar circuits damage both of which must have occurred, according to Mishkin, when amnesia is severe and permanent. Polysensory association cortex receives inputs from most or all sensory modalities, and these inputs will already have received considerable amounts of processing. The polysensory association cortices projecting to the amygdala include orbitofrontal, insular and anterior temporal cortices. Polysensory association cortices project to the hippocampus largely via the entorhinal cortex, and almost two-thirds of the projections come from the perirhinal and parahippocampal cortices, which lie in the medial temporal lobes near to the entorhinal cortex and hippocampus. The frontal regions depicted include the cingulate cortex, which is in the hippocampal circuit, and the orbitofrontal cortex (also a polysensory association cortex region), which is in the amygdalar circuit.

in the medial temporal lobes and then from the amygdala both directly and indirectly to the dorsomedial thalamus and other thalamic midline nuclei. The dorsomedial thalamus projects to the orbitofrontal cortex, which completes the circuit back to the amygdala. These circuits are illustrated in Figure 4.2. Finally, both the hippocampus and amygdala project to and receive cholinergic projections from the basal forebrain (i.e. those that are mediated by the neurotransmitter acetylcholine), which also projects to and receives projections from association neocortex and midline thalamic nuclei. This is illustrated in Figure 4.3

Precise localization of the lesions that are critical in amnesia is hard in humans because structures that are unrelated to amnesia are usually also disrupted. In recent years, the search for the critical lesions has been helped by the use of a monkey model of amnesia that has examined the effects of different lesions on animals' performance on an analogue of a recognition task as well as on a range of further memory tasks believed to be either sensitive or insensitive to amnesia in humans. Two views about the locations of the critical lesions underlying amnesia have emerged from this work, and both these views have received some corroboration from the human literature.

The first view is that of Mishkin and his colleagues (see Mishkin and Appenzeller 1987) and states that severe, permanent amnesia only occurs when there is damage to both hippocampal and amygdalar circuits just described or to the parts of the cholinergic basal forebrain that modulate both the hippocampal and amygdalar circuits (see Figures 4.2 and 4.3). On this view, severe temporal lobe amnesia should only occur if both the hippocampus and amygdala are damaged, although milder amnesia may result if only one of these structures is lesioned. Similarly, a severe midline diencephalic amnesia only occurs either if there is conjoint damage to the anterior thalamus and dorsomedial thalamus (or other thalamic nuclei that receive amygdalar projections), the thalamic projections to these nuclei, or to the mammillary bodies and the dorsomedial thalamus (or other thalamic nuclei that receive amygdalar projections). Damage to diencephalic structures in only one of the circuits should cause at most only a mild amnesia.

The second view derives from recent work of Zola-Morgan and his colleagues (Zola-Morgan, Squire, Amaral and Suzuki 1989; Zola-Morgan, Squire and Amaral 1989). These researchers have found that destruction of the amygdala that does not extend into underlying association cortex neither causes amnesia in monkeys nor does it exacerbate amnesia caused by hippocampal lesions. In contrast, lesions of the perirhinal and parahippocampal cortex (the underlying polysensory association cortex regions damaged coincidentally by earlier combined hippocampal and amygdalar lesions) caused a severe amnesia. A plausible interpretation of these results depends on a knowledge of the projections to the entorhinal cortex. The entorhinal cortex receives projections from polysensory association cortex regions such as the orbitofrontal, insular and superior temporal cortices, but above all from perirhinal and parahippocampal cortices which supply nearly two-thirds of its input. As most cortical input reaches the hippocampus from the entorhinal cortex, damage to perirhinal and parahippocampal cortices massively reduces the projection of processed cortical information into the hippocampus. Although the hippocampus does project to the midline diencephalon, in primates its projections back to polysensory association cortex via the entorhinal cortex probably assume greater importance. Polysensory association cortices, such as the perirhinal cortex, also project to midline thalamic nuclei that are

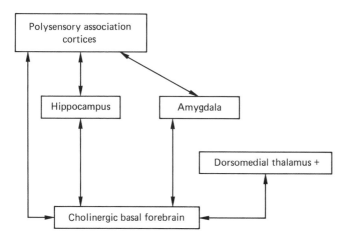

Figure 4.3 The connections of the cholinergic basal forebrain with the other regions implicated in amnesia.

both implicated in amnesia and may work relatively independently of the hippocampus. The following view therefore emerges: damage to the hippocampus causes a moderate amnesia largely because this damage disrupts activity in a hippocampal–entorhinal–polysensory association cortex loop. Damage to certain midline diencephalic structures causes amnesia because it disrupts activity in a relatively independent diencephalic–polysensory association cortex loop and also perhaps in a hippocampo–diencephalic–hippocampal loop. The effect on recognition memory of damage to these two loops should be additive although their contributions to memory are likely to be different. Damage to the basal forebrain causes amnesia because it disrupts modulation of both hippocampal and diencephalic systems. Finally, damage to polysensory association cortices, and particularly the parahippocampal and perirhinal cortices, which lie just under the hippocampus in the medial temporal lobes, causes a more severe amnesia because it disrupts activity in both hippocampal loops and in the diencephalic–polysensory association cortex loop. The circuits involved in this hypothesis about the anatomy of amnesia are illustrated in Figures 4.3 and 4.4.

It is currently not possible to rule conclusively between these two views (and both may be incorrect). Although both groups of researchers agree that parahippocampal and perirhinal cortex lesions cause severe amnesia, the evidence is not conclusive that the amygdala plays no role in amnesia. Tranel and Hyman (1990) have recently described a woman with Urbach–Wiethe disease in whom there appeared to be a selective bilateral lesion of the amygdala caused by a mineralization process typical of the disease. Although intelligence and verbal memory were preserved in this woman, she was significantly impaired on several non-verbal visual memory tasks, so the possibility that the amygdala plays a role in recall and recognition memory in humans cannot be ruled out. It is not disputed that hippocampal lesions alone can cause a moderate amnesia in humans, as several cases have been reported with lesions more or less specific to the hippocampus, of which the best described is case R.B. (Zola-Morgan et al. 1986). This patient had a moderate anterograde amnesia and, at most, a very mild retrograde amnesia. More extensive medial temporal lobe lesions that extend into polysensory association cortices, as occurs after Herpes simplex encephalitis, are associated with more severe anterograde and retro-grade amnesias. More research needs to be done to identify the critical diencephalic lesions in amnesia and to work out the extent to which the lesioned regions receive hippocampal and polysensory association cortex projections. It also remains possible that amnesia can be caused or exacerbated by lesions to modulatory systems other than the cholinergic basal forebrain. One such system is the noradrenergic pathway from the locus coeruleus, which projects to medial temporal lobe structures as well as association cortex, and which is often disrupted in Korsakoff patients (see Mayes, Meudell, Mann and Pickering 1988). A key issue, yet to be resolved with either humans or non-human primates, is the extent to which different lesions have additive disruptive effects on memory. For example, it is not known whether hippocampal and various kinds of diencephalic lesions have additive effects, and whether the effects of these lesions are exacerbated by locus coeruleus lesions. Also, as will be discussed in the next section, lesions of various parts of association neocortex are likely to exacerbate the retrograde amnesia and possibly even the anterograde amnesia found in patients.

IS AMNESIA CAUSED BY ONE OR SEVERAL FUNCTIONAL DEFICITS?

Although it is well-established that left hemisphere lesions can cause an amnesia specific to verbalizable material and that right hemisphere lesions can cause an amnesia specific to non-verbalizable material (Milner 1971), it seems likely that the damaged left and right hemisphere systems perform basically the same kind of operation on the different kinds of information that are processed by the left and right association cortices. Other and more controversial proposed dissociations of the syndrome carry the more radical implication that there are several brain systems processing the same kinds of information in different ways that are important for recalling and recognizing that information. The proposal that is currently best supported is that there is a partial dissociation between retrograde and anterograde amnesia. In many patients there is a poor correlation between the severity of the two kinds of amnesia, and, in particular, between anterograde amnesia and degree of impairment for more remote premorbid memories (for example, see Shimamura and Squire 1986). More dramatically, there are patients like R.B., who has a moderately severe anterograde amnesia, but no measurable retrograde amnesia, and contrastingly, patients have been reported with no measurable disturbance of new learning, but severe retrograde amnesia (see Mayes 1988 for a review). These latter cases are rare and although there is evidence that they have brain damage, perhaps affecting the anterior temporal association cortex (Kapur, personal communication), it is important to eliminate the possibility that such amnesias are hysterical.

It seems possible that many amnesics have damage to two processing systems. Damage to the first system causes an anterograde amnesia and a mild retrograde amnesia that is steeply temporally graded, whereas damage to the second system disrupts premorbid memories equally regardless of how long ago in the past they were formed. In support of the first system, Zola-Morgan and Squire (1990) have shown that hippocampal lesions in monkeys not only cause moderate anterograde amnesia, but also cause a steeply temporally graded retrograde amnesia such that memories formed more than 4 weeks prior to surgery are unaffected. The temporal duration of retrograde amnesia in human patients with

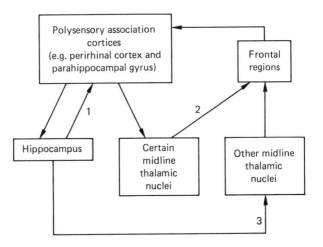

Figure 4.4   The connections of the structures damage which causes amnesia, according to the view that can be derived from the work of Zola-Morgan and his colleagues. Three circuits, damage to which causes amnesia, which are mentioned in the text are labelled 1, 2 and 3. Involvement of the cholinergic basal forebrain is illustrated in Figure 4.3.

hippocampal lesions remains a matter for debate, but could be anything between a few weeks and a year or so. Interestingly, Salmon, Zola-Morgan and Squire (1987) found that monkeys with combined hippocampal and amygdalar lesions, in whom damage extended into the perirhinal and parahippocampal cortices, showed retrograde amnesia with no temporal gradient over a period of 32 weeks. Similarly, with humans, more severe retrograde amnesia that extends back for decades is found after more widespread medial temporal lobe lesions that include parts of the temporal association cortex. This region could constitute the second system, which could be concerned with the long-term storage of episodic and semantic information. But as signs of frontal lobe damage have been found to correlate with degree of remote memory impairment in Korsakoff patients (Kopelman 1989), this brain region may also be concerned with the storage or retrieval of remote memories.

Several points about this hypothesis remain unclear. First, it is unknown whether damage to the second system only causes a retrograde amnesia or whether it also leads to an anterograde amnesia. If it causes an anterograde amnesia, this may not be like that found in most amnesics. For example, Kapur, Young, Bateman and Kennedy (1989) have described a patient with a selective retrograde amnesia and periodic attacks of transient global amnesia, some of which had clear epileptic features. Although this patient performed at normal levels on standard tests of anterograde memory (except during attacks), he had poor memory for events since the onset of his illness 10 years before. As Kapur (personal communication) has seen similar patients whose poor memory only becomes apparent several days following learning, one interpretation of these results is that the patient had normal initial memory, but showed a pathological decline over a period of days or weeks. If right, then hippocampal lesions prevent initial storage and also prevent relatively new memories being transferred to a site that may be in the anterior temporal lobes. Many temporal lobe amnesics will also have damage to this second site, so their retrograde amnesia will be much more extensive. It seems probable that heavily rehearsed memories are eventually transferred to other association cortex regions and these memories are immune to the brain disruption found in patients such as the one described by Kapur and his colleagues. New memories for episodes and facts may be dependent initially on hippocampal storage, cease to be so with time as storage in the anterior temporal lobe becomes important, and eventually

101

with rehearsal may cease to depend on either structure as storage is transferred to other association cortex regions.

Second, if the hypothesis is correct, then lesions that affect only the midline diencephalon should cause retrograde amnesias that are at least as steeply temporally graded as those caused by hippocampal lesions. The evidence from human patients is currently confusing and conflicting (see Butters and Stuss 1989) although, using an animal model of amnesia, Winocur (1985) found a short temporal gradient for rats with dorsomedial thalamic lesions

There are two further proposals about dissociations of the amnesic syndrome. The first proposal, which is derived from Mishkin's anatomical hypothesis, is that damage to the amygdalar circuit causes one set of functional deficits whereas damage to the hippocampal circuit causes a different set of deficits, so that severe amnesics must be suffering from two kinds of functional deficits each of which contributes to the amnesia observed. The applicability of this hypothesis to amnesia clearly depends on the correctness of Mishkin's anatomical hypothesis. Nevertheless, there is evidence from research with monkeys that amygdalar lesions disrupt cross-modal recognition memory, memory for temporal order information and for certain kinds of stimulus–reinforcement associations (see Mayes 1988 for a review), whereas hippocampal lesions have little effect on these kinds of memory but do disrupt spatial memory.

The second proposal is that amnesia caused by medial temporal lobe lesions is not functionally identical to that caused by midline diencephalic lesions (although usually ignored, basal forebrain lesions might be expected to produce both kinds of deficit). The plausibility of this second proposal depends on which neuroanatomical account of amnesia is correct. If Mishkin's account is correct, then both large medial temporal lobe and large midline diencephalic lesions will disrupt the same pair of amygdalar and hippocampal circuits and so might be expected to have identical effects. On the view that can be derived from the experiments of Zola-Morgan and his colleagues, large lesions in both regions might be expected to have similar effects except that the medial temporal lobe lesion will also disrupt the hippocampal–entorhinal–cortex–polysensory–cortex loop. In other words, large lesions in the two locations should have similar effects, but medial temporal lobe lesions may cause some additional memory disruption. One suggestion has been that only medial temporal lobe lesions cause a pathological acceleration of forgetting. This suggestion has been tested with unclear results over delays between 10 minutes and 1 week (see Mayes 1988 for a review), but some recent evidence indicates that patients with large medial temporal lobe lesions may forget faster in the period immediately after distraction up to a delay of a few minutes (Hart, Kwentus, Harkins and Taylor 1988). The issue needs further investigation as does the pattern of retrograde amnesia seen after lesions in the two regions. In general, dissociations that some researchers have claimed to exist are more plausible if they can be related to the anatomy of amnesia. In other words, belief in a dissociation between two deficits is better founded if one deficit can be shown to be caused by lesions in one brain region whereas the other deficit can be shown to be caused by lesions in another brain region.

THE MEMORY DEFICITS FOUND IN AMNESIA

Amnesics do not seem to be equally impaired at all kinds of memory. Not only is there evidence that they are unimpaired at certain kinds of memory task, but there is also evidence that their recall and recognition impairments for various kinds of information are not all of the same degree of severity. In particular, there is evidence that recognition of recently presented target information to which patients attended during learning is less severely impaired than is their free recall and also their memory for various kinds of background contextual information. Before discussing this evidence in more detail, two problems with its interpretations need to be considered.

The first problem is that the disproportionate deficits that amnesics seem to show for various kinds of memory may be unrelated to their amnesia and arise because of extra damage found in patients that does not contribute to their amnesia. The most influential version of this proposal is that many amnesics have damage to certain parts of the prefrontal association neocortex, which does not contribute to their amnesia, but does cause various cognitive deficits and specifically disrupts free recall of target material to which attention has been given during learning and memory for context, which typically falls on the periphery of attention and provides the background for target material. According to the proposal, amnesia disrupts recognition and free recall of target material and memory for various kinds of context to an equal degree. If amnesia occurs in conjunction with frontal lobe damage, however, patients will show greater deficits for target free recall and context memory than they will for target recognition (which is only affected in amnesia). The hypothesis is hard to test because the frontal lobes are large and comprise a functionally heterogeneous region so if damage to lesioned regions does not affect free recall or context memory, it can always be argued that effects would be found if other frontal lobe regions were damaged. This argument can, of course, be extended to other brain regions outside the frontal lobes, which makes it very difficult to refute because so few amnesics have lesions completely confined to structures believed to be critical to the syndrome.

The second problem relates to the method that needs to be used to demonstrate that certain forms of memory are more impaired in patients than is target recognition. If amnesics and controls were tested on, for example, target free recall and recognition under identical conditions, then floor and ceiling effects would almost certainly make the results uninterpretable. Even if such effects were avoided, the two groups would be performing at radically different points on the measurement scale, so that one could have no confidence that numerically equivalent differences truly indicated the same change. The only way to avoid these difficulties is to test amnesics under easier conditions than their controls so as to match the recognition performance of the two groups and then see whether under these same conditions the amnesics show worse free recall. If they do, then it is argued that their free recall is more impaired than their recognition. This inference is only valid provided that the manipulation used to match recognition across the groups (typically this involves varying the learning exposure, the length of the learning list, the delay before test, or some combination of these) has an equal or lesser effect on target recognition than it does on target free recall or context memory when it is applied to normal subjects. Although it is unlikely that the matching manipulation has less effect on free recall and context memory than it does on recognition, this possibility has rarely been formally tested.

In two studies, Hirst and his colleagues (1986, 1988) have found evidence that amnesics are more impaired at free recall than at recognition of word lists. These effects were found both in Korsakoff patients and amnesics of mixed aetiologies although the effect was only significant for Korsakoff patients with word lists comprising words in several different semantic categories. The effects were found when recognition scores between patients and controls were matched both by varying presentation time and delay to test. They also accord with clinical intuition. It remains possible, however, that the effect may be secondary to incidental frontal lobe damage, as Shoqeirat (1989) has found that although amnesic free recall is more impaired than their recognition in a task where subjects have to remember nameable shapes presented in different positions on a grid, that this disproportionate deficit correlated with performance on a test sensitive to frontal lobe damage. The disproportionate free recall deficit effect is, however, unlikely to be an artefact of the matching procedure because, in an unpublished study, we have found an amnesic group of mixed aetiology to be more impaired on free recall of a list of categorically organized words than they were at a recognition test of a list of uncategorized words. The matching procedure had an equivalent effect on the free recall and recognition of normal subjects. This task was also interesting because the difficulty of the free recall and recognition tasks was the same in normal subjects, so it cannot be said that the patients were simply worse at the harder task. Nevertheless, in further unpublished work, we have not always found amnesics to show a disproportionate deficit in free recall. This need not be too surprising. Both recognition and free recall will depend on several overlapping processes, and with different tasks the dependency on these processes may vary. Amnesics may be more impaired at a process that normally makes a greater contribution to free recall.

There is evidence using the matching procedure that amnesics are less impaired at target recognition than they are at several forms of independent context and at interactive context. Independent context is information about the spatiotemporal location of attended items and about the sensory modality via which items are presented, that does not affect the meaningful interpretation of the items, and which typically falls on the periphery of attention. In contrast, interactive context affects the meaningful interpretation of items although it falls on the background of attention (Baddeley 1982).

There is still no published evidence using the matching procedure that spatial memory is more impaired than target recognition, but we have found this result in five unpublished studies (Pickering 1987; Shoqeirat 1989). The effect was found both when spatial information was attended to and when it was incidentally encoded. Others (MacAndrews 1990; Squire, personal communication) have not found the effect, however, so the sources of the conflicting results need to be identified. As with the free recall deficits, it could be that under some circumstances spatial memory is disproportionately impaired and under others it is not. What these circumstances are, remains to be explored.

With respect to temporal memory, it has been shown by Squire (1982) that Korsakoff patients were more impaired at remembering from which of two lists recognized sentences came than they were at recognizing the words themselves. He argued that this effect correlated with frontal lobe damage and did not occur in all amnesics. In an unpublished study, we have, however, found the effect using a similar task in a large group of amnesics of mixed aetiology and failed to find that the effect correlated with signs of frontal lobe dysfunction. The issue is unresolved. Interestingly, Sagar, Gabrieli, Sullivan and Corkin (1990) have shown that the temporal lobectomy patient, H.M., is less impaired at within-list recency judgments than he is at recognition judgments. In further work with other amnesics using the same and similar tasks, much the same kind of results have emerged, so it may be that there are different kinds of temporal order memory and that amnesics can manage some kinds much better than others.

Pickering, Mayes and Fairbairn (1989) showed, using the matching procedure with a group of Korsakoff amnesics, that the patients were more impaired at remembering whether words had been presented visually or auditorily than they were at recognizing the words. The degree of the patients' impairment correlated with the severity of their amnesia, but not with signs of frontal lobe damage. In an unpublished study, we have replicated these findings with a larger group of amnesics with mixed aetiologies so that some patients had medial temporal lobe damage and others had midline diencephalic damage.

In one unpublished study, we used the matching procedure in two experiments in which subjects were required to remember homonyms. Each homonym was presented within a rectangle on a card with an interactive context word beneath it that was designed to bias subjects' interpretation of the homonym towards its less dominant meaning. Subjects' attention was directed towards the homonym during learning. In one experiment, subjects' recognition was tested for half of the homonyms in isolation and for half in the presence of the interactive context word. In the other experiment, subjects' recognition was tested separately for the target homonyms and interactive context words. In this second experiment, amnesics were more impaired at recognizing the context words than at recognizing the target words. In the first experiment, amnesics' recognition was not helped by the presence of context words whereas that of controls was. The disproportionate context memory deficit did not seem to be associated with the presence of signs of frontal lobe damage although its association with severity of amnesia remains to be proved.

KINDS OF MEMORY PRESERVED IN AMNESIA

One of the most interesting features of amnesia is that patients show preservation of certain kinds of memory in addition to short-term memory and information that was well-learned a long time prior to brain damage. Patients have been shown to be normal at acquiring and retaining simple forms of classical conditioning (Daum, Channon and Canavan 1989) and at the acquisition and retention of various forms of perceptual, motor and even cognitive skills (see Mayes 1988 for a review). Patients typically show these kinds of preserved memory, but deny having had the learning experiences that made them possible. Preservation of these kinds of memory in patients is not surprising because there is evidence that at least some forms of conditioning depend on the cerebellum and that skill memory involves the basal ganglia. Both of these structures are intact in amnesics.

More interesting theoretically is preservation of what many call priming, which is a form of item-specific indirect memory. Priming occurs when subjects process an item differently or more efficiently after having examined it earlier. When priming occurs in amnesics, unlike in controls, they usually fail to recognize the item to which they may have successfully primed. For example, if subjects are shown a series of words and later given the first three letters of those words and others that they have not been shown, and are asked to complete the openings with the first word that comes to mind, then amnesics complete as many stems as their controls with words that they have previously been shown (this is known as word completion priming). But they do not recognize those words as well as their controls. What is interesting about this is that the amnesics are displaying normal indirect memory for the same items that they are very impaired at recognizing. It becomes plausible to argue, therefore, that patients can store item information, but are unable to recognize and recall it.

There is good evidence that amnesics show preserved priming to a variety of kinds of information that were familiar prior to the priming experience. In other words, amnesics seem to prime normally when they already have memory representations for primed information.

Such representations exist most obviously for verbal information. In addition to word completion priming, amnesics have also been found to prime normally to previously familiar information in several other priming paradigms (see Mayes 1988 for a review). For example, Jacoby and Witherspoon (1982) presented subjects with the less common variant of a series of homophones (e.g. 'reed' instead of 'read'), and later asked them to spell the word. Both patients and controls tended to use the less common variant to the same extent despite the fact that patients had problems identifying these variants as recently experienced.

There is rather more controversy about whether patients show preserved priming for information that was novel prior to the training experience. This was originally demonstrated by Graf and Schacter (1985) using a paradigm that was designed to enhance word completion priming by associating the primed word with another and previously unrelated word during training. For example, if 'Mountain–Stamp' and 'Window–Reason' had been shown during training, then word completion priming was greater with pairings like 'Mountain–Sta—' than 'Window–Sta—'. Graf and Schacter found this enhancement in amnesics and controls and concluded that it depended on indirect memory for novel verbal associations. Subsequent work has more often than not failed to find an enhancement effect in amnesics (for example, Mayes and Gooding 1989), so that there is a serious doubt about whether this form of priming occurs at all in amnesics, let alone that it shows normal preservation. In unpublished studies with novel verbal information priming, we have generally been unable to find normal amnesic performance although, like Moscovitch, Winocur and McLachlan (1986) we have found that patients seem to show a normal reading speed-up effect on later re-exposure to novel verbal material.

Findings with novel non-verbal information have been more encouraging for the view that amnesics should show preserved priming for novel information. Schacter and his colleagues (see Schacter 1990) have developed a task in which subjects are shown novel shapes, half of which correspond to real three-dimensional objects and half of which are impossible objects. In normal subjects, the accuracy with which briefly displayed real objects can be identified as real can be increased by prior exposure although, for not clearly understood reasons, this improvement does not occur for impossible objects. Initial experimental findings suggest that patients show a speed-up of comparable size. Gabrieli, Milberg, Keane and Corkin (1990) have created another task in which subjects copy a drawing of a novel shape comprising lines that join five dots that are differently located for each shape. Subjects are later shown each of the dot arrays again and asked to join them up in the first way that comes to mind (this is like a non-verbal version of word completion priming). The previous exposure to the shapes biases normal subjects towards joining the dots together so as to reproduce what they have just seen. This tendency was shown to the same extent by the severely amnesic temporal lobectomy patient, H.M., despite the fact that his recognition of the shapes was very impaired. In unpublished work, Gooding has repeated this study with ten amnesic patients of mixed aetiology and found a basically similar result in so far as the patients had very impaired recall of the shapes and normal priming, at least on one of the measures that was used.

Several comments on these findings are warranted. First, no theory of the functional deficit(s) that causes amnesia can convincingly explain how global amnesics can show preserved priming for previously familiar information and for novel non-verbal information, but not for at least some kinds of novel verbal information. Second, if amnesics do show preserved priming and this indirect memory is based on the same memory representation that underlies recall and recognition of the same information, then one would expect priming to last for a comparable time to that found for recall and recognition of the same information learnt under the same conditions. If priming only lasts for a much shorter time than does recall and recognition, then it is likely to be based on a different kind of memory representation that is more transient than that which is responsible for recall and recognition. No one has yet shown that amnesic priming is preserved using a task where normal priming has been shown to last for weeks and/or for a comparable time to that found for recall and recognition. Third, performance in priming tasks is supposed to depend on a kind of automatic memory process, but it is hard to be sure that this is the case in normal subjects. Despite experimental instructions to the contrary, normal subjects could be boosting their performance using intentional recollective processes that are not available to amnesics. When amnesics do not show preserved priming, then this argument can always be used. It therefore becomes important to find a means of directly assessing the contribution of automatic and recollective processes to memory performance. Jacoby and Kelley (in press) have recently proposed a method for doing this.

It remains unresolved whether amnesics show preserved automatic memory for all those kinds of information for which they show impaired recall and recognition. It also remains unclear how this kind of memory operates. Tulving and Schacter (1990) have argued for a view according to which automatic memory depends on the continuing activation of a relatively abstract perceptual or semantic representation. In order to explain automatic memory for previously novel information, this view needs to be extended to state that sometimes a new abstract representation has to be created and to remain active. A contrasting view proposes that priming depends on automatic access to episodic memory (for example, see Allen and Jacoby 1990). If this view is correct, then even priming of previously familiar information depends on creating new memories for the contextual markers of the episodes in which the previously familiar information was presented. The theoretical implications of preserved priming in amnesia are clearly dependent on which of these views is nearer to the truth.

THEORIES OF THE FUNCTIONAL DEFICIT UNDERLYING AMNESIA

Amnesia can be characterized as a disorder in which patients may show indirect evidence of remembering things (to an extent that may even be normal), but are impaired at consciously realizing that they have remembered. In other words, remembering is not associated with a feeling of familiarity in amnesics. Not surprisingly, one theory of the syndrome is that patients have an intact memory system for facts and episodes which has become disconnected from a conscious awareness system (see Schacter 1990). This theory assumes that conscious awareness of all kinds is mediated by the activities of a single system. Whether this is true or whether different kinds of awareness depend on the activities of different systems, it is clear that amnesics are aware of things, but fail to recognize that they are familiar. It is the loss of this sense of familiarity for previously experienced facts and episodes that requires explanation. If patients are merely showing a disconnection of an intact memory system from the brain system that produces a feeling of familiarity for what is retrieved, then it is hard to see why amnesics should be more impaired at free recall and context memory than they are at recognition. Such findings, if valid, are inconsistent with a simple disconnection account of the syndrome.

One view of amnesia that can explain disproportionate deficits for free recall and context memory and, perhaps also, the loss of a feeling of familiarity, postulates that amnesics have a primary, selective memory deficit for contextual information which causes a secondary and less severe recognition deficit for the target information that was attended to during learning (see Mayes 1988). Schacter (1990) has argued that an item will not be recognized unless its encoding re-evokes the episodic context in which it previously occurred. Whether this can explain the loss of a feeling of familiarity for previously experienced facts as well as episodes is unclear. The context-memory deficit hypothesis is not usually specified with respect to what kinds of context are involved and whether the memory deficit is caused by encoding, storage, or retrieval problems. If memory for both independent and interactive context are primarily affected, then work on context-dependent forgetting in normal subjects would lead one to expect that free recall should be more impaired than recognition of target information (Mayes 1988). Amnesics do not appear to have problems registering information normally, and Shoqeirat (1989) has shown that amnesics can encode spatial and also semantic information as well as controls. The hypothesis must therefore postulate that patients either fail to consolidate context or cannot consciously recollect it. If the latter possibility obtains, then amnesics would be expected to show normal priming for all kinds of information. But if they fail to consolidate contextual information, the expectation is unclear because it depends critically on the correct account of how automatic memory works in normal people.

In contrast to the context-memory deficit hypothesis, one of the oldest views of amnesia states that patients are impaired at consolidating into long-term memory all those kinds of information for which they have impaired recall and recognition (Squire, Shimamura and Amaral 1989). A currently influential version of this general consolidation failure hypothesis is that fact and episode memory is initially stored in structures that are damaged in amnesics (such as the hippocampus) and later memory is transferred to association neocortical structures (Zola-Morgan and Squire 1990). This version of the hypothesis broadly explains anterograde amnesia and retrograde amnesia that is steeply temporally graded. Retrograde amnesia that extends back for decades would have to be accounted for in terms of damage to the cortical storage site or damage to a recollective-retrieval system dependent on frontal lobe integrity. The consolidation version of the context-memory deficit hypothesis makes similar predictions although it also requires that both fact and episode memory becomes somehow decontextualized. Unlike the context-memory deficit hypothesis, the general consolidation failure hypothesis has some difficulty in explaining why amnesics should be less impaired at target recognition than they are at target free recall and various kinds of context memory. Also, on no currently available account of how automatic memory works can it explain preserved priming of novel information unless this is based on a completely different memory representation to that which underlies recall and recognition. If this hypothesis is correct, therefore, the appearance of disproportionate deficits in free recall and context memory, and of preserved novel information priming must be illusory.

It seems likely that none of the above three hypotheses about the functional deficit(s) underlying amnesia will prove to be completely correct. This may be true if only because more than one functional deficit will be found to underlie amnesia. The correct hypothesis will be based on a better understanding of normal recognition than we now possess. It has been proposed that normal recognition depends on an automatic process and an intentional recollective process operating in parallel (for example, see Jacoby and Kelley in press). If the automatic process operates normally in amnesics, it may be possible to train it and so enhance the level of recognition that patients can show. This may prove to be a feasible approach to rehabilitation, but if so, it has yet to be properly tried.

REHABILITATION AND MANAGEMENT OF MEMORY-DISORDERED PATIENTS

Amnesia, like other memory disorders, varies in severity, but when it is severe is a crippling disorder. The sufferer is incapable of independent existence and must either be supported in an institution or by relatives. If relatives are responsible for the necessary care, the need for constant vigilance, the emotional stress engendered by repeatedly being exposed to the same questions and remarks, and the effective loss of a previously close companion gives rise to an immense strain that typically does not improve with the passage of time. Any strategy of patient rehabilitation or management must, therefore, take into account not only the patients' needs, but also those of the carers. Anything that reduces the strain for either party is a benefit. If the patient has a milder amnesic problem, then the therapy or management strategy can have the goal of enabling him or her to achieve a greater degree of independence. Ideally, such a patient should be trained so as to be able to work in a suitably structured environment.

Spontaneous recovery from organic amnesia and other kinds of organic memory disorder is relatively unusual, but not unknown. Relatively little is known about the frequency of recovery from non-amnesic organic memory disorders, but Baddeley and Wilson (1988) have described a patient with a phonological short-term memory disorder (he had a digit span of two) and a problem with comprehending longer sentences. Relevant testing was performed up to 2 years after the problem initially developed as a complication of epilepsy. Four years later, the patient was retested and showed completely normal performance on phonological short-term memory tests (his digit span was nine) and sentence comprehension (Wilson and Baddeley, submitted for publication). This dramatic recovery is particularly interesting because it occurred some years after the initial trauma. How common it is in patients of this type remains to be properly explored. It is also unknown why it occurred, although brain scans failed to show evidence of structural brain damage so this may have been minimal allowing dysfunctional neurons eventually to return to normal levels of activity. It is also interesting that the patient did follow a memory rehabilitation programme, although recovery is not proof that this worked.

With respect to organic amnesia, recovery has been reported in cases of the disorder that have been caused by Herpes simplex encephalitis and operations for repairing ruptured aneurysms, and Victor *et al.* (1989) reported a high level of partial and even 'complete' recovery in Korsakoff's syndrome. In general, however, there have been few studies that have followed the progress of patients over several years, so little is known about whether the severity of the memory disorder remains stable, gets worse or reduces, and also about whether patients learn to compensate for their disorder in daily life. Wilson (in press) has recently described a long-term follow-up study of fifty patients, who had been referred for memory therapy to the Rivermead Rehabilitation Centre, Oxford. The follow-up took place between 5 and 10 years after the patients' cerebral pathology had been sustained and several years after their original assessment. Although the severity of the memory deficits of 60 per cent of the patients showed little or no change, just under one-third of the

113

patients showed improved performance on a memory test that had been used both on the initial and follow-up assessments. This suggests that a proportion of amnesic patients show some recovery of memory up to at least several years after brain damage was sustained. Quite a few subjects were leading relatively independent lives (fifteen were in full-time employment) despite their memory problems. Most interestingly, the majority of subjects had learnt coping methods to compensate for their memory problems, which involved the increased use of memory aids and strategies. It would seem then that some recovery can occur in a currently unknown proportion of cases, but that its causes are unknown. In Wilson's study, the patients were of several different aetiologies that included closed head injury, chronic alcoholism, encephalitis, vascular accidents and anoxia, but there was no clear evidence that these aetiologies were associated with different frequencies of recovery. Even if recovery does not occur, many patients learn to compensate for their memory deficits and achieve a greater degree of independence than they had shortly after the occurrence of their brain insult. The patients described by Wilson did receive memory therapy although that does not, of course, prove that the strategies they were later found to be using were influenced by the therapy.

If recovery of memory does not occur, as seems to be the case in the majority of people who develop amnesia, then the prospects of producing some improvement in memory functioning through the use of rehabilitation are not good at present. It is generally agreed that rehabilitation procedures that try to redevelop the damaged 'muscle' of memory are unsuccessful (Sohlberg and Mateer 1989). The prospects of developing therapeutic procedures that will actually improve memory obviously depend on what causes patients' memory deficits, and this is still uncertain. If amnesics do not consolidate new information normally, then their memory is unlikely to be greatly improved by behavioural training procedures, but may respond to drug treatments or, in the longer term, to grafts of the appropriate kinds of foetal brain tissue (see Mayes 1988 for a discussion). If amnesia is caused by some kind of failure to use consolidated information so as to achieve recall and recognition, then it may be possible to improve memory both via drugs and via behavioural training procedures.

Some success in using drugs to treat amnesia has been reported, but the ameliorative effects are relatively slight and no practical treatment is yet available. Drugs that affect the activity of acetylcholine, noradrenaline and serotonin have been reported to have beneficial effects on memory in amnesics with particular aetiologies. Some success has been found with the anticholinesterase, physostigmine, in treating post-encephalitic amnesics (Catsman-Berrevoets, van Harskamp and Appelhof 1986) although this drug often has unpleasant autonomic side-effects. Improvement may depend on aetiology as this drug has been reported not to improve memory in a group of Korsakoff amnesics (see McEntee and Mair 1990). In contrast, the noradrenergic agonist, clonidine, and the specific serotonin uptake inhibitor, fluvoxamine, have been reported to improve memory in Korsakoff patients (see McEntee and Mair 1990 for a review). If effective drugs that do not have unacceptable side-effects can be developed, there is a good chance that milder amnesics will be enabled to achieve some degree of independence, and the memory of severe amnesics may be improved sufficiently to make their management much easier.

Behavioural treatment of memory disorders is either basically concerned to help patients make better use of their existing memory abilities or to train them on some skill that will increase their ability to live relatively independently. These aims are not totally distinct, because, if existing memory abilities are to be better used, then skills must be acquired. A good example of training a skill in a patient to give greater independence is provided by Giles and Morgan (1989). They trained a post-encephalitic amnesic, who not only had a severe amnesia but also semantic memory and organizational problems, to carry out a series of washing and dressing activities that he had not been reliably performing. The training programme involved chaining nine discrete activities (for example, washing face, shaving, dressing and checking hair) by getting the patient to spontaneously use linking phrases (although initially he needed to be cued by these phrases). After 14 weeks of training the patient was washing effectively on his own initiative and, at 3 months follow-up, he was showing generalization of the skill in washing effectively in a shared bathroom rather than in his own bathroom area. The training programme drew not only on forms of skill learning likely to be preserved in the patient, but also on verbal learning that was severely impaired. The length of training was probably important not only to establish the verbal learning, but also to ensure that the verbal cues consistently triggered the appropriate behaviours. Previous studies may have failed to achieve this because they were not continued long enough. The study demonstrates that complex reliable skills can be trained even in extremely impaired amnesic patients.

Patients have also been taught to acquire new skills and knowledge by trying directly to exploit what may be a preserved ability to show automatic kinds of memory for new materials. The use of this route is possibly illustrated by the vanishing cues technique (for example, see Glisky and Schacter 1989) in which, as training progresses, subjects are given smaller and smaller cues until eventually they can produce the correct answer with no cues at all. This procedure was found to be more effective than rote learning in enabling patients to acquire a vocabulary of computer terms and simple programming abilities that lasted over a six week period. The fact that small changes in the wording of definitions which the patients were required to recall disrupted their ability to remember the words, suggested to the experimenters that learning had depended on a priming-like process rather than intentional recollection. In the future, the patients who can be helped by the technique need to be identified, as does its range of effective use. The longer-term hope is that patients may be trained to use the automatic processes that underlie their experience of familiarity so as to improve their recognition and recall to an even greater degree. Jacoby and Kelley (in press) has suggested that the automatic process may involve an attribution of familiarity that is based on more fluent processing of the remembered item, so training might aim at increasing the ability to make this attribution when it is appropriate and items have indeed been processed fluently.

Patients can be helped to make better use of their remaining memory abilities *either* by the provision of external memory supports such as diaries and, more recently, of electronic memory aids that cue subjects when to do things that are indicated by the aid *or* by training them to use more elaborative encoding strategies and/or visual mnemonics (a futuristic example of this kind is given at the end of the preceding paragraph). External aids have the potential to improve the reality orientation of patients and as such help with their management, although there is still a problem in getting patients to use aids in a consistent fashion. This is a greater problem when it comes to attempts to improve patients' learning performance through the use of more efficient processing strategies. Nevertheless, patients do learn to use better processing strategies either spontaneously or as a result of training (as Wilson's long-term follow-up study showed) and they can also be trained to use external memory aids in a consistent fashion.

A demonstration of the effective use of an external memory aid has recently been reported by Sohlberg and Mateer (1989). They taught an amnesic patient to use a memory book to help him remember what he should be doing, to identify what he had done in the recent past, to recall people's names, and to find his way around neighbourhood and work places. This was achieved using a theoretically motivated training programme, which incorporated principles of learning theory as well as drawing on kinds of memory that are usually preserved in amnesics (notably skill learning). The procedures with the memory book were initially explained repeatedly so that the patient could explicitly recall them, then he was trained to use the book in the training sessions by a process that used gradually lessening amounts of cueing, and, finally, he was taught to use the book in a variety of natural settings. It required six months training before the patient learned to use the memory book independently, but he succeeded in doing so spontaneously and reliably in naturalistic settings and this considerably increased his independence. The basic message is clear: effective use of external memory aids not only needs principled training, but also patients need to be continuously exposed to the external aids over a long period of time. Many attempts to train the use of aids are ineffective because training is inconsistent and not continued for long enough.

Patients can also be taught to process information more efficiently so as to compensate for their impairment. A good example is provided by a study of Stern and Stern (1989). They taught an intelligent patient with a severe amnesia specific to verbal material, that was caused by a left frontotemporal lobe lesion, so that his verbal memory performance markedly improved and approached normal levels, enabling him to continue his training as an architect. The patient was trained to translate verbal material into a series of visual images and then at retrieval to translate these images back into words. The procedure was particularly effective because the patient had a high visual imaging ability, and doing something at which he was very successful not only had a direct impact on his verbal memory but also an indirect impact because it improved his morale. There was no problem in ensuring that he continued to use the translation procedures. In general, however, there is a problem in ensuring that patients continue to use more effective processing strategies, particularly if they have frontal lobe damage as is common after head injury (see Leng and Copello 1990). The evidence suggests that this problem will be less severe if training is made more principled, consistent and is continued for longer. Even if patients cannot be trained to use an effective strategy spontaneously in a reliable fashion it should be possible to get relatives to prompt them in situations where its use will be beneficial. Not only might the relatives play the role of the missing or damaged frontal lobes, but persistent regular use of the strategy may eventually make its use relatively automatic.

There needs to be far more investigation not only of the use of new memory training procedures, but also of the effectiveness of currently available procedures. One new procedure that may be effective with some memory impaired patients is the use of training to improve attention. This is often impaired in memory impaired patients, particularly those with closed head injury, and poor attention is likely to aggravate the memory problems caused by an independent amnesic deficit. It is therefore encouraging that Mateer, Sohlberg and Youngman (1990) have reported an attention training procedure that appears to have been effective with a group of closed head injury patients. There have also been some attempts to evaluate less novel memory training procedures. In one such study, Deelman, Berg and Koning-Haanstra (1990) compared the effects on memory-impaired head-injury patients of a procedure that involved instructing and exercising memory strategies with a no-treatment condition. There was evidence at follow-up of improvement on memory test performance even in the no-treatment patients, although effects tended to be larger for patients given memory training. More importantly, there was evidence that the patients given memory training showed post-therapy improvements in their coping behaviour with everyday memory problems, improvements in their vocational and social activities, and a more relaxed attitude to their memory deficits.

Memory therapy is often carried out with groups of patients rather than individuals, not only because of the shortage of therapists' time but also because of the possibility that patients may benefit from interacting with others having similar difficulties. Wilson and Moffat (in press) have reported an initial evaluation of groups of this kind. The evaluation of the Rivermead-based groups involved a comparison of a memory training group with another group given less specific problem-solving training. Patients showed improved performance on memory tests even one year after treatment, but this was not significantly greater in the memory training group although it tended to be greater. Consistent with Wilson's (in press) other results, memory aids were more likely to be used one year after treatment than before treatment was begun. It was not possible to predict which patients would show a favourable response to treatment. This study emphasizes the need to develop good evaluation procedures to help determine how specific are the effects of particular training procedures.

Work concerned with the rehabilitation of the non-amnesic memory disorders has scarcely begun. The most debilitating such disorder is the forgetting of previously very well-established semantic memories. If this disorder is general and severe, it clearly makes independent life extremely difficult. If it is combined with an amnesia, the prospects of independence are non-existent. Work needs to focus on the conditions, if any, under which it is possible to retrain patients to relearn the knowledge that has been lost. Certainly, with some conditions, such as anomia and prosopagnosia, there is evidence that patients do not spontaneously reacquire what has been lost (see Mayes 1988). The question is whether there are any training conditions that can overcome this block.

REFERENCES

Allen, S.W. and Jacoby, L.L. (1990) 'Reinstating study context produces unconscious influences of memory', *Memory and Cognition* 18: 270–8.

Baddeley, A.D. (1982) 'Domains of recollection', *Psychological Review* 89: 708–29.

Baddeley, A.D. and Wilson, B. (1988) 'Comprehension and working memory: A single case neuropsychological study', *Journal of Memory and Language* 27: 479–98.

Becker, J.T., Furman, J.M.R., Panisset, M. and Smith, C. (1990) 'Characteristics of the memory loss of a patient with Wernicke–Korsakoff's syndrome without alcoholism', *Neuropsychologia* 28: 171–9.

Bowen, D.M. (1990) 'Treatment of Alzheimer's disease: Molecular pathology versus neurotransmitter-based therapy', *British Journal of Psychiatry* 157: 327–30.

Butters, N. and Stuss, D.T. (1989) 'Diencephalic amnesia', in F. Boller and J. Grafman (eds) *Handbook of Neuropsychology*, vol. 3, Amsterdam: Elsevier.

Catsman-Berrevoets, C.E., van Harskamp, F. and Appelhof, A. (1986) 'Beneficial effect of physostigmine on clinical amnesic behaviour and neuropsychological test results in a patient with post-encephalitic syndrome', *Journal of Neurology, Neurosurgery and Psychiatry* 49: 1088–90.

Daum, I., Channon, S. and Canavan, A.G.M. (1989) 'Classical conditioning in patients with severe memory problems', *Journal of Neurology, Neurosurgery and Psychiatry* 52: 47–51.

Deelman, B.G., Berg, I.J. and Koning-Haanstra, M. (1990) 'Memory

119

strategies for closed head injured patients. Do lessons in cognitive psychology help?' in: R.L1. Wood and I. Fussey (eds) *Cognitive Rehabilitation in Perspective*, London: Taylor and Francis.

Delbecq-Derouesne, J., Beauvois, M.F. and Shallice, T. (1990) 'Preserved recall versus impaired recognition', *Brain* 113: 1045–74.

Gabrieli, J.D.E., Milberg, W., Keane, M.M. and Corkin, S. (1990) 'Intact priming of patterns despite impaired memory', *Neuropsychologia* 28: 417–27.

Giles, G.M. and Morgan, J.H. (1989) 'Training functional skills following Herpes Simplex encephalitis: A single case study', *Journal of Clinical and Experimental Neuropsychology* 11: 311–18.

Glisky, E.L. and Schacter, D.L. (1989) 'Extending the limits of complex learning in organic amnesia: computer training in a vocational domain', *Neuropsychologia* 27: 107–20.

Graf, P. and Schacter, D.L. (1985) 'Implicit and explicit memory for new associations in normal and amnesic subjects', *Journal of Experimental Psychology: Learning, Memory and Cognition* 11: 501–18.

Hart, J., Berndt, R.S. and Caramazza, A. (1985) 'Category-specific naming deficit following cerebral infarction', *Nature* 316:439–40.

Hart, R.P., Kwentus, J.A., Harkins, S.W. and Taylor, J.R. (1988) 'Rate of forgetting in mild Alzheimer's-type dementia', *Brain and Cognition* 7: 31–8.

Hasher, L. and Zacks, R.T. (1979) 'Automatic and effortful processes in memory', *Journal of Experimental Psychology: General* 108: 356–88.

Heindel, W.C., Butters, N. and Salmon, D. (1987) 'Impaired motor skill learning associated with neostriatal function', *Journal of Clinical and Experimental Neuropsychology* 9: 18.

Hirst, W. (1985) 'Use of mnemonic in patients with frontal lobe damage', *Journal of Clinical and Experimental Neuropsychology* 9: 18.

Hirst, W., Johnston, M.K., Kim, J.K., Phelps, E.A., Risse, G. and Volpe, B.T. (1986) 'Recognition and recall in amnesics', *Journal of Experimental Psychology: Learning, Memory and Cognition* 12: 445–51.

Hirst, W., Johnson, M.K., Phelps, E.A. and Volpe, B.T. (1988) 'More on recognition and recall', *Journal of Experimental Psychology: Learning, Memory and Cognition* 14: 758–62.

Hodges, J.R. and Warlow, C.P. (1990) 'Syndromes of transient amnesia: towards a classification. A study of 153 cases', *Journal of Neurology, Neurosurgery and Psychiatry* 53: 834–43.

Jacoby, L.L. and Kelley, C. (in press) 'Unconscious influences of memory: Dissociations and automaticity', in D. Milner and M. Rugg (eds) *The Neuropsychology of Consciousness*, London: Harcourt Brace Jovanovich.

Jacoby, L.L. and Witherspoon, D. (1982) 'Remembering without awareness', *Canadian Journal of Psychology* 36: 300–24.

Kapur, N., Young, A., Bateman, D. and Kennedy, P. (1989) 'Focal retrograde amnesia: a long term clinical and neuropsychological follow-up', *Cortex* 25: 387–402.

Kopelman, M.D. (1989) 'Remote and autobiographical memory, temporal context memory and frontal atrophy in Korsakoff and Alzheimer patients', *Neuropsychologia* 27: 437–60.

Kritchevsky, M. (1989) 'Transient global amnesia', in Boller, F. and Grafman, J. (eds) *Handbook of Neuropsychology*, vol. 3, Amsterdam: Elsevier.

Leng, N.R.C. and Copello, A.G. (1990) 'Rehabilitation of memory after brain injury: is there an effective technique?' *Clinical Rehabilitation* 4: 63–9.

Levin, H.S. (1990) 'Deficit after closed head injury', *Journal of Clinical and Experimental Neuropsychology* 12: 129–53.

Lye, R.H., O'Boyle, D.J., Ramsden, B.T. and Schady, W. (1988) 'Effects of unilateral cerebellar lesion on the acquisition of eye-blink conditioning in man', *Journal of Physiology* 403: 58P.

MacAndrews, S.B.G. (1989) 'The structure of recall in amnesia', unpublished PhD thesis, University of Warwick.

McEntee, W.J. and Mair, R.G. (1990) 'The Korsakoff syndrome: a neurochemical perspective', *Trends in Neurosciences* 13: 340–4.

Martone, M., Butters, N., Payne, M., Becker, J.T. and Sax, D.S. (1984) 'Dissociation between skill learning and verbal recognition in amnesia and dementia', *Archives of Neurology* 41: 965–70.

Mateer, C.A., Sohlberg, M.M. and Youngman, P.K. (1990) 'The management of acquired attention and memory deficits', in R.Ll. Wood and I. Fussey (eds) *Cognitive Rehabilitation in Perspective*, London: Taylor and Francis

Mayes, A.R. (1988) *Human Organic Memory Disorders*, Cambridge: Cambridge University Press.

Mayes, A.R. and Gooding, P. (1989) 'Enhancement of word completion priming in amnesics by cueing with previously novel associates', *Neuropsychologia* 27: 1057–72.

Mayes, A.R., Meudell, P.R., Mann, D. and Pickering, A. (1988) 'Location of lesions in Korsakoff's syndrome: neuropsychological and neuropathological data on two patients', *Cortex* 24: 1–22.

Milner, B. (1971) 'Interhemispheric differences in the localization of psychological processes in man', *British Medical Bulletin* 27: 272–7.

Milner, B., Petrides, M. and Smith, M.L. (1985) 'Frontal lobes and the temporal organization of memory', *Human Neurobiology* 4: 137–42.

Mishkin, M. and Appenzeller, T. (1987) 'The anatomy of memory', *Scientific American* 256: 62–71.

Moscovitch, M. (1982) 'Multiple dissociations of function in amnesia', in L.S. Cermak (ed.) *Human Memory and Amnesia*, Hillsdale, NJ: Erlbaum, pp. 337–70.

Moscovitch, M., Winocur, G. and McLachlan, D. (1986) 'Memory as assessed by recognition and reading time in normal and memory-impaired people with Alzheimer's disease and other neurological disorders', *Journal of Experimental Psychology: Learning, Memory and Cognition* 115: 331–47.

Pickering, A. (1987) 'Does amnesia arise from a specific deficit in memory for contextual information?', unpublished doctoral dissertation, Manchester University.

Pickering, A., Mayes, A.R. and Fairbairn, A.F. (1989) 'Amnesia and memory for modality information', *Neuropsychologia* 27: 1249–59.

Richardson, J.T.E. (1989) 'Performance of free recall following rupture and repair of intracranial aneurysm', *Brain and Cognition* 9: 210–26.

Roth, M. and Iversen, L.L. (eds) (1986) 'Alzheimer's disease and related disorders', *British Medical Bulletin*, 42: 1–114.

Sagar, H.J., Gabrieli, J.D.E., Sullivan, E.V. and Corkin, S. (1990) 'Recency and frequency discrimination in the amnesic patient H.M.', *Brain* 113: 581–602.

Salmon, D.P., Zola-Morgan, S. and Squire, L.R. (1987) 'Retrograde amnesia following combined hippocampus–amygdala lesions', *Psychobiology* 15: 37–47.

Schacter, D.L. (1990) 'Toward a cognitive neuropsychology of awareness: Implicit knowledge and anosognosia', *Journal of Clinical and Experimental Neuropsychology* 12: 155–78.

Schacter, D.L. (in press) 'Consciousness and awareness in memory and amnesia: critical issues', in D. Milner and M. Rugg (eds) *Consciousness and Cognition: Neuropsychological Perspectives*, London: Academic Press.

Shallice, T. (1989) *From Neuropsychology to Mental Structure*, Cambridge: Cambridge University Press.

Shallice, T. and Warrington, E.K. (1979) 'Auditory-verbal short-term memory impairment and conduction aphasia', *Brain and Language* 4: 479–91.

Shimamura, A.P. (1989) 'Disorders of memory: the cognitive science perspective', in *Handbook of Neuropsychology*, vol. 3, Amsterdam: Elsevier.

Shimamura, A.P., Jernigan, T.L. and Squire, L.R. (1988) 'Korsakoff's syndrome: radiological (CT) findings and neuropsychological correlates', *Journal of Neuroscience* 8: 4400–10.

Shimamura, A.P. and Squire, L.R. (1986) 'Korsakoff's syndrome: the relationship between anterograde amnesia and remote memory impairment', *Behavioral Neuroscience* 100: 65–100.

Shoqeirat, M.A. (1989) 'Contextual memory deficits and rate of forgetting in amnesics with different aetiologies', unpublished PhD thesis, University of Manchester.

Sohlberg, M.M. and Mateer, C.A. (1989) 'Training use of compensatory memory books: A three stage behavioral approach', *Journal of Clinical and Experimental Neuropsychology* 11: 871–91.

Solomon, P.R., Stowe, G.T. and Pendlbeury, W.W. (1989) 'Disrupted eyelid conditioning in a patient with damage to cerebellar afferents', *Behavioral Neuroscience* 103: 898–902.

Squire, L.R. (1982) 'Comparison between forms of amnesia: some deficits are unique to Korsakoff syndrome', *Journal of Experimental Psychology: Learning, Memory and Cognition* 8: 560–71.

Squire, L.R. (1987) *Memory and Brain*, New York: Oxford University Press.

Squire, L.R., Shimamura, A.P. and Amaral, D.G. (1989) 'Memory and the hippocampus', in J. Byrne and W. Berry (eds) *Neural Models of Plasticity*, New York, Academic Press.

Squire, L.R., Slater, P.C. and Chace, P.M. (1981) 'Retrograde amnesia following ECT: Long-term follow-up studies', *Archives of General Psychiatry* 38: 89–95.

Stern, J.M. and Stern, B. (1989) 'Visual imagery as a cognitive means of compensation for brain injury', *Brain Injury* 3: 413–19.

Stillhard, G., Landis, T., Schiess, R., Regard, M. and Sialer, G. (1990) 'Bitemporal hypoperfusion in transient global amnesia: 99m-Tc-HM-PAO SPECT and neuropsychological findings during and after an attack', *Journal of Neurology, Neurosurgery and Psychiatry* 53: 339–42.

Stuss, D.T. and Benson, D.F. (1984) 'Neuropsychological studies of the frontal lobes', *Psychological Bulletin* 95: 3–28.

Tranel, D. and Hyman, B.T. (1990) 'Neuropsychological correlates of bilateral amygdala damage', *Archives of Psychiatry* 47: 349–55.

Tulving, E. and Schacter, D.L. (1990) 'Priming and human memory systems', *Science* 247: 301–6.

Vallar, G. and Baddeley, A.D. (1984) 'Fractionation of working memory: Neuropsychological evidence for a phonological short-term store', *Journal of Verbal Learning and Verbal Behavior* 23: 151–61.

Victor, M., Adams, R.D. and Collins, G.H. (1989) *The Wernicke–Korsakoff Syndrome and Related Neurological Disorders due to Alcoholism and Malnutrition*, 2nd edn, Philadelphia: F.A. Davis.

Warrington, E.K. and Shallice, T. (1984) 'Category specific semantic impairments', *Brain* 107: 829–55.

Wilson, B. (in press) 'Long term prognosis of patients with severe memory disorders', *Neuropsychological Rehabilitation*.

Wilson, B. and Baddeley, A.D. (submitted for publication) 'Spontaneous recovery of impaired memory spans: Does comprehension recover?'.

Wilson, B. and Moffat, N. (in press) 'The development of group memory therapy', in: B. Wilson and N. Moffat (eds) *Clinical Management of Memory Problems*, 2nd edn, London: Chapman and Hall.

Winocur, G. (1985) 'The hippocampus and time', *Behavioural and Brain Sciences* 8: 512–13.

Yankner, B.A., Duffy, L.K. and Kirschner, D.A. (1990) 'Neurotrophic and neurotoxic effects of amyloid B protein reversal by Tachykinin neuropeptides', *Science* 250: 279–82.

Zola-Morgan, S. and Squire, L.R. (1990) 'The primate hippocampal formation: evidence for a time-limited role in memory storage', *Science* 250: 288–90.

Zola-Morgan, S., Squire, L.R. and Amaral, D.G. (1986) 'Human amnesia and the medial temporal region: enduring memory impairment following a bilateral lesion limited to field CA1 of the hippocampus', *Journal of Neuroscience* 6: 2950–67.

Zola-Morgan, S., Squire, L.R. and Amaral, D.G. (1989) 'Lesions of the amygdala that spare adjacent cortical regions do not impair memory or exacerbate the impairment following lesions of the hippocampal formation', *Journal of Neuroscience* 9: 1922–36.

Zola-Morgan, S., Squire, L.R., Amaral, D.G. and Suzuki, W.A. (1989) 'Lesions of perirhinal and parahippocampal cortex that spared the amygdala and hippocampal formation produce severe memory impairment', *Journal of Neuroscience* 9: 4355–70.

5

MEMORY AND AGING

Deborah M. Burke

> Blossoms will run away
> Cakes reign but a Day,
> But Memory like Melody
> is pink Eternally.
> (Emily Dickinson in Johnson 1960: 654–5)

Emily Dickinson wrote this poem in 1883 when she was 53 years old. It expresses her sense that her memory is a valued and pleasurable possession, and one of the few that would endure throughout her life. Her optimistic assessment of the ability of her memory to withstand the ravages of time stands in sharp contrast to the views of many older adults today, over one hundred years later. A decline in memory ability with aging seems to be widely accepted by older adults (e.g. Hultsch, Hertzog, Dixon and Davidson 1988) and is well established in empirical research (e.g. Burke and Light 1981).

Age-related changes in memory, however, are not uniform across different memory functions. Laboratory studies have shown that some aspects of memory performance are unchanged or even improved, while others suffer a decline (Light and Burke 1988). Consistent with this, while older adults give lower self-ratings than young adults for their ability to remember proper names and numbers such as postal codes, young and older adults give equivalent assessments of their memory for factual and personal information, such as experiences in childhood or with friends (Cohen and Faulkner 1984; Martin 1986). Indeed, young and older adults' recall and description of specific incidents from their past lives are similar in specificity and completeness (Winthorpe and Rabbitt 1988), and older adults rate the vividness of such memories higher than do young adults (Cohen and Faulkner 1987). Thus Dickinson may, in fact, be in agreement with current research and with older adults today: What she treasured in her memory was undoubtedly her rich store of personal experiences and this aspect of memory may remain 'pink'.

This example makes clear that the evaluation of memory changes in old age is a complex endeavour that requires distinctions among different kinds of memory. Moreover, identification of the mechanisms underlying memory change in old age requires the assessment of non-cognitive, as well as cognitive factors associated with aging because of the enormous difference between the lifestyle of young and older adults. In this chapter, we examine the pattern of spared and impaired memory functions in old age, and evaluate some cognitive and non-cognitive explanations of these changes.

We focus on two memory functions that figure prominently in older adults' memory complaints: namely, memory for new information, and production of well-known words, especially proper names. We consider why these two quite different memory functions, one involving the ability to form new memory representations and the other involving the ability to retrieve well-established pre-existing representations for words, should decline in old age. We describe an explicit model of memory and language which provides a framework for analyzing these aging effects. The model postulates specific memory representations and processing mechanisms, and views age-related deficits as the result of an impairment in a particular mechanism that is basic to all learning and memory. Finally, we consider the extent to which non-cognitive factors are able to account for these age differences in memory.

AGING AND MEMORY FOR NEW INFORMATION

One of the strongest patterns found in cognitive aging research is older adults' decline in performance on tasks that require new learning, but not on tasks that require already learned information (Light and Burke 1988; Salthouse 1988). This dissociation of aging effects on new and old learning tasks was neatly demonstrated by Charness (1981) in his evaluation of the contribution of age and skill to chess performance. He found that skill, but not age, predicted the quality of a move chosen for a particular chess board and the accuracy of an evaluation of an end-game position. Performance on these tasks draws on knowledge of chess that is acquired over years of practice and is apparently relatively immune to aging effects. However, recall of all the specific board positions was tested at the end of the session and was negatively affected by age. Memory for this new information was impaired in older adults compared with younger adults. A similar dissociation in the effects of aging was demonstrated by Welford (1985) on practice of new and familiar tasks: On tasks involving new learning, older adults improved with practice more slowly than young adults whereas, on familiar tasks, older adults improved at least as rapidly as young adults.

A parallel aging pattern is found in psychometric studies of intellectual abilities where the classification of fluid and crystallized abilities overlaps with the distinction between new and old learning. For example, vocabulary subtests involve long-term knowledge and are thought to test *crystallized abilities*; they show relatively little decline in old age. In contrast, subtests such as digit–symbol substitution, which requires learning arbitrary associations between digits and symbols, involve new learning and are thought to test *fluid abilities*; these show substantial age-related decline (e.g. Horn 1982; Horn and Cattell 1966; Salthouse 1985).

Perhaps because of the substantial age deficits found in memory for new information, this is one of the most intensive areas of research in memory and aging (for reviews see Burke and Light 1981; Hultsch and Dixon 1990; Light 1991; Salthouse 1985). Age decrements in memory for new information have been found for a broad range of materials and methods of testing, including the traditional measures of paired associate learning, serial recall, free recall and prose recall. For example, for each of these measures Salthouse (1985) gathered results from a number of studies and calculated a negative correlation with age ranging from -0.21 to -0.48. Thus, the differential effects of age on establishing new memory representations versus using already-established representations must be addressed by any model of cognitive change in old age.

AGING AND WORD-FINDING FAILURES

Older adults' increased difficulties in producing well-known words is an exception to the generalization that existing knowledge or old learning is relatively immune to aging. Older adults complain that failures in retrieving well-known words increase dramatically in old age and become an irksome problem (e.g. Cohen and Faulkner

1986). There are at least four sources of evidence that suggest an age-linked deficit in word retrieval.

First, there are age-related decreases in the *accuracy* of naming pictures of objects or actions (e.g. Borod, Goodglass and Kaplan 1980; Nicholas, Obler, Albert and Goodglass 1985), and age-related increases in the *time* to name pictures (Thomas, Fozard and Waugh 1977). These differences appear to reflect deficits in access to the *sounds* of words – that is, phonological information – because the age difference decreases for naming accuracy when phonological cues are provided (Nicholas *et al.* 1985), and for naming latency when the picture is preceded by its name (Thomas *et al.* 1977).

Second, older adults are slower and less accurate than young adults in producing a target word corresponding to a definition (Bowles and Poon 1985). On timed fluency tests, older adults usually produce fewer words starting with a specified letter or in a specified category than do young adults (Burke and Light 1981; Borod *et al.* 1980).

Older adults' greater word-finding difficulty is also reflected in their spontaneous speech. Relative to young adults, older adults produced proportionately more pronouns than common or proper nouns in describing a memorable experience, suggesting a problem in accessing the names of people and things (Ulatowska, Hayashi, Cannito and Fleming 1986). In a study of young and older adults' descriptions of pictures, older adults used more indefinite words such as 'thing', apparently because they were less able than younger adults to retrieve the appropriate words (Cooper 1990).

The tip-of-the-tongue experience

Finally, one of the most dramatic instances of word-finding difficulty is the tip-of-the-tongue (TOT) state in which a person is unable to produce a word although absolutely certain that the word is known. The sense of imminent retrieval is like being on '. . . the brink of a sneeze' (Brown and McNeill 1966; 326). Despite the inaccessibility of the TOT target, people can typically report the initial letters of the target or the numbers of syllables, and often a persistent alternate, a wrong word phonologically similar to the target that comes persistently to mind (e.g. Brown and McNeill 1966; Burke, MacKay, Worthley and Wade 1991).

In a series of studies, my colleagues and I have examined young and older adults' TOT experiences in everyday life and in the laboratory (Burke *et al.* 1991; Burke, Worthley and Martin 1988). In our naturalistic study, we asked 130 young, midage, and older adults to use structured diaries to record spontaneous TOTs as they occurred during a 4 week interval in their everyday life. This technique allowed us to examine the characteristics of TOT states, such as partial information available about the inaccessible word, the nature of the TOT words themselves and how and when TOTs are resolved, while avoiding the constraints of a laboratory study where potential TOT targets are selected by the experimenter.

Because naturalistic data may be subject to reporting biases, we also attempted to replicate our diary study findings with laboratory induced TOTs. We developed a set of 100 questions that were the most successful in inducing TOTs; a sample of seven of these questions is shown in Table 5.1 (and the answers are shown on the bottom of Table 5.3). These questions were presented one at a time on a computer and twenty-two young and twenty-two older adults indicated whether they knew the answer, did not know the answer, or had the answer on the tip of their tongue. In the case of a TOT response, they reported any partial phonological information or persistent alternates that were available.

Table 5.1 Examples of TOT-inducing questions

- What do you call a word or sentence that reads the same backward or forward, such as 'Madam, I'm Adam'?
- What is the name of the process by which plants make their food?
- What do you call a stone building (often found in a cemetery) with places for entombment of the dead above ground?
- What word means to deposit (something valuable) as security for money borrowed?
- What word means to formally renounce a throne?
- What is the last name of the man who assasinated Robert Kennedy?
- What is the name of the islands off the coast of Ecuador that Darwin visited to study unique species of birds and animals?

Note: Answers are listed at the bottom of Table 5.3

As can be seen in Table 5.2, we found that the frequency of both spontaneous and lab-induced TOTs increased with age. Persistent alternates, however, decreased with age. These persistent alternates were related to the targets in very consistent ways. As can be seen in the examples, they were generally phonologically and semantically similar to the target, and they were virtually always in the same grammatical class as the target. Partial information about the target that was accessed, such as its number of syllables and initial phonemes, also decreased significantly with age for spontaneous TOTs but not laboratory-induced TOTs.

Table 5.2 Mean number of naturally occurring and lab-induced TOTs and percentage of TOTs with persistent alternates

TOT	Age	Mean number of TOTs	Percentage of TOTs with persistent alternates
Naturally occurring	Young	3.9*	66.7
	Midage	5.4	57.9
	Old	6.6	48.3
Lab-induced	Young	9.9†	40.9
	Old	11.9	9.9

Examples:	Target	Persistent alternates
	mausoleum	mortuary
	eccentric	exotic
	metastasis	metaphor
	pomegranate	persimmon
	blender	vibrator
	Shatner	Shakespeare

*Mean number during 1 month
†Mean number for 100 questions

The corpus of TOT targets from the diary study revealed that, not surprisingly, the words had very low frequency of occurrence and, in the case of acquaintance names, were words that had not been used recently. The frequency of most TOT target words was too low to be listed in frequency of occurrence norms (e.g. Francis and Kucera 1982). Proper names accounted for about 68 per cent of all TOT targets and of these from one-third to one-half, depending on age, were names of acquaintances. As can be seen in Table 5.3, these acquaintances were people who had been known for some time, with the duration depending on age, but who had not been contacted recently. Thus, TOT targets can be described as words which occur infrequently in the language or as the names of people who have not been contacted recently, especially for older adults.

In sum, older adults experience more TOTs, have fewer alternative words come persistently to mind, and access less information about the target (in spontaneous TOTs) than young subjects (see also Maylor 1990). Thus, our data are consistent with the reports of older adults that, in the throes of a TOT, their minds simply

Table 5.3 Naturally occurring TOTs for acquaintance names

Age	Length of acquaintance	Recency of contact
	years	years
Young	1.1	0.3
Midage	4.2	0.4
Old	17.7	4.0

Answers to Questions in Table 5.1: palindrome, photosynthesis, mausoleum, pawn, abdicate, Sirhan, Galapagos

go blank. It also took longer for older adults than young adults to resolve a TOT. The most frequent method of resolution of spontaneous TOTs in everyday life was for the target word to pop into mind when the person was no longer trying to retrieve it. These spontaneous retrievals took about twice as long in older adults compared with young and midage adults.

In the next section, we present a model of the memory system that specifies the cognitive mechanisms underlying older adults' increasing word-finding problems, as well as their deficits in memory for new information.

THEORETICAL FRAMEWORK FOR MEMORY CHANGES IN OLD AGE

Current models of memory postulate a vast network of pathways connecting representational units called nodes. Nodes are organized into a *semantic system* which represents word meanings and a *phonological and orthographic system* which represents word sounds and spellings (e.g. Baddeley 1982; Collins and Loftus 1975; Dell 1986; MacKay 1987; McClelland and Rumelhart 1981). Figure 5.1 illustrates a portion of the representation of *dragon* in the semantic and phonological systems within interactive activation models (e.g. Burke *et al.* 1991; Dell 1986; MacKay 1982, 1987). Lexical nodes do not store either phonological or semantic information, but rather are connected, in the phonological system, to hierarchically organized nodes which represent syllables, phonological compounds and features, and in the semantic system, to nodes which represent aspects of meaning or experience corresponding to the word. For example, the lexical node for *dragon* is connected to the syllables *dra* and *gon*, and to nodes representing conceptual information about dragons such as the fact that they are imaginary. Representational nodes in the phonological and semantic system are types, not tokens, because they are connected to all lexical nodes whose words include that component.

Activation of nodes to threshold causes retrieval of information and may occur in one system independently of the others. Activation spreads along connections within and between systems to related nodes, increasing subthreshold levels of excitation, called priming, which increases the availability of the information at these nodes. Retrieval of a word sound occurs only when nodes at the lowest level, i.e. phonological features, have been activated to threshold.

The strength of connections between nodes, called linkage strength, determines the rate and amount of priming transmitted between them (MacKay 1987). Thus, linkage strength is an important determinant of what information represented in memory becomes available. Within the present model, linkage strength is influenced by three factors: recency and frequency of activation, and age of the subject. Linkage strength of connections is increased by frequent and recent activation of nodes which enables more efficient transmission of priming. Thus linkage strength explains a variety of practice effects: Highly practised connections have greater linkage strength and therefore a greater rate of priming producing more rapid and accurate behaviour (MacKay 1982). According to the Transmission Deficit Hypothesis, age weakens linkage strength so that the transmission of priming across connections is decreased (Burke *et al.* 1991; MacKay and Burke 1990).

Aging effects on TOT experiences: The Transmission Deficit Hypothesis

Within this model, TOTs originate when a lexical node becomes activated, causing a strong 'feeling of knowing' for the target word, but at least some of its connected phonological nodes remain unactivated because insufficient priming is transmitted to enable activation and retrieval of the phonology. This transmission deficit is related to frequency and recency of use, and thus TOTs involve words used infrequently or not recently. For example, a TOT for *dragon* would occur if the lexical node *dragon* became activated, but

131

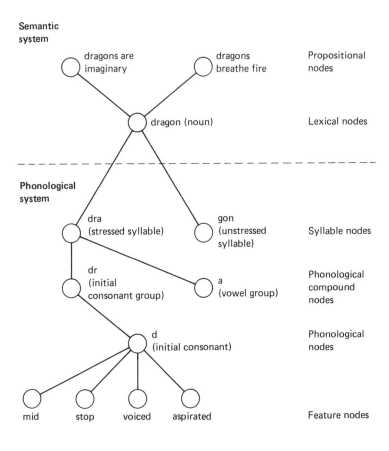

Figure 5.1 Nodes representing 'dragon' in the semantic and phonological systems. Many modes necessary for producing this word have been left out to simplify the figure.

connections to the phonology were weakened in linkage strength from disuse so that there was insufficient transmission of priming to enable some of the connected phonological nodes to become activated (see Figure 5.1).

The TOT can be resolved by the target's popping into mind if there is an externally delivered boost in priming to the appropriate phonological nodes. It has been suggested that this boost may arise when the TOT target is no longer in mind and the critical phonological components occur accidentally during internal speech or everyday language comprehension (Burke *et al.* 1991; Yaniv and Meyer 1987). For example, hearing the word *dragnet*, increases activation levels of the relevant nodes shared with *dragon*, so that a pop-up can occur.

This transmission deficit hypothesis must explain why TOT experiences and their resolution time increase with age, whereas persistent alternates and information available about the TOT target decrease with age (see Burke *et al.* 1991; Maylor 1990). All four phenomena are consistent with the transmission deficit hypothesis. If aging reduces the priming delivered to nodes in the phonological system, phonological information will be less primed, leading to reduced information retrieval about the target, as observed. Older adults would also retrieve fewer persistent alternates (as observed) because the spread of priming 'bottom-up' from phonological nodes shared by the alternate and target and 'top-down' from shared semantic nodes would both be reduced. Finally, the time required for TOT targets to pop into mind would be longer for older adults (as observed) because more input would be required to raise priming levels to a point where the target nodes could be activated. The transmission deficit hypothesis therefore explains how TOTs arise and are resolved in general, and how TOTs change with age.

Aging effects on memory for new information

We have been discussing the activation of information that is already represented in memory. The representation of new information – that is, new learning – requires new connections between existing nodes and a commitment of new 'uncommitted' nodes to link these connections. For example, no pre-established nodes represents the phrase *dragons eat fudge* in Figure 5.2, although there are pre-existing lexical nodes representing each of the words. This would be true for a person who has not experienced or processed this particular noun phrase before, or at least not to the extent required for permanent commitment learning. The node labelled *X* is an uncommitted node and new learning occurs to the extent that it becomes committed, i.e. represents the proposition *dragons eat fudge*.

This process of commitment of a node so that it represents new information requires *prolonged activation* under the present model (MacKay and Burke 1990). Thus, strong transmission of priming is essential for the retention of new information or novel combinations of old information within this model. If insufficient priming is delivered to the uncommited node, commitment cannot occur. This means that if aging reduces priming transmission, as postulated under the Transmission Deficit hypothesis, then uncommitted nodes in older adults will be more likely to fail to achieve commitment, and new learning will fail to occur. As a result, memory for new information will suffer greater age-related deficits than memory for old or committed information because new learning requires

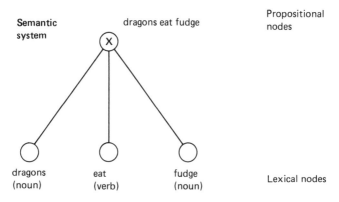

Figure 5.2 A sample of nodes representing 'dragons', 'eat', 'fudge' and their connections. The uncommitted node making a new connection between these words, and representing new learning, is marked with an X.

considerably more summation of priming than does retrieval of old information.

Aging effects on direct versus indirect memory tasks

A currently popular dimension for describing memory tasks is the involvement or non-involvement of conscious recollection. Direct memory tasks such as recall or recognition require conscious recollection of prior experiences. Indirect memory tasks show effects of prior experience without seeming to require conscious recollection of those experiences. For example, in the fragment completion task, subjects are asked to complete a fragment of a word (e.g. given BE—VI—, the correct response is BEHAVIOUR). Improved performance after recent previous exposure to the words forming the completions is taken as evidence of memory for the previous experience and is called repetition priming. Young and older adults show equivalent levels of repetition priming in a variety of indirect tasks, although the older adults show deficits when memory is tested directly through recall (e.g. Light and Singh 1987; Moscovitch 1982; Howard 1988).

Does this dissociation between the effects of aging on direct and indirect memory tasks constitute an exception to the generalization that older adults show declines in new learning? The transmission deficit hypothesis accounts for these findings using the same cognitive mechanisms that we have applied to a range of memory phenomena, not just age differences in direct versus indirect memory tasks. Predictions here parallel predictions for practice effects in general: Repetition increases linkage strength of existing connections and the rate of increase should be unaffected by aging. Thus previous exposure to a word such as BEHAVIOUR will strengthen its availability equivalently in young and older adults. The larger age deficits obtained in direct than indirect memory tasks (e.g. Howard 1988) reflect the greater number of new connections typically required in direct tasks. That is, conscious recall or recognition of a target word requires new connections in memory linking the word to the specific episodic context in which it occurred (MacKay and Burke 1990).

However, the transmission deficit hypothesis does predict age differences for indirect memory tasks in so far as they require new connections. A similar analysis of direct and indirect memory tasks in terms of the degree to which new associations are involved has been suggested in research on amnesia. Shimamura and Squire (1989) have recently demonstrated, for example, that amnesics who showed preserved repetition priming, were impaired in priming involving new associations. Further, the size of priming effects for new associations was related to the degree of residual direct memory ability (see also Schacter and Graf 1986).

Similarly, there is now growing evidence that older adults show decrements in performance on indirect memory tasks when new learning is involved and conditions are not optimal for learning. For example, Howard, Fry and Brune (1991) required subjects to complete a word stem (e.g. STA—) with the first word that came to mind after generating sentences using unrelated word pairs (e.g. QUEEN–STAIRS). When the word stem was presented with a word from the original pair, subjects used the target word to complete the stem more often than when a different word preceded it. This effect, demonstrating a new connection between the two words, was the same for young and older adults, although older adults had poorer cued recall. However, under more impoverished or time-constrained study conditions, the effect was obtained for young but not older adults (see also Howard 1988.)

Thus, within the present theoretical framework, the age deficit in direct recall is consistently more pronounced than in indirect memory tasks such as repetition priming because direct recall typically requires more new learning. Age deficits have been obtained in indirect memory tasks that require new learning, under conditions that reduce learning. (See Light 1991 for a review of other explanations which have been offered to account for the dissociation of aging effects on direct and indirect memory.)

CONTRIBUTIONS OF NON-COGNITIVE MECHANISMS TO MEMORY DECLINE

Attributing memory decline in old age to changes in fundamental cognitive processes is only tenable if we can eliminate explanations based on differences between young and older adults in non-cognitive factors such as lifestyle, personality processes or health. Thus we consider the extent to which these non-cognitive factors may provide an alternative explanation for age differences in new learning and word-finding deficits.

Cohort effects

Young and older participants in aging research often differ in age by fifty years or more, raising the possibility that they also differ in generational and cultural experiences. Such differences in common experiences are called cohort differences and are clearly related to year of birth. The effect of certain cohort differences must be carefully evaluated before attributing differences in young and older adults' memories to age. For example, although memory researchers usually attempt to equate years of education across age, young adults participating in their studies tend to be college students while older adults are not. Because of their current experience as students, young adults may be more adept at test taking and more comfortable in having their performance evaluated. However, age differences in remembering new information remain when neither young nor older adults are students (e.g. Salthouse, Kausler and Saults 1988; West and Crook 1990), and when both age groups are currently students (Parks, Mitchell and Perlmutter 1986).

Motivation

A related point is that older adults may be less motivated to perform well on unfamiliar, artificial and seemingly irrelevant laboratory tasks such as remembering lists of random numbers, words, or shapes (Perlmutter and Monty 1989). Thus, their performance on such tasks may be a poor indication of memory ability outside the laboratory (e.g. Sinnott 1989); memory tasks involving naturalistic materials or settings may provide a more accurate index of memory ability. Indeed, studies using such tasks have been a critical source of information for development of general memory theory and data (see Baddeley 1989).

Although everyday memory studies provide important data for defining age-related changes, they have not eliminated memory deficits for older adults. Substantial age declines remain when memory for new information in a familiar format is tested in the laboratory – for example, memory for stories or cartoons (Pratt, Boyes, Robins and Manchester 1989), telephone numbers (West and Crook 1990), groceries on a shelf (Read 1987), names of people on a videotape (Crook and West 1990), and medication instructions on prescription medicine bottles (Morrell, Park and Poon 1990). Hartley and Walsh (1980) attempted to increase motivation on a laboratory memory task by offering an incentive (money) for proficient performance, but the size of the age deficit in performance was unaffected.

Similarly, naturalistic studies of memory failures in everyday life report age differences. Older adults were less accurate than young adults in recalling experiences in their daily life during $2^1/2$ days of testing at a research centre (Sinnott 1986). Age-related increases in word-finding failures in everyday life have also been reported: Older adults reported more TOT experiences than young adults and the age discrepancy was more pronounced for TOTs occurring spontaneously during everyday life than for TOTs induced in the laboratory (Burke et al. 1991). In general, age differences in memory for new information or well-known words remain on naturalistic or everyday memory tasks (see Hultsch and Dixon 1990).

Self-efficacy

Because of the clear evidence for memory decline in old age, it is hardly surprising that in some studies older adults report lower memory self-efficacy or self-evaluation of abilities than young adults. For example, Berry, West and Dennehey (1989) asked subjects to indicate the level of difficulty at which they could perform specific memory tasks (e.g. 'If a friend asked me to do 10 errands, 5 minutes later I could remember 2 [or 4 or 6 or 8 or 10] of the errands I had to do'). Older adults indicated lower levels of expected performance than young adults (see Rebok and Balcerak 1989 for a similar finding). It has been argued that such self-evaluations not only derive from performance, but can also reduce or enhance performance (Berry 1989). According to Bandura's (1986, 1989) model of the relation of self-efficacy to cognition, beliefs about one's ability influence the effort exerted in performing tasks and this affects the level of performance. Within this model, older adults' diminished expectations for their performance may act as a self-fulfilling prophesy mediated by reduced effort or motivation.

There is, at this time, insufficient data for evaluating the adequacy of Bandura's model for explaining memory decline in old age. However, the early evidence is not encouraging. For self-efficacy to reduce memory performance, older adults' self-evaluations must be lower than the level of performance they are capable of. This is not necessarily indicated by age-related reductions in predicted performance levels *per se*, because they may accurately reflect the observed age-related reductions in memory performance; it is indicated by older adults underestimating the level of memory performance they actually obtain to a greater extent than young adults. This result, however, is rarely found (e.g. Rebok and Balcerak 1989).

Health

There is mounting evidence that poor physical health has a negative impact on memory and other cognitive abilities (e.g. Manton, Siegler and Woodbury 1986). Because age is a risk factor for most diseases, poor health is certain to contribute to memory decline in old age. Indeed, some researchers challenge the view that memory decline is inexorably linked to aging, arguing that health factors may account for the decline rather than age *per se* (Elias, Elias and Elias 1990; Perlmutter and Nyquist 1990).

It is unsurprising that catastrophic illness has a deleterious effect on cognition. This effect has been vividly demonstrated by a 'terminal drop' in cognitive performance shortly before death: Participants in longitudinal studies who are deceased showed a precipitous decline in memory scores at the last testing session before death relative to their own previous performance and to that of survivors (e.g. Johansson and Berg 1989; Siegler 1975).

More surprising, perhaps, are reports that even slow-acting, progressive diseases negatively affect memory. For example, declines in older adults' vocabulary between two tests 5 years apart were predicted by the number of medical problems (e.g. high blood pressure, diabetes, arthritis) reported at the first test (Lachman and Leff 1989). Indeed, high blood pressure negatively affects memory performance in young and older adults, even at levels not clinically defined as hypertension (e.g. Elias, Robbins, Schultz and Pierce 1990).

Alzheimer's disease and other dementias

Perhaps the greatest health threat to memory functioning in old age is from dementia, especially Alzheimer's disease which constitutes about one-half of dementia cases and affects perhaps 10 per cent of people over age 65, although estimates of incidence vary widely (Botwinick 1984; Cohen 1986). Older adults are cognizant of the increased risk of Alzheimer's disease in old age: Fear of Alzheimer's is probably responsible for the recent large increase in the number of older adults requesting neuropsychological evaluation of their memories (LaRue 1991). No doubt adding to the worry about Alzheimer's disease is the fact that the early symptoms bear some similarity to cognitive changes associated with normal aging – namely, declines in new learning and in word finding (e.g. Huff 1988; Reisberg *et al.* 1986).

Identification of memory changes that deviate from normal aging is essential for several reasons. First, understanding the extent of normal age changes will enable older adults to seek treatment for pathological changes. And 20–30 per cent of people referred for memory evaluation have a reversible dementia that can be effectively treated (Cohen 1986). Although Alzheimer's disease is irreversible, accurate diagnosis is necessary for development of an appropriate care plan. Finally, researchers must identify the boundary between normal and pathological aging if they are to identify mechanisms producing normal cognitive change in old age.

Recent research has clarified the boundary between normal and pathological aging by identifying clinical assessment instruments and psychometric and laboratory tests of cognitive performance that differentiate these two conditions (e.g. Bayles *et al.* 1989; Reisberg *et al.* 1986). Indeed, a diagnosis of Alzheimer's disease need no longer be made by exclusion of other diseases causing mental decline, such as multi-infarct dementia or geriatric depression, but is now defined by both inclusion and exclusion phenomena (Reisberg *et al.* 1986). For example, the Global Deterioration Scale is a rating scale of clinical characteristics that differentiates normal aging and Alzheimer's disease and defines stages of Alzheimer's disease (Reisberg, Ferris, de Leon and Crook 1982). Complaints about forgetting well-known names or where familiar objects have been placed are considered within the range of normal aging; early stages of Alzheimer's disease are indicated by deficits in everyday activities such as shopping or handling finances, and in everyday memory tasks such as remembering one's own telephone number or postal code, or the names of close relatives and friends. Laboratory tests showing the largest differences between normal older adults and adults with early Alzheimer's disease involve new learning, such as recall of stories, paragraphs or paired associates, as well as memory for well-known information such as the meaning of vocabulary words (Bayles *et al.* 1989; Reisberg *et al.* 1986).

Thus, adults with early-stage Alzheimer's disease show memory deficits that are not characteristic of normal aging – for instance, their decreased recall of old information such as the meaning of words on vocabulary tests. However, both normal older adults and adults with early-stage Alzheimer's disease show declines relative to young adults in memory for well-known names and for new information, although the extent of the decline differs very significantly between the two older groups. Is it possible that a small proportion of undiagnosed, dementing older adults in research samples of presumed normal older adults could be responsible for age declines in the average performance on these memory functions? If this were the case, older adults' distributions of memory scores should be bimodal, with the dementing group producing a cluster of scores below the normal older adults' scores which should overlap the young adults' scores. However, I have never seen such a result reported.

CONCLUSIONS

Memory declines with normal aging are not uniform across all functions, but rather some aspects of memory are impaired while others are spared. We have focused on two of the most prominent memory changes in old age: namely, decline in new learning, and increased word-finding problems. Normal older adults describe memory declines as irksome, but there is little evidence that these changes significantly impair their ability to function in everyday life. Indeed, pathological memory changes in Alzheimer's disease affect these same functions but are indicated by a magnitude of decline that is noticeable to family and friends and that interferes with everyday activities.

The Transmission Deficit hypothesis postulates an age-related deficit in a cognitive mechanism involved in both the retrieval of existing knowledge and the creation of new knowledge – namely, the transmission of priming among memory representations. Thus, this hypothesis provides a means of integrating age declines in the seemingly disparate memory functions of new learning and word finding. One of the problems for non-cognitive explanations of memory declines in old age is that they are unable to account for the involvement of specific memory functions and not others.

Although the Transmission Deficit hypothesis views cognitive aging as an inexorable part of human development, non-cognitive variables may modify performance inasmuch as they influence the frequency and recency of relevant experiences. The model postulates that recency and frequency, as well as aging, affect the strength of memory connections and thus can compensate for aging declines. This has been dramatically demonstrated, for example, in training studies where older adults are practised on mnemonic strategies that substantially improve face–name recall (Gratzinger, Sheikh, Friedman and Yesavage 1990) or serial recall of words (Kliegl, Smith and Baltes 1989) above the unpractised levels of young adults. Similarly, continuation of hobbies such as chess in old age maintains performance levels (Charness 1981). It remains for future research to further specify the relevant experiences that compensate for age-linked declines in fundamental memory processes and thus maintain vulnerable memory functions in healthy older adults.

ACKNOWLEDGEMENTS

The research reported in this chapter was supported by grant AGO2452 from the National Institute on Aging.

I thank Dr Cristanne Miller in the Pomona College English Department for helpful discussions of the Dickinson poem. I alone, however, am responsible for any errors in interpretation.

REFERENCES

Baddeley, A.D. (1982) 'Domains of recollection', *Psychological Review* 89: 708–29.

Baddeley, A. (1989) 'Finding the bloody horse', in L.W. Poon, D.C. Rubin and B.A. Wilson (eds) *Everday Cognition in Adulthood and Late Life*, pp. 104–15, Cambridge: Cambridge University Press.

Bandura, A. (1986) *Social Foundations of Thought and Action: A Social Cognitive Theory*, Englewood Cliffs, New Jersey: Prentice-Hall.

Bandura, A. (1989) 'Regulation of cognitive processes through perceived self-efficacy', *Developmental Psychology* 25: 729–35.

Bayles, K.A., Boone, D.R., Tomoeda, C.K., Slauson, T.J. and Kaszniak, A.W. (1989) 'Differentiating Alzheimer's patients from the normal elderly and stroke patients with aphasia', *Journal of Speech and Hearing Disorders* 54: 74–87.

Berry, J.M. (1989) 'Cognitive efficacy across the life span: Introduction to the special series', *Developmental Psychology* 25: 683–6.

Berry, J.M., West, R.L. and Dennehey, D.M. (1989) 'Reliability and validity of the memory self-efficacy questionnaire', *Developmental Psychology* 25: 701–13.

Borod, J.C., Goodglass, H. and Kaplan, E. (1980) 'Normative data on the Boston Diagnostic Aphasia Examination, Parietal Lobe Battery, and the Boston Naming Test', *Journal of Clinical Neuropsychology* 2: 209–15.

Botwinick, J. (1984) *Aging and behavior*, New York: Springer.

Bowles, N.L. and Poon, L.W. (1985) 'Aging and retrieval of words in semantic memory', *Journal of Gerontology* 40: 71–7.

Brown, R. and McNeill, D. (1966) 'The "tip-of-the-tongue" phenomenon', *Journal of Verbal Learning and Verbal Behavior* 5: 325–37.

Burke, D.M. and Light, L.L. (1981) 'Memory and aging: The role of retrieval processes', *Psychological Bulletin* 90: 513–54.

Burke, D.M., MacKay, D.G., Worthley, J.S. and Wade, E. (1991) 'On the tip of the tongue: What causes word finding failures in young and older adults', *Journal of Memory and Language* 30:

Burke, D.M., Worthley, J. and Martin, J. (1988) 'I'll never forget what's her name: Aging and tip of the tongue experiences in everyday life', in M.M. Gruneberg, P.E. Morris and R.N. Sykes (eds) *Practical Aspects of Memory: Current Research and Issues*, vol. 2, pp. 113–18, Chichester: Wiley.

Charness, N. (1981) 'Aging and skilled problem solving', *Journal of Experimental Psychology: General*, 110: 21–38.

Cohen, D. (1986) 'Psychopathological perspectives: Differential diagnosis of Alzheimer's disease and related disorders', in L. Poon *et al.* (eds) *Handbook for Clinical Memory Assessment of Older Adults*, pp. 81–107, Washington, DC: American Psychological Association.

Cohen, G. and Faulkner, D. (1984) 'Memory in old age: "good in parts"', *New Scientist* 11: 49–51.

Cohen, G. and Faulkner, D. (1986) 'Memory for proper names: Age differences in retrieval', *British Journal of Developmental Psychology* 4: 187–97.

Cohen, G. and Faulkner, D. (1987) *Life Span Changes in Autobiographical Memory* (Tech. Rep. No. 24), Milton Keynes: The Open University, Human Cognition Research Laboratory.

Collins, A.M. and Loftus, E.F. (1975) 'A spreading-activation theory of semantic processing', *Psychological Review* 82: 407–28.

Cooper, P.V. (1990) 'Discourse production and normal aging: Performance on oral picture description tasks', *Journal of Gerontology: Psychological Sciences* 45: P210–14.

Crook, T.H. and West, R.L. (1990) 'Name-recall performance across the adult life-span', *British Journal of Psychology* 81: 335–49.

Dell, G.S. (1986) 'A spreading-activation theory of retrieval in sentence production', *Psychological Review* 93: 283–321.

Elias, M.F., Elias, J.W. and Elias, P.K. (1990) 'Biological and health influences on behavior', in J.E. Birren and K.W. Schaie (eds) *Handbook of the Psychology of Aging*, pp. 79–102, San Diego: Academic Press.

Elias, M.F., Robbins, M.A., Schultz, N.R. and Pierce, T.W. (1990) 'Is blood pressure an important variable in research on aging and neuropsychological test performance?', *Journal of Gerontology* 45: P128–35.

Francis, W.N. and Kucera, H. (1982) *Frequency Analysis of English Usage: Lexicon and Grammar*, Boston: Houghton Mifflin.

Gratzinger, P., Sheikh, J.I., Friedman, L. and Yesavage, J.A. (1990) 'Cognitive interventions to improve face–name recall: The role of personality trait differences', *Developmental Psychology* 26: 889–93.

Hartley, J.T. and Walsh, D.A. (1980) 'The effect of monetary incentive on amount and rate of free recall in older and younger adults', *Journal of Gerontology* 35: 899–905.

Horn, J.L. (1982) 'The aging of human abilities', in B. Wolman (ed.) *Handbook of Developmental Psychology*, pp. 847–870, Englewood Cliffs, New Jersey: Prentice-Hall.

Horn, J.L. and Cattell, R.B. (1966) 'Age differences in primary mental ability factors', *Journal of Gerontology* 21: 210–20.

Howard, D.V. (1988) 'Implicit and explicit assessment of cognitive aging', in M.L. Howe and C.J. Brainerd (eds) *Cognitive Development in Adulthood: Progress in Cognitive Development Research*, pp. 3–37, New York: Springer.

Howard, D.V., Fry, A.F. and Brune, C.M. (1991) 'Aging and memory for new association: Direct and indirect measures', *Journal of Experimental Psychology: Learning, Memory and Cognition* 17.

Huff, F.J. (1988) 'The disorder of naming in Alzheimer's disease', in L.L. Light and D.M Burke (eds) *Language, Memory and Aging*, pp. 209–20, New York: Cambridge University Press.

Hultsch, D.F., Hertzog, C., Dixon, R.A. and Davidson, H. (1988) 'Memory self-knowledge and self-efficacy in the aged', in M.L. Howe and D.J. Brainerd (eds) *Cognitive Development in Adulthood: Progress in Cognitive Development Research*, pp. 65–92, New York: Springer.

Hultsch D.F. and Dixon, R.A. (1990) 'Learning and memory and aging', in J.E. Birren and K.W. Schaie (eds) *Handbook of the Psychology of Aging*, pp. 258–74, San Diego: Academic Press.

Johansson, B. and Berg, S. (1989) 'The robustness of the terminal decline phenomenon: Longitudinal data from the digit-span memory test', *Journal of Gerontology* 44: P184–6.

Johnson, T.J. (ed.) (1960) *The Complete Poems of Emily Dickinson*, Boston: Little, Brown & Co.

Kausler, D.H. and Hakami, M.K. (1983) 'Memory for activities: Adult age differences and intentionality', *Developmental Psychology* 19: 889–94.

Kliegl, R., Smith, J. and Baltes, P.B. (1989) 'Testing-the-limits and the study of adult age differences in cognitive plasticity of a mnemonic skill', *Developmental Psychology* 25: 247–56.

Lachman, M.E. and Leff, R. (1989) 'Perceived control and intellectual functioning in the elderly: A 5-year longitudinal study', *Developmental Psychology* 25: 722–8.

LaRue, V. (1991, March) 'Age-associated memory impairments: Diagnostic criteria and longitudinal patterns', Paper presented at the Claremont Conference on Applied Cognitive Psychology, Claremont, CA.

Light, L.L. (1991) 'Memory and aging: Four hypotheses in search of data', in M.R. Rosenzweig and L.W. Porter (eds) *Annual Review of Psychology*, pp. 333–76, Palo Alto: Annual Reviews.

Light, L.L. and Burke, D.M. (1988) 'Patterns of language and memory in old age', in L.L. Light and D.M. Burke (eds) *Language, Memory and Aging* pp. 244–71, New York: Cambridge University Press.

Light, L.L. and Singh, A. (1987) 'Implicit and explicit memory in young and older adults', *Jouranl of Experimental Psychology: Learning Memory and Cognition* 13: 531–41.

McClelland, J.L. and Rumelhart, D.E. (1981) 'An interactive model of context effects in letter perception: Part 1. An account of basic findings', *Psychological Review* 88: 375–407.

MacKay, D.G. (1982) 'The problems of flexibility, fluency, and speed-accuracy trade-off in skilled behavior', *Psychological Review* 89: 483–506.

MacKay, D.G. (1987) *The Organization of Perception and Action: Theory for Language and other Cognitive Skills*, New Yori: Springer.

MacKay, D.G. and Burke, D.M. (1990) 'Cognition and aging: new learning and the use of old connections', in T.M. Hess (ed.) *Aging and Cognition: Knowledge Organization and Utilization*, pp. 213–63, Amsterdam: North Holland.

Manton, K.G., Siegler, I.C. and Woodbury, M.A. (1986) 'Patterns of intellectual development in later life', *Journal of Gerontology* 41: 486–99.

Martin, M. (1986) 'Aging and patterns of change in everyday memory and cognition', *Human Learning* 5: 63–74.

Maylor, E.A. (1990) 'Recognizing and naming faces: Aging, memory retrieval and the tip of the tongue state', *Journal of Gerontology: Psychological Sciences* 45: P215–25.

Morrell, R.W., Park, D.C. and Poon, L.W. (1990) 'Effects of labeling techniques on memory and comprehension of prescription information in young and old adults', *Journal of Gerontology* 45: P166–72.

Moscovitch, M. (1982) 'A neuropsychological approach to perception and memory in normal and pathological aging', in F.I.M. Craik and S. Trehub (eds) *Aging and Cognitive Processes*, pp. 55–78, New York: Plenum Press.

Nicholas, M., Obler, L., Albert, M. and Goodglass, H. (1985) 'Lexical retrieval in healthy aging', *Cortex* 21: 595–606.

Parks, C.W., Jr., Mitchell, D.B. and Perlmutter, M. (1986) 'Cognitive and social functioning across adulthood: Age or student status differences?', *Psychology and Aging* 1: 248–54.

Perlmutter, L.C. and Monty, R.A. (1989) 'Motivation and aging', in L.W. Poon, D.C. Rubin and B.A. Wilson (eds) *Everyday Cognition in Adulthood and Late Life*, pp. 373–93, Cambridge: Cambridge University Press.

Perlmutter, M. and Nyquist, L. (1990) 'Relationships between self-reported physical and mental health and intelligence performance across adulthood', *Journal of Gerontology* 45: P145–55.

Pratt, M.W., Boyes, C., Robins, S. and Manchester, J. (1989) 'Telling tales: Aging, working memory, and the narrative cohesion of story retellings', *Developmental Psychology* 25: 628–35.

Read, D.E. (1987) 'Neuropsychological assessment of memory in the elderly', *Canadian Journal of Psychology* 41: 158–74.

Rebok, G.W. and Balcerak, L.J. (1989) 'Memory self-efficacy and performance differences in young and old adults: The effect of mnemonic training', *Developmental Psychology* 25: 714–21.

Reisberg, B., Ferris, S.H., de Leon, M.J. and Crook, T. (1982) 'The Global Deterioration Scale for the assessment of primary degenerative dementia', *American Journal of Psychiatry* 139: 1136–9.

Reisberg, B., Ferris, S.H., Borenstein, J., Sinaiko, E., de Leon, M.J. and Buttinger, C. (1986) 'Assessment of presenting symptoms', in L. Poon *et al.* (eds) *Handbook for Clinical Memory Assessment of Older Adults*, pp. 108–28, Washington, DC: American Psychological Association.

Salthouse, T.A. (1985) *A Theory of Cognitive Aging*, Amsterdam: North-Holland.

Salthouse, T.A. (1988) 'Initiating the formalization of theories of cognitive aging', *Psychology and Aging* 3: 3–16.

Salthouse, T.A., Kausler, D. and Saults, J.S. (1988) 'Investigation of student status, background variables, and feasibility of standard tasks in cognitive aging research', *Psychology and Aging* 3: 29–37.

Schacter, D.L. and Graf, P. (1986) 'Preserved learning in amnesic patients: Perspectives from research on direct priming', *Journal of Clinical and Experimental Neuropsychology* 6: 727–43.

Shimamura, A.P. and Squire, L.R. (1989) 'Impaired priming of new associations in amnesia', *Journal of Experimental Psychology: Learning, Memory and Cognition* 15: 721–8.

Siegler, I.C. (1975) 'The terminal drop hypothesis: fact or artifact?', *Experimental Aging Research* 1: 169–85.

Sinnott, J.D. (1986) 'Prospective/intentional and incidental everyday memory: Effects of age and passage of time', *Psychology and Aging* 1: 110–16.

Sinnott, J.D. (1989) 'Prospective/intentional memory and aging: Memory as adaptive action', in L.W. Poon, D.C. Rubin and B.A. Wilson (eds) *Everyday Cognition in Adulthood and Late Life*, pp. 59–70, Cambridge: Cambridge University Press.

Thomas, J.C., Fozard, J.L. and Waugh, N.C. (1977) 'Age-related differences in naming latency', *American Journal of Psychology* 90: 499–509.

Ulatowska, H.K., Hayashi, M.M., Cannito, M.P. and Fleming, S.G. (1986) 'Disruption of reference in aging', *Brain and Language* 28: 24–41.

Welford, A.T. (1985) 'Practice effects in relation to age: A review and a theory', *Developmental Neuropsychology* 1: 173–190.

West, R.L. and Crook, T.H. (1990) 'Age differences in everyday memory: Laboratory analogues of telephone number recall', *Psychology and Aging* 5: 520–9.

Winthorpe, C. and Rabbitt, P. (1988) 'Working memory capacity, IQ, age and the ability to recount autobiographical events', in M.M. Gruneberg, P.E. Morris and R.N. Sykes (eds) *Practical Aspects of Memory: Current Research and Issues*, pp. 175–9, New York: Wiley.

Yaniv, I. and Meyer, D.E. (1987) 'Activation and metacognition of inaccessible stored information: Potential bases for incubation effects in problem solving', *Journal of Experimental Psychology: Learning, Memory, and Cognition* 13: 187–205.

6

THE FACILITATION OF
MEMORY PERFORMANCE

Douglas J. Herrmann and Mark Palmisano

INTRODUCTION

Historically, the study of memory has been approached in several ways (Herrmann and Chaffin 1988). One approach has attempted to *identify key memory phenomena* that illustrate how human memory operates. A second approach has attempted to *explain* memory phenomena within a framework or according to a model or theory. A third approach has attempted to *improve* a person's ability to perform memory tasks. A fourth, and less recognized, approach has attempted to *facilitate* the performance of memory tasks, i.e. by producing transitory improvements in the individual's capability to acquire, retain, and remember information or events.

For a variety of reasons, research has focused almost exclusively on the first three approaches. However, the lack of attention to the fourth approach, memory facilitation, should not imply that it is an unimportant topic.

The primary goal in many applied situations is memory facilitation. This goal is especially important when someone needs to get another person to *learn* something, while not needing the learner to acquire the facilitating process. For example, a helmsman must comprehend and retain the commands necessary to steer a ship long enough to execute them. Facilitation is important also when someone needs to get another person to *remember* something that presumably he or she already knows. For example, government agencies gather information about the economy by asking people to recall information such as how many hours they worked in a particular time period, or how long they have been out of work,

147

or what kind of, and how many, purchases of a specific type they made in a designated time period (Biennias, Dippo and Palmisano 1987; Palmisano 1988).

Administrators, instructors, supervisors, and teachers have such facilitation goals frequently. In these instances, the persons in authority hope to create conditions that merely facilitate (i.e. temporarily improve) the other person's memory performance (without permanently altering the person's capability to acquire, retain, or remember information). Of course, a person need not be in a position of authority in order to facilitate another person's memory performance. Spouses may want to facilitate each other's memory performance; similarly, parents may want to do the same with their children and children may want to do likewise with their parents.

Since little research has focused specifically on this topic, it is necessary to point out that 'facilitation' is sometimes confused with other memory constructs. First, since facilitation affects memory processing temporarily, it may be mistaken for *short-term memory* phenomena. Second, because facilitation may result in the formation or retrieval of long-term memories, it may be mistaken with *long-term memory* phenomena. For example, a person may be instructed to rehearse in a way known to lead to durable learning (i.e. a long-term memory) but not in a way that the person acquires a new rehearsal skill. Third, since facilitation leads to better performance on a particular occasion, it is sometimes seen as interchangeable with, or as a subset of, *memory improvement*. However, as noted above, facilitation constitutes just a temporary adoption, or an increased use of, an effective memory process. For better performance to constitute memory improvement, it is necessary that the adoption or increased use of facilitation procedures be relatively *permanent* (Ericsson 1985).

Although facilitation and improvement may be distinguished in the abstract, many situations involve both of these processes and sometimes make it difficult to assess when performance represents one or the other of them. For example, suppose someone is told to rehearse a particular phone number just once and to do so in a certain way that will facilitate the learning of the number. By using the recommended facilitation strategy, the person may learn the number faster than he or she normally would. Later when required to learn another number, the person may revert to their normal learning processes. Alternatively, the person may make use of the facilitation instruction taught earlier, demonstrating an improved memory skill. It must be acknowledged that sometimes memory improvement may result from an attempt to facilitate memory performance. However, the research literature indicates that such a result is very unlikely. For example, reviews of memory-training research have found that even intensive memory-improvement courses (in some cases lasting a month) typically do not induce a permanent use of the mental manipulations taught (Herrmann and Searleman 1990, 1992; see also Druckman and Swets 1988). (For an explanation of how durable memory improvement may be achieved, see Chapter 7.)

Purpose

This chapter first distinguishes between two types of memory facilitation and their subtypes and examines the properties of each subtype. Secondly, the chapter discusses the theoretical perspective on memory suggested by facilitation findings.

Types of facilitation

On the basis of our examination of the literature, we have concluded that basically there are two types of facilitation. These two types are: the *optimization of memory processing* (through instructions; mental manipulations; providing appropriate prior performance; making use of environmental cues) and the *optimization of non-memory factors* that influence memory processing (such as physical and emotional states). The procedures used to achieve these two kinds of facilitation are described in detail in the sections that follow.

THE OPTIMIZATION OF MEMORY-PROCESSING

The performance of memory tasks may be facilitated by the transient activation of internal processes that enhance an individual's memory performance. First, people may temporarily achieve better performance when instructions direct them to orient to or mentally manipulate material which is to be learned or remembered. Second, people may temporarily optimize memory performance by processing certain information prior to the memory task of interest.

Third, better memory performance may be achieved temporarily by making use of environmental cues. These ways to optimize memory processing are discussed below.

Instructions

Orienting instructions

Instructions may facilitate memory performance by providing a person with information about the nature of material that is to be learned or remembered. The instructions may also orient a person to the best sequence in which to learn or remember parts of the material (Gagne and Paradise 1961). In the case of prose learning, instructions that provide clues ahead of time about a passage's organization facilitate learning. Similarly, instructions about how to remember something, such as an event that you witnessed, can also be facilitated by instructions that provide clues relevant to the organization and the context of a memory (Tulving 1983; Meyer, Young and Bartlett 1989). Although it has not been addressed by the research in these areas, the presumption has been that advance organizers and retrieval instructions/cues facilitate and do not result in an improvement in memory skills.

Instructional set

Instructions may also include information to familiarize a person with the gist of the material to be encountered in a memory task and to the procedures of the task. Such instructions provide a mental set that gives direction and purpose to learning and remembering by preparing the person for the kinds of mental processing called for by the task (Hagman 1983; Shuell 1983; Tyler, Hertel, McCallum and Ellis 1979). Pre-training, pre-tests, and pretest-instructions are examples of procedures that create a mental set conducive to memory performance.

Mental manipulations

Besides calling attention to information to be learned or to cues to aid remembering, instructions may attempt to get a person to mentally manipulate information or experience in a particular way. Many kinds of mental manipulations have been extensively investigated in the literature (Underwood 1978; Weinstein, Goetz and Alexander 1988). The use of such manipulations to improve memory is examined by Gruneberg in this text; below we provide a few examples of how mental manipulations may be used to facilitate memory.

Learning manipulations

Different kinds of learning manipulations function in different ways. Regardless of the manner of their functioning, their ultimate purpose is to form long-term memories of whatever is studied. While it is true that people can have their memory skills improved by being trained in the use of learning manipulations, it is equally true that they can be instructed or guided in the use of a manipulation without ever acquiring its habitual use. We will consider here three kinds of learning manipulations that may be used to facilitate learning.

Dating back more than two thousand years, *mnemonics* are probably the best-known learning manipulations that may be used to facilitate memory performance (Herrmann and Chaffin 1988). For example, people may acquire the vocabulary of a foreign language by associating an image that represents how a foreign word is to be pronounced with the English word. People may engage repeatedly in this 'linkword' memory technique, at the direction of an instructor, a computer software program, or a book (e.g. Gruneberg 1987), without adopting the use of the technique for other memory tasks. Similarly, neurologically impaired patients may have their memory performance facilitated by being guided through the use of certain imagery mnemonics while not learning how to use these manipulations on their own (Schacter and Glisky 1986; Wilson 1987).

Facilitation may enhance learning by *chunking* information into clusters. For example, a list of words may be learned by organizing the words according to sensory properties, such as by clustering words that sound similar. Or words may be organized semantically, such as by clustering words which belong to the same category. Teachers and instructors frequently present information to their students in an organized form to facilitate learning, without intending to change the students' memory skills (Bower, Clark, Lesgold and Winzenz 1969).

Learning may be facilitated by *elaborating* the information to be learned, i.e. thereby providing additional cues to be used later in retrieval. For example, the phrase 'Every Good Boy Does Fine' is an elaboration of the notes of the 'treble clef' of sheet music (EGBDF) that has helped many beginning music students learn and remember these notes. Learning may also be assisted by the *reduction* of information from what is to be learned. Acronyms are the usual outcome of reduction (e.g. UNICEF is an acronym which reduces the phrase 'The United Nations International Childrens Fund'). Usually acronyms are much easier to learn than the phrases that lead to the acronyms.

Retrieval manipulations

While learning manipulations have been extensively investigated, retrieval manipulations have not (Morris 1977). Nevertheless, it is clear that when people are instructed to recall an event from start to finish, to break the event down into its parts, and to recall again, accurate recall increases (Adams 1985; Geiselman, Fisher, MacKinnon and Holland 1986; Means *et al.* 1989). Such instructions, sometimes called 'guided interviewing', were explicitly formulated to facilitate memory, not to improve it.

Transient processes versus memory skills

Mental manipulations may foster temporary retention or relatively permanent retention (Craik and Tulving 1975). Many manipulations have been created by researchers in recent years. Ostensibly, these manipulations have been devised to use in the development of permanent memory skills. However, as noted earlier, the vast amount of memory training has not imparted sustained improvement. It may be that most mental manipulations are designed to process information in a way that leads to the facilitation of memory rather than to memory improvement.

Prior processing

The performance of memory tasks can be facilitated by having a person experience part or all of the material to be learned prior to the onset of a learning or remembering task. By processing specific contents of presented information, the person activates words and relevant concepts in long-term memory, sometimes including the concepts to be encountered in the memory task.

Warm-up

Familiarization with materials to be learned or with cues to aid remembering has long been known to enhance memory processing. Warming-up apparently has a facilitating effect on learning because exposure to materials temporarily activates task-specific information in memory (Thune 1951). It has a facilitating effect on retrieval as well, since it apparently enables access to memory information that otherwise would have remained hidden (Hunter 1955).

Repetition

Rehearsal or repeated attempts to recall may facilitate memory performance by activating the processes in encoding or retrieval and by activating information already present in memory. The literature generally holds that repetition is necessary to achieve proficiency at all but the simplest verbal and perceptual-motor tasks. Two or more repetitions beyond those necessary for achieving minimum task proficiency promote overlearning, increase retention, and reduce the need for frequent refresher training (Farr 1986). The greatest transfer of training is obtained when the number of repetitions is intermediate (Cormier and Hagman 1987; Hagman 1980).

Massed versus distributed study

Since Ebbinghaus (1885), it has been generally accepted that distributed study, i.e. which provides rest between study sessions, improves acquisition and retention. There are essentially two explanations for why massed study, i.e. which does not provide breaks when studying, is less effective than spaced study. The first is that massed study produces mental fatigue, for mental processing and for the subject matter under study. The second explanation is that spaced study allows more opportunity for variable encoding to occur which, in proper amounts, may facilitate learning (Underwood 1969). However, spaced study can sometimes lead to poorer learning than massed study. For example, an unusually long interval between spaced practice trials disposes the learner to encode different mental representations on different trials and not to integrate the learning of the spaced trials.

Transient processes versus memory skills

Prior processing may be provided by warming up, repetition, and an appropriate amount of distributed rehearsal. It is true that memory training may get people to increase their use of these procedures. Nevertheless, in the hands of a teacher or an instructor, warming-up, directions to rehearse, or distribution of study trials is intended, pure and simple, to only facilitate memory. It is doubtful that engaging in these activities permanently disposes a person to warm-up more, rehearse more, or distribute their study trials differently than they did before participating in the situation in which the facilitating procedure was used.

Environmental cues

External memory aids

People may externally manipulate memory to assist their 'retrospective memory', i.e. for past events (Graumann 1985), and their 'prospective memory', i.e. for events to occur in the future (Dorner, 1987; Intons-Peterson and Fournier 1986). Virtually every normal adult assists memory with non-technical memory aids, e.g. such as by writing notes or by placing objects in conspicuous places as reminders (Harris 1984; Intons-Peterson and Fournier 1986; Intons-Peterson and Newsome 1992).

An important reason for why external aids facilitate memory is that the physical presence of an object usually stimulates memory more than imagining or thinking about the object. Because of the superior capability to stimulate memory, external aids have been developed to serve diverse memory functions (Harris 1984; Herrmann and Petro 1991), e.g. devices to find lost objects (such as one's car keys at home, or one's car in a parking lot), to remind you to do things (such as to meet an appointment or water one's plants), or to perform home chores which otherwise you would have to remember (such as to turn on one's lights, furnace, sprinklers, and other appliances).

External aids clearly facilitate memory, without improving memory skills. Indeed, it has been argued that the use of external aids reduces memory skills. By using external aids, a person has less experience using mental manipulations; as experience at using these manipulations decreases, memory skills presumably diminish (Herrmann and Chaffin 1988; Herrmann and Petro 1991). It is unclear whether a loss in memory skills is actually produced by using external memory aids, since the appropriate research has yet to be conducted.

Information delivery systems

A complex computerized training device, the information delivery system, presents information to be learned at optimum exposure durations, optimum inter-stimulus intervals, and in perceptually salient displays. These systems have been found to facilitate the performance of memory tasks in classroom instruction (Stolurow 1969). These systems may be central to instruction, such as the case with computerized training devices (e.g. driving and flight simulators; Farr 1986). The benefit of using an information delivery system is that it allows the information being presented to the student to be structured in a particular fashion. For example, an information delivery system and an instructional strategy may be employed together to structure information in ways conducive to acquisition, retention, and remembering. Used in this manner, the goal of informational delivery systems is to facilitate memory performance, not to improve it.

OPTIMIZATION OF NON-MEMORY FACTORS

The functioning of other components of the psychological system (Royce 1973) is known to affect memory performance (Herrmann and Searleman 1990, 1992; Herrmann, Weingartner, Searleman and McEvoy 1992; McEvoy 1992). For the most part, non-memory factors facilitate memory performance by rectifying deleterious states that impair memory function.

Memory performance may be facilitated by affecting a person's (1) physical state (2) emotional state (3) environmental condition and (4) social environment. Theoretically these factors affect memory performance, influencing *arousal* by influencing a person's disposition to *selectively pay attention* to a memory task (Eysenck 1984; Hockey 1983, 1984; Weingartner 1984), by influencing *neurochemical* processes which directly affect acquisition, retention and/or retrieval (Lawlor, Sunderland, Martinez, Molchan and Weingartner in press), and by eliminating conditions that otherwise might bias a person to respond incorrectly.

Physical state

A less-than-optimal physical state may impair memory (Cutler and Grams 1988; Herrmann and Searleman 1990). This impairment apparently occurs because diminished physical state reduces a person's arousal and capacity to selectively pay attention (Jennings 1986). Going without sufficient sleep interferes with memory performance. Poor nutrition is believed to diminish memory activity, and the eating of an extra large meal has been shown to impair memory (Smith 1988). Physical fitness may affect memory performance. Of course, while a good nights sleep, a nutritious meal in moderate amounts, and exercise may facilitate memory performance on a particular occasion, such facilitation will end as soon as sleep, eating, and exercise becomes inadequate. Thus, facilitation will not result in memory improvement unless the behaviours in which a person engages are accompanied by training that makes these behaviours habitual.

Emotional state

Stress

Memory performance in everyday life may be impaired to varying degrees by stress (Broadbent, Cooper, Fitzgerald and Parkes 1982; Reason and MyCielska 1983; Reason 1988). The removal of stressors or the reduction of their influence on the individual (e.g. either through stress reduction or other techniques, such as meditation, yoga, or exercise) can be expected to facilitate the performance of memory tasks; Yesavage, Rose and Spiegel (1982) found that relaxation training yielded improvements in memory performance comparable to that produced by memory training.

Mood

It is well established that people remember pleasant experiences better than unpleasant ones (Matlin and Stang 1978). Thus, remembering may be facilitated if pleasant associations are developed during encoding. Also, retrieval may be facilitated by attempting to reinstate the mood experienced during encoding (Bower 1981; Singer and Salovey 1988). Regardless of the content of a memory, a depressed mood impairs memory performance, both at encoding and at retrieval (Blaney 1986; Johnson and Magaro 1987). Consequently, treatments that temporarily alleviate depression will facilitate memory performance.

Attitudes

People hold attitudes about the memory tasks that they like or dislike performing. These attitudes affect memory performance. People are likely to attempt a memory task and to perform it well when they believe that they typically succeed at this task (Herrmann 1990; Klatzky 1984; Morris 1984). Hence, memory performance may be changed for the better by changing attitudes about a task. For example, attitudes will change if a person estimates his or her ability at a memory task and then attempts to perform this task (Herrmann, Grubs, Sigmundi and Grueneich 1986). Such a procedure usually changes the original attitude to reflect the level of proficiency demonstrated by the person when he or she performed the task. In that attitudes are not easily changed in a permanent fashion, any manipulation that produces a temporary change in relevant attitudes will facilitate, but not improve, memory performance.

Environmental conditions

Climate

Decrements in human motor and cognitive performance have been associated with environmental extremes and are well documented. Extremely cold and wet environments have been shown to produce physiological stress and fatigue that lead to decrements in both short-term and long-term memory, as well as in response accuracy (Wittmers 1991). Extremely hot temperatures also impair memory (Wyon, Anderson and Lundqvist 1979). Clearly, memory performance will be facilitated by removing people from extreme climates or working places with extreme temperatures and humidity. Obviously, a climate change does not produce an improvement in memory skills.

Neurochemical agents

Numerous substances impair memory performance through their neurochemical effects (McGaugh 1989; Petty and Cacioppo, 1981; Squire 1987). Such substances include alcohol (Birnbaum and Parker 1977; Hashtroudi and Parker, 1986), tobacco (when smoked) (Peeke and Peeke 1984; Spilich 1986; Wittenborn 1988), coffee (Petros, *et al.* 1987), marijuana (Block and Wittenborn 1984; Darley *et al.* 1973), and medications such as tranquilizers and antidepressants (Curran, Sakulsriprong and Lader 1988). Abstinence from such substances facilitates memory without manipulating either the contents of memory or the cues intended to activate memory. However, such abstinence obviously does not result in permanent improvements to a person's memory-system physiology. Thus, this kind of neurochemical facilitation eliminates an impaired state as long as the agent is not used or used less. A cessation in the use of the agent obviously does not result in permanent improvements in a person's memory-system physiology.

Facilitation may also be accomplished by taking an agent which temporarily enhances normal memory processes. According to psychophysiological theory, this kind of neurochemical facilitation also eliminates an impaired state. For example, Gold (1987) and colleagues have recently reported that ingestion of glucose right before learning results in improved learning. Similarly, recent research indicates that ingestion of glycine also enhances learning (Schwartz *et al.* 1991). Also, inhalation of appropriate amounts of oxygen has been found to facilitate memory performance in certain elderly (Jacobs, Winter, Alvis and Small 1969). No suggestion has been made indicating that these agents permanently improve a person's memory-system physiology.

Living cycles

Memory performance may be facilitated by having the learner or rememberer perform a task at certain times of the day. Although the optimal time differs across tasks and people, memory performance is subnormal after waking and after lunch, peaking in the mid afternoon (Folkard and Monk 1978; Tilley and Statham 1989).

The social environment

A person's inclination to register and remember information depends on how the information meets his or her social goals (Wyer and Srull 1989). Thus memory performance may be facilitated by fostering a student's awareness with an instructor's expertise and by increasing rapport between the instructor and student. Also, information will be learned and remembered better if it is consistent with the student's beliefs (Levine and Murphy 1943; Roberts 1985) and cultural values (Cole and Scribner 1974).

Learners and rememberers also may fail to learn or remember accurately because social pressures distort information to be learned and/or cues to aid remembering (Bruner and Postman 1947a, 1947b; Zeller 1951). Additionally, people sometimes claim to know less or more than they actually do in order to achieve social goals (Gentry and Herrmann 1990; Goffman 1961). Consequently, memory performance may be facilitated by altering the social factors that may lead a person to distort what they know or by reducing the social pressures that may encourage a person to misrepresent what they have learned or remembered. Changes in social pressures, while facilitative of memory performance, would not be expected to improve a person's memory aptitude.

DISCUSSION

This chapter has reviewed a wide range of findings that demonstrate that the performance of memory tasks can be temporarily enhanced by optimizing mental manipulations and non-memory factors that affect memory processes. The findings reviewed here are consistent with the conclusion that facilitation procedures typically produce a transient change in memory performance.

Facilitation versus improvement

The theoretical mechanisms involved in facilitation presumably overlap with those involved in memory improvement. Nevertheless, the mechanisms of facilitation are not identical with those of memory improvement; the nature of this difference has not been elucidated previously. We propose that this difference is that genuine memory improvement is based on the acquisition of *habitual use of facilitative behaviours* (James 1890; Shiffrin and Schneider 1977; Watson 1925) and an *appropriate belief system* (Hertzog 1991; Pressley, Borkowski and Schneider 1987). Effective memory training, i.e. that achieves permanent improvement, invariably includes extensive practice in order to impart appropriate habits. Effective training also includes experience at bridging tasks (which enable transfer from the training tasks to target tasks in everyday life), as well as procedures that foster an appropriate belief system (by correcting deleterious attitudes and teaching information about the appropriate use of the manipulations imparted by training). Facilitation procedures do not endeavour to create the conditions essential to memory improvement, i.e. procedures which give rise to habitual memory processing and an appropriate belief system which supports this processing.

Modelling facilitation

It is our opinion that most models of cognition and memory are not sufficiently broad to incorporate the facilitation findings reviewed here. It is also our opinion that it would be premature to propose a theory of facilitation. Instead, we feel that what would be useful at the present time would be a general conceptual framework within which facilitation may be understood.

The type of framework which we feel could account for facilitation phenomena is one that holds that memory performance is optimized both by variables identified with the memory system (e.g. rehearsal, presentation rate) and also by variables identified with other processing modes of the psychological system (e.g. physiological, perceptual, motoric, emotional, motivational, and social; see Royce 1973). Such a *multi-modal* model has recently been proposed to account for the effectiveness of many new procedures for improving memory ability (Herrmann and Searleman 1990, 1992; McEvoy 1992). It seems plausible that this kind of model, minus any assumptions about the habitual use of manipulations, might provide a good account of temporary changes in memory processing.

The multi-modal model of memory improvement assumes that some psychological processing modes involve thought processes that are in some sense under the subject's *control*. These modes include mental manipulations, as well as manipulations of the physical environment and the social environment to better process information in memory tasks. The model also assumes that certain non-memory factors can increase a person's *arousal* and readiness for, basic memory processes and control processes (Herrmann and Searleman 1990, 1992; Herrmann, Weingartner, Searleman and McEvoy 1992; McEvoy 1992; Poon 1980).

The multi-modal model can be extended to memory facilitation, first, by assuming that subjects may put their mental manipulations under the control of someone else (such as a teacher, instructor, or a friend). Second, the model also can be extended to facilitation by having the person who attempts to achieve facilitation (e.g. the teacher, instructor, or a friend) affect the learner/rememberer's level of arousal by manipulating other psychological processing modes (e.g. physical state, emotional state, mood, attitudes, social interaction) in ways that produce better memory processing.

Conclusions

Memory facilitation is important practically. Whenever it is necessary to get another person to learn or remember something (while not having to get this person to acquire a learning or remembering process), facilitation procedures are called for. Such facilitation goals obviously occur frequently in both professional and personal situations. Additionally, memory facilitation is theoretically important. By defining the conditions by which memory processing is enhanced only temporarily, facilitation research helps to identify the boundary conditions for permanent improvement in memory processing and, thereby, elucidate the mechanisms responsible not only for memory facilitation but also for memory improvement.

REFERENCES

Adams, L.T. (1985) 'Improving memory: Can retrieval strategies help?', *Human Learning* 4: 281–97.

Biennias, J., Dippo, C.S. and Palmisano, M. (1987) *A Cognitive Approach to Survey Research Methodology*, Washington, DC: US Bureau of Labor Statistics.

Birnbaum, I. and Parker, E. (eds) (1977) *Alcohol and Human Memory*, Hillsdale, New Jersey: Erlbaum.

Blaney, P.H. (1986) 'Affect and memory: A review', *Psychological Bulletin* 99: 229–46.

Block, R.I. and Wittenborn, J.R. (1984) 'Marijuana effects on semantic memory: Verification of common and uncommon category members', *Psychological Reports* 55: 503–12.

Bower, G.H. (1981) 'Mood and memory', *American Psychologist* 36: 129–48.

Bower, G.H., Clark, M.C., Lesgold, A.M. and Winzenz, D. (1969). 'Hierarchical retrieval schemes in recall of categorized word lists', *Journal of Verbal Learning and Verbal Behavior* 8: 323–43.

Broadbent, D.E., Cooper, P.F., Fitzgerald, P. and Parkes, K.R. (1982) 'The Cognitive Failures Questionnaire (CFQ) and its correlates', *British Journal of Psychology* 21: 1–16.

Bruner, J.S. and Postman, L. (1947a) 'Tension and tension release as ongoing factors in perception', *Journal of Personality* 15: 300–8.

Bruner, J.S. and Postman, L. (1947b) 'Emotional selectivity in perception and reaction', *Journal of Personality* 16: 69–77.

Cole, M. and Scribner, S. (1974) 'Culture and thought: A psychological introduction', New York: Wiley.

Cormier, S. and Hagman, J. (eds) (1987) *Transfer of Learning*, San Diego: Academic Press.

Craik, F.I.M. and Tulving, E. (1975) 'Depth of processing and the retention of words in episodic memory', *Journal of Experimental Psychology: General* 104: 286–94.

Curran, H.V., Sakulsriprong, M. and Lader, M. (1988) 'Antidepressants and human memory: An investigation of four drugs with different sedative and anticholinergic profiles', *Psychopharmacology* 95: 520–7.

Cutler, S.J. and Grams, A.E. (1988) 'Correlates of self-reported everyday memory problems', *Journal of Gerontology* 43: 582–90.

Darley, C.F., Tinklenberg, J.R., Hollister, T.E. and Atkinson, R.C. (1973) 'Marihuana and retrieval from short term memory', *Psychopharmacology* 25: 231–8.

Dorner, D. (1987) 'Memory systems and the regulation of behavior', In E. van der Meer and J. Hoffmann (eds) *Knowledge Aided Information Processing*, Amsterdam: North Holland.

Druckman, D. and Swets, J.A. (1988) *Enhancing Human Performance*, Washington, DC: National Academy Press.

Ebbinghaus, H. (1885/1964) *Memory*, A. Ruger and C.E. Bussenius (translators), New York: Dover; (original work published in 1885).

Ericsson, K.A. (1985) 'Memory skill', *Canadian Journal of Psychology* 39: 188–231.

Eysenck, M.W. (1984) *A Handbook of Cognitive Psychology*, Hillsdale, New Jersey: Erlbaum.

Farr, M. (1986) *The Long-Term Retention of Knowledge and Skills*, Alexandria, Virginia: Institute for Defense Analysis (Log No. HQ 86–31217).

Folkard, S. and Monk, R. (1978) 'Time of day effects in immediate and delayed memory', M.M. Gruneberg, P.E. Morris and R.N. Sykes (eds) *Practical Aspects of Memory*, London: Academic Press.

Gagne, R.M. and Paradise, N.E. (1961) 'Abilities and learning sets acquisition', *Psychological Monographs* 75, No. 14 Whole No, 518. 308.

Geiselman, R.E., Fisher, R.P., MacKinnon, D.P. and Holland, H.L. (1986) 'Enhancement of eyewitness memory with cognitive interview', *American Journal of Psychology* 99: 385–401.

Gentry, M. and Herrmann, D.J. (1990) 'Memory contrivances in everyday life', *Personality and Social Psychology Bulletin*.

Goffman, E. (1961) *Encounters*, Indianapolis: Bobbs-Merrill.

Gold, P.E. (1987) 'Sweet memories', *American Scientist* 75: 151–5.

Graumann, C.F. (1985) 'Memorabilia, mementos, memoranda: Towards an ecology of memory', F. Klix and Hagendorf (eds) *Human Memory and Cognitive Capabilities*, Part A, Amsterdam: North Holland.

Gruneberg, M.M. (1987) *Link Word Language System: French; German; Spanish; Italian*, London: Corgi Books.

Hagman, J.D. (1980) 'Effects of training task repetition on retention and transfer of maintenance skill' (Research Rep. No. 1271), Alexandria, Virginia: US Army Research Institute for the Behavioral and Social Sciences (ADA 101 859).

Hagman, J.D. (1983) 'Presentation and test-trial effects on acquisition and retention of distance location', *Journal of Experimental Psychology* 9: 334–45.

Harris, J.E. (1984) 'Methods of improving memory', in B.A. Wilson and N. Moffatt (eds) *Clinical Management of Memory Problems*, London: Croom Helm.

Hashtroudi, S. and Parker, E.S. (1986) 'Acute alcohol amnesia: what is remembered and what is forgotten', in H.D. Cappell, F.B. Glaser, Y. Isreal, H. Kalant, W. Schmit, E. Sellers and R.C. Smart (eds) *Research Advances in Alcohol and Drug Problems*, New York: Plenum.

Herrmann, D.J. (1990) 'Memory self perceptions', in W.K. Shaie, J. Rodin and C. Schooler (eds) *Self-directedness and Efficacy: Cause and Effects through the Life Course*, Hillsdale. New Jersey: Erlbaum.

Herrmann, D.J. and Chaffin, R. (1988) *Memory in Historical Perspective*, New York: Springer.

Herrmann, D.J. and Petro, S. (1991) 'Commercial memory aids', *Applied Cognitive Psychology* 4: 439–50.

Herrmann, D.J. and Searleman, A. (1990) 'A multimodal approach to memory', in G. Bower (ed.) *Advances in Learning and Motivation*, New York: Academic Press.

Herrmann, D.J. and Searleman, A. (1992) 'Memory improvement and memory theory in historical perspective', in D. Herrmann, H. Weingartner, A. Searleman, C. McEvoy (eds) *Memory Improvement: Implications for Memory Theory*, New York: Springer.

Herrmann, D.J., Grubs, L., Sigmundi, R. and Grueneich, R. (1986) 'Aware ness of memory ability before and after relevant memory experience', *Human Learning* 5: 91–108.

Herrmann, D., Weingartner, H., Searleman, A., and McEvoy, C. (eds) (1992) *Memory Improvement: Implications for Theory*, New York: Springer.

Hertzog, C., (1991) 'Improving memory: The possible roles of meta-memory', in D. Herrmann, A. Searleman and C. McEvoy (eds) *Memory Improvement: Implications for Memory Theory*, New York: Springer.

Hockey, R. (1983) *Stress and Fatigue in Human Performance*, Chichester: Wiley.

Hockey, R. (1984) 'Varieties of attentional state: The effects of the environment', in R. Parasuraman and D.R. Davies (eds) *Varieties of Attention*, New York: Academic Press.

Hunter, I.M.L. (1955) 'The warming-up effect in recall performance', *Quarterly Journal of Experimental Psychology*, 7: 166–75.

Intons-Peterson, M.J. and Fournier, J. (1986) 'External and internal memory aids: When and how often do we use them?', *Journal of Experimental Psychology: General* 115: 267–80.

Intons-Peterson, M.J. and Newsome, G.L., III (1992) 'External memory aids: Effects and effectiveness', in D. Herrmann, H. Weingartner, A. Searleman and C. McEvoy (eds) *Memory Improvment: Implications for Memory Theory*, New York: Springer.

Jacobs, E.A.S., Winter, P.M., Alvis, H.J. and Small, S.M. (1969) 'Hyperoxygenation effect on cognitive functioning in the aged', *New England Journal of Medicine* 28: 753–7.

James, W. (1890) *The Principles of Psychology*, vol. 1, New York: Holt.

Jennings, J.R. (1986) 'Bodily changes during attending', in M.G.H. Coles, E. Donchin and S.W. Porges (eds) *Psychophysiology: Systems, Processes and Applications*, New York: Guilford.

Johnson, M.H. and Magaro, P.A. (1987) 'Effects of mood and severity on memory processes and mania', *Psychological Bulletin* 101: 28–40.

Klatzky, R.L. (1984) 'Memory and awareness: Information processing perspective', New York: W.H. Freeman.

Lawlor, B.A., Sunderland, T., Martinez, R.A., Molchan, S.E. and Weingartner, H. (in press) 'Drugs and memory', in T. Yamagihara and R.C. Petersen (eds) *Memory Disorders in Clinical Practice*, Rochester, Minnesota: Mayo Foundation.

Levine, K. and Murphy, G. (1943) 'The learning and forgetting of contro-versial material', *Journal of Abnormal Social Psychology* 38: 507–17.

McEvoy, C.L. (1992) 'Memory improvement in context: Implications for the development of memory improvement theory', in D. Herrmann, H. Weingartner, A. Searleman and C. McEvoy (eds) *Memory Improvement: Implications for Memory Theory*, New York: Springer.

McGaugh, J.L. (1989) 'Modulation of memory processes', in P.R. Solomon, G.R. Goethals, C.M. Kelley and B.R. Stephens (eds), *Memory: Inter-disciplinary Approaches*, pp. 33–64, New York: Springer.

Matlin, M. and Stang, D. (1978) *The Pollyanna Principle*, Cambridge, Massachusetts: Schenkman.

Means, B., Nigam, A., Zarrow, M., Loftus, E.F. and Donaldson, M.S.

(1989) 'Autobiographical memory for health-related events', *Vital and Health Statistics, Series 6, No. 2, Cognition and Survey Measurement*, Hyattsville, Maryland: National Center for Health Statistics.

Meyer, B.J.F., Young, C.J. and Bartlett, B.J. (1989) *Memory Improved: Reading and Memory Enhancement across the Life Span through Strategic Text Structures*, Hillsdale, New Jersey: Erlbaum.

Morris, P. (1984) 'The cognitive psychology of self reports', in J. Harris and P. Morris (eds) *Everyday Memory and Action and Absentmindedness*, London: Academic Press.

Morris, P. (1977) 'Practical strategies for human learning and remembering', in M. Howe (ed.) *Adult Learning: Psychological Research and Applications*, London: Wiley.

Palmisano, M. (1988) 'Understanding key labor force concepts used in the Current Population Survey (CPS)', *Proceedings of the American Statistical Society*, Washington, DC.

Peeke, S.C. and Peeke, H.V. (1984) 'Attention, memory, and cigarette smoking', *Psychopharmacology*, 84: 205–16.

Petros, T., Beckwith, B.E., Erickson, C.G., Arnold, M.E. and Sternhagen, S. (1987). 'The effects of caffeine on working memory', Presented at the annual meeting of the American Psychological Association, New York.

Petty, R.E. and Cacioppo, J.T. (1981) *Attitudes and Persuasion: Classic and Contemporary Approaches*, Dubuque, Iowa: W.C. Brown.

Poon, L.W. (1980) 'A systems approach for the assessment and treatment of memory problems', in J.M. Ferguson and C.B. Taylor (eds) *The Comprehensive Handbook of Behavior Medicine*, vol. 1, pp. 191–212.

Pressley, M., Borkowski, J.G. and Schneider, W. (1987) 'Good strategy users coordinate metacognition, strategy use and knowledge', in R. Vasta and G. Whitehurst (eds) *Annals of Child Development*, 4.

Reason, J.T. (1988) *Human Error*, Cambridge: Cambridge University Press.

Reason, J.T. and MyCielska, M. (1983) 'Absentmindedness', Hillsdale, New Jersey: Prentice-Hall.

Roberts, J. (1985) 'The attitude–memory relationship after 40 years', *Basic and Applied Social Psychology*, 6: 212–41.

Royce, J.R. (1973) 'The present situation in situational psychology', in B.B. Wolman (ed.) *Handbook of General Psychology*, Englewood Cliffs, New Jersey: Prentice-Hall.

Schacter, D.L. and Glisky, E.L. (1986) 'Memory remediation: Restoration alleviation, and the acquisition of domain-specific knowledge', in B. Uzzell and Y. Gorss (eds) *Clinical Neuropsychology of Intervention*, Boston: Nijhoff.

Schwartz, B.L, Hashtroudi, S., Herting, R.L., Handerson, B.A. and Deutsch, S.I. (1991) 'Glycine production(?) facilitates memory retrieval in humans', unpublished manuscript, Washington, DC.

Shiffrin, R.M. and Schneider, W. (1977) 'Controlled and automatic human information processing: II, Perceptual learning, automatic attending and a general theory', *Psychological Review* 84: 127–90.

Singer, J.A. and Salovey, P. (1988) 'Mood and memory: evaluating the network theory of affect', *Clinical review* 8: 211–15.

Shuell, T.J. (1983) 'The effect of instructions to organize for good and poor learners, *Intelligence* 7: 271–86.

Smith, A. (1988) 'Effects of meals on memory and attention', in M.M. Gruneberg, P.E. Morris and R.N. Sykes (eds) *Practical Aspects of Memory*, Chichester: Wiley.

Spilich, G. (1986) 'Cigarette smoking and memory: Good news and bad news', in G.J. Spillich (Chair) *Symposium on Cognitive and Environmental Agents: Theoretical and Pragmatic Implications*, New York: American Psychological Association.

Squire, L. (1987) *Memory*, New York: Oxford University Press.

Stolurow, L.M. (1969) 'Instructional strategies in computer assisted instruction' (Report No. T44709, p. 28), Alexandria, Virginia: *Defense Technical Information Center*.

Thune, L.E. (1951) 'Warm-up effect as a function of level of practice in verbal learning', *Journal of Experimental Psychology* 51: 111–16.

Tilley, L. and Statham, D. (1989) 'The effect of prior sleep on retrieval', *Acta Psychologica* 70: 199–203.

Tulving, E. (1983) *Elements of Episodic Memory*, New York: Oxford University Press.

Tyler, S.W., Hartel, P.T., McCallum, M.C. and Ellis, H.C. (1979) 'Cognitive effort and memory', *Journal of Experimental Psychology: Human Learning and Memory* 5: 607–17.

Underwood, B.J. (1969) 'Attributes of memory', *Psychological Review* 76: 559–73.

Underwood, G. (1978) *Strategies of Information Processing*, London: Academic Press.

Watson, J.B. (1925) *Behaviorism*, London: Kegan Paul, Trench, Trubner.

Weingartner, H. (1984) 'Models of memory dysfunctions', in D.S. Olton, E. Gamzu and Corkin (eds) *Memory Dysfunctions: An Integration of Animal and Human Research from Preclinical and Clinical Perspectives*, New York: New York Academy of Sciences.

Weinstein, C.E., Goetz, E.T. and Alexander, P.A. (1988) 'Learning and study strategies: Issues in assessment, instruction, and evaluation', New York: Academic Press.

Wilson, B. (1987) *Rehabilitation of Memory*, New York: Guilford.

Wittenborn, J.R. (1988) 'Assessment of the effects of drugs on memory', *Psychopharmacology* 6: 67–78.

Wittmers, L.E. (1991) 'Evaluation of physiological and psychological impairments of human performance in cold' (Report No. T44709, p. 20). Alexandria, Virginia: Defense Technical Information Center.

Woodworth, R. (1938) *Experimental Psychology*, New York: Henry Holt.

Wyer, R., Jr and Srull, T. (1989) *Memory and Cognition in its Social Context*, Hillsdale, NJ: Erlbaum.

Wyon, D.P., Anderson, B. and Lundqvist, G.R. (1979) 'The effects of moderate heat stress on mental performance', *Scandinavian Journal of Work Environment and Health* 5: 352–61.

Yesavage, J.A., Rose, T.L. and Spiegel, D. (1982) 'Relaxation training and memory improvement in elderly normals: Correlations of anxiety ratings and recall improvement', *Experimental Aging Research* 8: 195–8.

Zeller, A. (1951) 'An experimental analogue of repression: III, The effect of induced failure and success on memory measured by recall', *Journal of Experimental Psychology* 42: 32–8.

7

THE PRACTICAL APPLICATION OF MEMORY AIDS

Knowing how, knowing when, and knowing when not

Michael M. Gruneberg

One of the more important areas of practical application of memory research in recent years has been that of memory aids. A number of recent reviews of the area, e.g. Bellezza (1981), Higbee (1988), indicate that a great deal of research has now been conducted in an area that at one time was regarded as somewhat trivial within psychology. It is now clear that not only do memory aids 'work' in the sense of enhancing recall, compared with normal 'rote' learning methods, they have considerable practical implications, as the studies of Morris, Jones and Hampson (1978) on face–name association, and of Raugh and Atkinson (1975) on foreign vocabulary learning, have demonstrated.

Yet a number of eminent psychologists are still sceptical of the practical value of mnemonic aids. Whilst there is no dispute that they work in laboratory studies, their generalizability to real-life situations has been questioned. Herrmann, Rea and Andrzejewski (1988), for example, found that memory improvement courses which teach various mnemonic strategies fail to show any significant effects of instruction over time. Again, Park, Smith and Cavenaugh (1990) found that even experts in the psychology of memory rarely used these methods in everyday life.

This chapter will aim to show that the concerns of Herrmann *et al.* (1988) and Park *et al.* (1990) are both justified, and unjustified. Katz (1987) makes the useful distinction between 'knowing how' to apply strategies and 'knowing when' to apply strategies. Instructing individuals on how mnemonic aids work in the context of the laboratory or memory improvement courses is a relatively simple procedure, as will be seen presently. Instruction on 'when', and as importantly, 'when not' to use such strategies is an area which has hardly been investigated, but which is critical to the successful implementation of these techniques. This chapter will argue that the failures to use mnemonic strategies referred to by Herrmann *et al.* (1988) and Park *et al.* (1990) are likely to reflect not that mnemonic strategies are of little use, but that little attention has been focused on knowing 'when' and when not to apply them. Indeed in the course of this chapter, a number of successful implementations which have been carried out will be described: in examinations, in foreign language learning in face–name association learning in the elderly and so on.

Mnemonic aids of the kind discussed above usually, but not exclusively, involve using visual imagery to enhance an interaction between two to-be-remembered items. For example, if elephant– chalk; book–floor and car–pig are to be associated, the learner is instructed to imagine in his or her mind's eye an elephant using chalk on a blackboard, a book lying on the floor and a car chasing a pig. Formal mnemonic systems which make use of this principle are the method of loci and the hook/peg system. However, imagery is also at the heart of mnemonic strategies which facilitate name–face association and foreign language vocabulary acquisition. Amongst non-imagery mnemonic strategies which facilitate retention are the digit–letter system which enhances retention of digit sequences, and the first letter mnemonic strategy, where the first letter of to-be-remembered material cues later recall. The most famous example of the latter is *R*ichard *O*f *Y*ork *G*ave *B*attle *I*n *V*ain for the colours of the rainbow. The rest of the chapter will not only examine how mnemonic aids work, but will discuss when they should and when they should not be used.

THE METHOD OF LOCI AND THE PEG SYSTEM

In her book *The Art Of Memory* Yates (1966) tells the story of how the Greek orator Simonedes is said to have invented the first mnemonic system. Simonedes was giving an oration in a banqueting hall when he was called outside by two messengers. While outside, the ban- queting hall collapsed killing all of those inside. If this was not bad enough – and presumably for those inside it was bad enough! – the bodies were so mangled that they could not be identified. However, Simonedes had pictured each person and where he was sitting at the banquet, and was therefore able to identify the bodies for the relatives – and thus be credited with inventing the first mnemonic aid – the method of loci or places. It's an ill wind that blows nobody any good!

The method of loci involves the learner fixing in his or her mind's eye a set number of locations, usually about ten, which are familiar. For example, learners may picture their bedrooms, starting with the bed, then next to the bed a table, next to the table a chair, and so on, until ten locations are fixed. When learning a set of new words, e.g., Elephant, Pencil, Hat, . . ., the learner first pictures an Elephant interacting with the first location, i.e. the bed, the Pencil on the second location, i.e. the table, the Hat on the third location, i.e. the chair, and so on. That this technique is highly effective in enhancing recall has been shown by, for example, Ross and Lawrence (1968) who found that retention after presentation of forty items for forty locations was 37.5 immediately after presentation. Groninger (1971) found that after 5 weeks, a group using the method of loci recalled twenty out of twenty-five words, compared with a control group who recalled only ten words. More recently DeBeni and Cornoldi (1985) confirmed the enhancing effects of the method of loci on retention and DeBeni (1988) found the method of loci to improve retention of orally presented passages and text. The effectiveness of this ancient technique, therefore, seems well established.

Related to the method of loci is the Hook or Peg system, in which learners are required to learn the poem, one is bun; two is shoe; three is tree; four is door; five is hive; six is sticks; seven is heaven; eight is gate; nine is wine; ten is hen. The Hook words, Bun, Shoe, etc. are associated in turn with to-be-remembered words, say Duck, Hand, Letter, etc. Thus Duck would be imaged interacting with peg-word one, i.e. Bun – say a Duck eating a bun. Peg-word two – shoe, would be pictured interacting with the second to-be-remembered word, i.e. Hand, perhaps a shoe stamping on a hand, and peg-word three – tree – interacts with the third word on the list and so on. The Peg system has the advantage over the method of loci in that to-be-remembered words can be recalled in any required order. Bugelski (1968) showed this technique to be highly effective in enhancing recall. Six lists of ten words presented using the Peg method were recalled at a significantly higher level than a control group, and there was little sign of any interference effects. Again not

170

only normal subjects benefit from this strategy. Elliot and Gentile (1986), for example, found that children with learning disabilities remembered twice as many words using the Peg method as without it. A number of further studies have shown the effectiveness of the Peg system: Morris and Reid (1970) again confirmed its superiority over control conditions using words, and both Higbee and Millard (1981) and Dyer and Meyer (1976) have found that it facilitated memory for ideas.

How, then, do the method of loci and the peg system work? In the case of the method of loci, the learner has a known list of cues – that is, cues well known to the learner. Usually these cues are of the locations in a well-known room, such as a bedroom, but other well-known geographical locations, such as a familiar golf course, street, or even parts of the body, can serve, provided one cue leads on to the next so that, for example, next to the bed the learner knows is perhaps a table, and next to the table a chair and so on.

The second main aspect of the method of loci is the use of visual imagery to relate the well-known cue to the new 'to-be-remembered' word. That imagery is a powerful tool in enhancing recall of word pairs has been well documented within psychology. In one well-known study, for example, Bower (1967) found that in a paired-associate learning task, the probability of recall of a word association increased by 60 per cent where subjects were required to image word pairs together, compared with a control group given no instruction. Imagery appears to work by strengthening the association between items, rather than the items themselves. Morris and Stevens (1974) found that where subjects were given word lists to learn and asked only to image each item as it came in, there was no increase in recall compared with a control group given no instruction. However, when subjects were asked to link one word to the next one coming in by using imagery in an interactive way – for example, the words 'dog' and 'book' would be remembered by perhaps imaging a dog eating a book – then recall increases substantially. It appears that the main factor affecting enhanced recall is that the image is vivid and interactive. Bower (1972), for example, found that in a study of paired associate learning, rated vividness of imagery correlated significantly with later recall. It is not clear, despite a number of investigations, that making an image bizarre is in fact important (see e.g. Higbee 1988), nor is it clear whether it is better for the individual to make up images or have them made up by the experimenter (Bellezza 1981).

At any rate, the method of loci employs two principles which enhance recall: the use of well-learned cues which allows newly learned material to be located in memory, and the use of imagery which strengthens the association between the well-learned cues and new incoming information. The pegword system also employs these two principles. As with the method of loci there is a retrieval plan. In this case the retrieval plan involves giving the order of cues by the number sequence 1, 2, 3 and so on. Added to this, each cue is related to its number by rhyme, e.g. one–bun. As with the method of loci, new material is related to the old by the use of imagery. The one major advantage of the peg system over the method of loci is that it allows new words to be recalled in any order. With the method of loci, remembering usually involves starting at the beginning and going through the list until the required word is located.

The question of course arises as to how useful it is to remember lists of unrelated words, however efficiently. Knowing how to remember more efficiently is of little value if it is not obvious when such knowledge should be applied. Hence the importance of the distinction made earlier, between 'knowing how' and 'knowing when'. 'Knowing when' is not, however, a simple matter, since it might well be the case that mnemonic strategies would be effective in a particular situation, but would simply not be worth the extra cognitive effort. Remembering shopping lists by means of mnemonic strategies is a case in point. It is sometimes suggested, for example, that mnemonic strategies such as the method of loci or the peg system are useful for remembering shopping lists. It seems to this writer a dubious suggestion since these can easily be written down and it is not clear that the extra mental effort involved in remembering them is therefore worthwhile. However, even this is not a simple matter. One individual who clearly finds imagery easy has reported to the author that shopping lists are easier to learn using mnemonics than writing them down. Again, it is not clear, as Cornoldi (1988) points out, that mnemonic strategies are useful in situations where individuals have to make a quick decision on how best to deal with new memory information. By the time the learner has decided to use a mnemonic strategy much of the to-be-learned material may have been presented. Again, there is evidence (see Bellezza 1981) that material being presented at rates faster than four per second are difficult to image, so that it may not be appropriate to apply mnemonic strategies to rapidly presented materials.

Yet there are situations where the use of the method of loci or peg system are indeed particularly useful. The writer, for example, uses such methods when driving to meetings, where ideas occur and it is not possible to write them down. For example, if the first point to be raised is 'Banking', the second point 'Accounts', the third point 'Date of Completion' and the fourth point 'The next meeting', the writer would imagine depositing buns (one) in his bank, giving his accountant a pair of shoes (two) for a present, picking dates from a tree (three) and throwing meat (meet) at a door (four). Several months after the writer gave a workshop on memory improvement to a computer company, the managing director reported that this was still the single most used aspect of the course. This use of mnemonic strategy, described by Higbee (1988) as the 'mental filing' application, can of course be extended to remembering ideas when in bed, and to the delivering of speeches, where the point to be made in the speech can be remembered by mnemonic strategies. Indeed before the age of pen and pencil, this was the classical use made of mnemonic strategies. The present writer, it must be said, prefers to write key-points down on a small note pad, just in case under the stress of the situation, he forgets a point!

One use to which the peg system can be put is remembering points to be made in examinations. Using the peg system for this purpose does, of course, often require the learner to make abstract words concrete. If, for example, the first topics to be discussed in an essay on ethics were

(a)   The concept of good
(b)   The concept of evil
(c)   Absolute values
(d)   Relative values

then 'Good' might be imagined as a priest, evil as Adolf Hitler, 'absolute' values as 'a salute' and 'relative' values as 'all your relatives'. To recall these, a priest would be imagined eating a bun (one), Hitler would be imagined throwing a shoe (two), you could imagine yourself giving 'a salute' to a tree (three) and imagine all your relatives banging on your door (four). As the example of a student who used this technique quoted below shows, this can be a highly effective method for those with a facility for imagery, but most students spontaneously appear to use the first-letter strategy (described later) in examinations (Gruneberg 1973).

That adaptations of the peg system can be used for exams is shown from this interview with a first year psychology student

(A.G.) who became interested in the use of mnemonic strategies as aids to examinations as a result of watching the BBC science programme 'QED' on the 'Magic of Memory'. A.G., as can be seen below, has high ability at imagery and could make concrete pictures of the numbers themselves, without having to use the peg words for numbers. Nevertheless he did use interactive visual imagery extensively.

M.M.G   Suppose the first thing you want to learn in relation to capital punishment is deterrence, what would you do?

A.G.   I would imagine a number 1 straying off my centre of vision, and as it got too close to the edge it would get an electric shock and jump back to the middle.

M.M.G.   So you actually use a visual image of the actual number, rather than the one–bun technique?

A.G.   I'm much better visually than auditorially.

M.M.G.   So to what extent do you have images for high numbers?

A.G.   For each essay I would have twenty or so ideas, all in a particular order, and I was giving up to 250 items for any one exam.

M.M.G.   Suppose you had to learn about democracy for your politics exams, and then about elections and the Tory Party, would you use the first twenty for democracy, then the second twenty for elections, and so on, or would you use the same numbers for the second lot of material to be learned?

A.G.   I wouldn't overlap, that would be confusing.

M.M.G.   So you would have an image, for, say the number 59? Say the fifty-ninth thing you wanted to remember was bye-elections. How would you do that?

A.G.   Well, the word 'bye-election' would conjure up some sort of image, so I might think of something I had seen on TV previously, like the announcement of a bye-election. So I might imagine some bloke wearing glasses and a bald head, reading from a piece of paper.

   I also play around with textures and colours. So I'd have '5' in a wooden, darkish colour – a rigid block – that would represent the podium. I could have the bloke turning into a number '9' and I could put glasses on him.

   So I would have the image of a Gothic digit looking like

a '5' in a brown colour and this boring drawing of a number '9' standing just behind the podium.

I would conjure up the image of someone standing at a lectern, reading out the numbers, which would then be my image of a bye-election.

It is not a very good image, you have just thrown this at me. If I was remembering something like that, I would remember talking about it in class, and there would be lots more images aside from what I have just used.

The above discussion, then, indicates clearly that the method of loci and the peg system are effective in enhancing recall of unrelated words. In order to use this knowledge, however, it is important to know when such strategies are likely to be useful in real-life situations and when they are not likely to be useful. Their practical application is probably best confined to those situations where writing down is impracticable, where preparation for their use is possible and where incoming information is not being presented at too fast a rate to make adequate imagery difficult.

FACE–NAME ASSOCIATION

As noted above, the strategy of using imagery to link together to-be-remembered material has been used to enhance face–name association. Both Morris, Jones and Hampson (1978) and McCarty (1980), for example, found that linking a name to a face by picturing the name associated with an outstanding feature of the face considerably enhanced recall of the name, given the face. For example, if someone's name is 'Fox' and they had a long nose, the learner should imagine Mr Fox with a long 'fox like' nose. Using this method Morris *et al.* found that there was an 80 per cent difference in mean recall for photographs for the imagery and control condition. Not only normal subjects, but elderly subjects have been shown to enhance face–name association by such techniques (Sheikh, Hill and Yesavage 1986). Sheikh *et al.* found that when linked to other strategies such as feature analysis, the benefits of an imagery strategy on an elderly population lasted for at least 6 months. Yet as Morris *et al.* point out, the practical value of such a technique is questionable because of the effort involved in its successful application in the first place – it takes time to make an image. Furthermore, in this writer's experience it is quite impossible for many people to create a useful image and to hold a sensible conversation at the same time. Many of those using this strategy, therefore, in normal social situations, may find it impossible to apply it, and therefore abandon its use. However, normal social interaction is not necessarily the place in which the application of such techniques are most appropriate. After all, at many social gatherings individuals are aware they are not going to meet again so the point of spending effort learning a name is fruitless. It can, however, be suggested that there are situations in which enhanced name–face association might be useful and practical. In one-day training courses, for example, it is often useful for a group of individuals to know each other's names, or for the trainer to know the names of trainees, and the effort of going through a list of names beforehand to familiarize oneself with possible images has been found by the present writer to be well worth the time invested. Similarly, after a meeting where one knows that a further meeting at a later date is likely, the present writer creates an image in the train going home, rather than at the time. In other words, whether it is worthwhile spending the effort making a name–face image cannot be determined on *a priori* grounds; it depends on the importance of remembering the names and the situation in which it is appropriate to apply such techniques. Furthermore, there may be specialist occupations, such as in police work, where name–face association is especially important and extra training might be needed to bring officers up to a level of expertise in the application of such strategies. Again the role of individual differences in speed and ability at making name–face associations is unknown, as is the role of training, so that for some individuals with a facility at imagery, the visual strategy of name–face association may indeed be practicable in ordinary social situations. Nevertheless for many individuals it is clearly not a practicable strategy in normal social situations because of the conflict between the needs of normal social interaction and the demands of processing visual interactions.

It can reasonably be argued therefore, that, in this area in particular, without adequate instruction in 'knowing when' and 'knowing when not' to, the strategy is likely to be prematurely abandoned as having no practical application. Indeed the work of Sheikh *et al.* in the elderly, and Wilson (1987) on the brain damaged, shows the considerable value of such strategies in socially useful situations. Wilson taught a group of four patients with memory difficulties the names of members of staff in a rehabilitation unit. Each patient had great difficulty in remembering the names of staff but the use of visual imagery very materially helped each subject to recall names.

A recent study by Gruneberg, Sykes and Hammond (1991) also showed that the strategy could be used to help learning-disabled adults. They found that such individuals failed on average (median) to recall a single name–face association when presented with eight such name–face pairs without any instruction on how to learn. When presented with an image linking the name to a face feature, the median retention was two, a highly statistically significant finding. These studies therefore indicate that a major social problem, that of remembering the names of new individuals, can be facilitated in groups with memory problems in this area. The Wilson and the Gruneberg *et al.* studies do not show that brain-damaged or learning-disabled individuals can generalize from the experimental situation to new situations where they themselves have to make up images unaided by the experimenter. Even if a failure to generalize were to be shown, however, the studies of Wilson and Gruneberg *et al.* are important in showing that, with the aid of nurses or helpers, who can supply images, brain-damaged or learning-disabled individuals can gain greater control over their social situation by the use of mnemonic strategies. These studies show that in the real world, where a major social problem is of learning names of significant individuals, then strategies which may be unimportant in normal social interaction may be powerful tools in enabling disadvantaged individuals to gain control over their social situation. As has been indicated above, however, these socially useful situations are not confined to the elderly, the brain damaged, or the learning disabled.

THE KEYWORD METHOD IN FOREIGN LANGUAGE LEARNING

Imagery has also been used to enhance foreign vocabulary learning. The keyword (or linkword) technique involves picturing an English word interacting with a foreign word which sounds like another English word. For example, the French for table-cloth is *nappe*; the learner is required to image him or herself having a *nap* on a *table-cloth*. The Spanish for cow is *vaca*. The learner is required to imagine a *cow* with a *vacuum* cleaner, cleaning a field.

The application of imagery mnemonics to language learning can be traced back at least to the nineteenth century. Bacon (1862) and

Loissette (1896) for example, both give accounts of the keyword method as an aid to foreign language learning. More recently, popular mnemonists such as Furst (1949) have outlined their use for this purpose. However, the scientific assessment of the keyword method can be said to have started in the 1970s with the publications of Ott, Butler, Blake and Ball (1973) and Raugh and Atkinson (1975). The latter publication has proved to be a highly influential spur to research, showing as it did that the use of the keyword method enhanced retention of Spanish words by a factor of about three.

The same authors (Atkinson and Raugh 1975) examined retention after 6 weeks using Russian vocabulary, and found that the keyword method does not lead to more rapid forgetting. This finding was confirmed by McDaniel, Pressley and Dunay (1987) who demonstrated that adult learners using the keyword method acquired foreign vocabulary significantly more rapidly than those not using it, but that once the non-users had learned to the same level as the keyword learners, there was then no difference in retention over a period of a week.

Furthermore, children have been shown in a number of studies to benefit from the use of keyword learning. Merry (1980) found 11- and 12-year-old British children performed significantly better on a French vocabulary learning task using the keyword method, than did a control group not instructed specifically to do so. Merry also found that one commonly raised objection to keyword learning, namely that it is liable to induce interference with the correct response, rarely occurred. Pressley (1977) also found the keyword method effective for elementary-school children.

A variation of the keyword method, the sentence keyword method, in which subjects generate a sentence to link the keyword and the to-be-learned word together, has also been found to be effective for children as young as 6 years old (Pressley, Levin and McCormick 1980). Furthermore, this adaptation has been shown to be effective in the learning of verbs as well as nouns (Miller, Levin and Pressley 1980).

One potential concern regarding the keyword method is that learning words in so-called isolation might lead to their not being understood within normal discourse. Two studies show this not to be the case. McDaniel and Pressley (1984) compared vocabulary learned by the keyword method with vocabulary learned where the meaning of a new item is inferred from a meaningful context.

They found the keyword method significantly better than the context method in terms of vocabulary retention. The keyword plus context condition was significantly superior to the context condition alone, but inferior to the keyword condition alone. In a second experiment they assessed the adequacy of the use of keyword-learned and context-learned vocabulary in sentences. They concluded 'both methods led to highly adequate use of vocabulary in sentences, but the keyword method produced higher recall of the word definitions.'

More recently, McDaniel and Pressley (1989) return to the question of whether learning vocabulary by keyword has deleterious effects on text comprehension. They note that 'the keyword method has proved more effective than any alternatives to date in terms of creating vocabulary-word-definition associations'. They go on to point out, however, that the keyword method is nevertheless often not recommended in vocabulary-instruction programmes, possibly because vocabulary instruction is embedded typically in concerns for enhancement of reading and comprehension skills. They therefore conducted an experiment which showed that the context method did not produce better reading comprehension than the keyword method. In fact the keyword method produced more accurate comprehension of the parts of the language containing new vocabulary. A second experiment failed to show differences in comprehension following keyword learning as compared to context learning. McDaniel and Pressley conclude that 'there is no evidence that the keyword-mediated gains in learning of vocabulary–definition associations are obtained at the expense of other information.'

Recent evidence in fact shows that the keyword strategy can enhance at least one aspect of 'other information' – gender acquisition. Desroches, Gelinas and Wieland (1989) found that not only the acquisition of German nouns but retention of genders was facilitated by use of keywords (they had their subjects associate the to-be-learned word with a man if it was masculine and a woman if feminine).

It should be added, however, that while some fifty or so studies have found considerable evidence for the facilitating effects of the keyword method on vocabulary acquisition, at least three have failed to provide positive results. Fuentes (1976) found no difference between the keyword and a control condition, but he provided only five words to learn in 10-minute sessions, and this allowed the control group time to learn to the level of the keyword group.

179

A study by Hall, Wilson and Patterson (1981) also failed to find the keyword method to be superior (though not inferior). But just as in the Fuentes study, a relatively long time was allowed for learning in both keyword and control conditions, and the presentation of images was unpaced, that is to say that no instruction was given on spending a set amount of time on each image.

Finally, Levin *et al.* (1979) failed to find any advantage associated with keyword learning in three experiments. However, when the researchers ensured that presentation rates were paced by the experimenters, so that learners spent a set amount of time on each image, the keyword method was shown to be highly effective with both small and large classroom groups.

The failure to find effects in these studies does not therefore detract from the positive findings in the overwhelming majority of studies. It is likely that the keyword method is ineffective when learners are not instructed to spend a set amount of time on each image. In almost all experiments involving presenting subjects with images at set time intervals – typically one image every 10 seconds – the keyword condition is superior.

Hall (1991) has recently argued, however, that the failure to find effects of the keyword method in his studies compared with other studies lay in the differences in task difficulty between studies. Hall's studies involved material on which it was difficult to use the keyword technique. It has to be said, however, that perceived difficulty is likely to vary from individual to individual and that failures in using the keyword method have been confined to experiments in which subjects have to generate their own linking images.

The present writer (Gruneberg 1985, 1987, 1988) has applied the keyword method in language courses which integrate vocabulary learning, grammar learning and sentence translation examples. Images are presented to the learner in sentences which include the keyword rather than the learner's having to generate his/her own images, a method of presentation which has seldom been investigated in the laboratory. Fieldwork studies, however, indicate that learners can 'tolerate' large amounts of vocabulary presented in this integrated manner. In one study, for example, five executives in a travel company learned a 400 word vocabulary and basic grammar to an almost faultless level in 12 contact hours, including translations into Spanish and into English. In another study, six bank employees learned at least a 600 word vocabulary and associated grammar in a 4 day period (Gruneberg and Jacobs 1991). As importantly, studies reported by Gruneberg and Jacobs and a study reported by Gruneberg and Sykes (1991) indicate that learners find the keyword method faster, easier and more enjoyable than conventional methods of language learning. These findings are in line with Higbee (1990) who found enhanced motivation when using the peg mnemonic to learn lists of errands and sayings.

The fieldwork and survey studies carried out by Gruneberg and Jacobs (1991) and Gruneberg and Sykes (1991) do not show that Linkword courses are superior to other courses since no direct comparison between such courses and other courses has been made. Such direct comparisons are invidious since different language courses are constructed in completely different ways to cater for completely different needs of learners. The needs of a learner who has to be in Bonn next Tuesday, and Madrid next Thursday are completely different from those of the student intent on an academic career in languages. Unfortunately the patent hostility of some linguists to the keyword method (see e.g. *Which* Report 1990; Pressley and McDaniel 1989) clearly indicates that linguists' concern with higher-order aspects of language learning is blinding them to the basic advantages of enhanced methods of vocabulary acquisition. In fact, the enhancing effects of the keyword method on retention is not confined to language learning. The method has been used successfully to enhance English vocabulary acquisition (Pressley and McDaniel 1989) and science facts. Rosenbeck, Levin and Levin (1989), for example, showed that the keyword method could facilitate the learning of botanical classifications. To teach that Angiosperms, for example, were flower producers, the word 'Angiosperm' is turned into something concrete, e.g. 'angels', and angels are then pictured surrounded by flowers. Rosenbeck *et al.* found that this method significantly enhanced the learning of plant classification. Yet one of the main problems faced by those wishing to apply memory research in general is the need to interact with professionals in other disciplines who regard memory improvement as a low-level, indeed a bizarre activity and who therefore discount the potential value of contributions to the learning of their discipline by psychologists. Unless psychologists are willing to interact with, and publicize the value of their findings to, professionals however, little value will come from the laboratory studies of psychologists.

THE DIGIT–LETTER SYSTEM

A further good example of the difference between 'knowing how', 'knowing when' and 'knowing not to' is in the use of the digit–letter transformation system. This system was partly devised for the learning of digit sequences. Learners are required to overlearn the following digit–letter equivalence:

1	=	t	(there is *one* downstroke in *t*)
2	=	n	(there are *two* downstrokes in *n*)
3	=	m	(there are *three* downstrokes in *m*)
4	=	r	(*r* is the last letter of *four*)
5	=	l	(l is 50 in the Roman numbers)
6	=	sh	(*six* has a sort of '*sh*' sound)
7	=	k	(number *7* is embedded in *k*)
8	=	f	(both *8* and *f* have two loops)
9	=	p	(*9* is *p* the wrong way round)
0	=	s	(zero starts with an *s* sound)

To remember any digit sequence such as 2 1 0, i.e. n t s, the learner can use vowels any way he or she likes in order to make a word, e.g. 'Nets or Nuts'. So the Telephone number 21023 could be 'Nuts in May'. That the use of this strategy is effective in learning digit sequences has been shown by Morris and Greer (1984) They found that subjects remembered twice as many two-digit numbers using this system as a control group not instructed in the system. The present writer does use this system for learning telephone numbers and bank pin numbers, but the effort of making up such sequences and the speed of forgetting makes their use as a matter of course simply not worthwhile. On the other hand, the writer does use this method for remembering his wife's birthday: 19 January – t p – top. The writer pictures his wife *top*-less on her birthday – this image was well worth the effort of making it up, as it prevents confusion between the 19th and 20th, which happened prior to the adoption of this particular method!

Apart from this somewhat idiosyncratic use, the digit–letter system has been reported to the writer as being used by a supermarket manager to remember prices of goods. If, for example, a tin of beans cost 21p, this would be NUT, so that a large nut would be pictured balanced on top of a tin of beans! Changes in prices of goods did not apparently cause any problems.

A second use of the digit–letter transformation system is for the extension of the pegword method. For example, the number 12 = tn, which could be TIN, is represented by the concrete word TIN as a peg. The number 113 TTM could be TOTEM, so that the peg for the number 113 could be represented by a totem pole, and so on. It is not clear exactly how useful such an extension of the peg word system is, although the student A.G. reported using numbers up to 250 for his examination preparation. For the great majority of people, however, it does not seem obvious how an extended peg system is going to be useful in everyday situations.

THE FIRST-LETTER STRATEGY

A final mnemonic strategy considered here – the first-letter strategy – paradoxically would appear to suffer from the reverse problem to those considered above – that is, when it should be applied is obvious; how it should be applied is more complex. The first-letter strategy involves using the first letter of to-be-remembered items to cue the to-be-remembered items at a later stage. For example, ROYGBIV gives the colours of the rainbow. Sometimes the first letters are used to make a meaningful sentence, such as *Richard of York Gave Battle In Vain.*

That this kind of first letter cueing can be effective has been in some doubt when dealing with poorly learned material, but as Gruneberg (1978) notes, when dealing with well-learned material, there is reasonable evidence that such strategies enhance recall (see e.g. Higbee 1988; Cook 1989). Gruneberg (1978), for example, found that when dealing with large amounts of related material where recall was delayed for 20 minutes, both order and item recall was significantly better using the first-letter strategy. It could reasonably be argued that learning large amounts of related materials where recall is delayed, mimics examination conditions to a reasonable degree. In fact, there is evidence that such strategies are used spontaneously by students in appropriate situations. Gruneberg (1973) asked students who had taken finals examinations in psychology at a Welsh University about the mnemonic strategies they had employed. About one-third of these reported that they used mnemonic strategies 'at least sometimes' in finals examinations. The most frequently used strategy was the first-letter strategy (the students had been given no instructions on their use). One reason for this might be that first-letter cueing has been shown to be effective in overcoming memory blocks (Gruneberg and Monks 1974) and students could have found this to be the case in their own experience. Clearly such a strategy is useful when in examinations, for example, where points to be made in essays need to be recalled, and where blocking under stress may occur.

The question is, however, how best should such strategies be used. In the first place, they are not suitable for everyone. Gruneberg (1978) reports for example, that one student took 20 minutes to make up one six-letter mnemonic phrase! Second, as large quantities of such phrases need to be retained for examination purposes, the possibility of interference and forgetting is likely to be high. A strategy for taking this into account is therefore necessary. The writer's own suggested strategy involves: (1) making an initial thorough review of the field; (2) some 2 weeks before the examination selecting out perhaps ten to twelve major points per topic; (3) making up either one or two mnemonic words or mnemonic phrases for each topic; (4) ensuring that these words and phrases and what they stand for are well learned; (5) the evening before the examination the mnemonic words and their associates should be gone over again until memory is perfect; (6) students should then arrive at the examination centre half an hour before the examinations, talk to no one, but again go over the mnemonic letters/words and their associations; (7) finally, once in the examination room, students should inspect the questions and then immediately write down the relevant mnemonics and their associated points. That this strategy can be effective for high-level performance is seen from the report by Gruneberg (1978) of one of his students (M.O.) who was interviewed immediately after having been awarded a first-class degree. Gruneberg had suggested to M.O. . . . that she use first-letter mnemonic aids, after coming across her crying during her second psychology exam.

Int.   Would you say that using mnemonics gives you more confidence?

M.O.   Yes certainly. Because I started doing it, because for the first few exams I didn't use it at all and I was just a nervous wreck because I could not remember anything and I knew I had learnt things. And I got into the exam and couldn't remember.

Int.   What were those first few papers?

M.O.   Oh, the Abnormal paper and then Basic Processes and Social. And it was only in the Social I started. I only used one mnemonic for that, that's when I started because I knew

184

I could not get anywhere if I didn't start to make a conscious effort to remember things. Because in the beginning, I said 'Oh, how silly, I am not using those things', and then I found I could not remember anything so I got home and said 'Right, make up some mnemonics', and it worked.

Int.   Did you use them before?

M.O.   I used them in school sometimes, but I used to think, 'Oh, you've gone past that stage now', but it's amazing you haven't, it does give you a lot of confidence, because you can go in, write them down, and you feel that you are ready to write an answer.

The importance of this section is that it suggests that users of mnemonic techniques might gain confidence in their memory abilities. Whether mnemonic techniques are actually more efficient than rote learning or other techniques might therefore not be such an important matter. If the student thinks they are helpful and gains confidence in his or her studying ability, then they might well be more efficient as learning aids.

Again the student claimed that the process of making up mnemonics was an enjoyable one, that it took place in a social context in which the mnemonics were often related to ongoing activity, and that it increased the amount of time she thought about the work that the mnemonics related to. These, too, might increase the value of using mnemonic aids. Of course, as indicated earlier, such strategies are not of value for everyone in all situations. But at least for individuals who find the memory load of examinations stressful or who find that memory problems arise in examinations, this strategy can be offered as one which has empirical backing.

OVERCOMING MEMORY BLOCKS

A question related to how best to prepare materials for an examination, is that of how best to overcome a memory block if it occurs during an examination, or indeed at any other time. Almost everyone has had the feeling at some time or other, that a response was just about to come, in other words was on the 'tip of the tongue' (TOT), but just could not be produced. In examinations this can be especially distressing as it might lead to an inability to write the answer which does justice to the knowledge stored.

There is considerable evidence that one of the most important categories which induces TOT states is proper names (Brown 1991). The problems seems to get worse with age, with Burke, MacKay, Worthley and Wade (1991) reporting one TOT incident per week for younger adults and one to seven incidents per week for older adults. Nevertheless it is common experience that in emotionally stressful situations such as in examinations, TOT states can occur for younger individuals.

Whilst the psychological significance of the TOT state was pointed out by James (1890), the first systematic investigation of the phenomenon was by Brown and McNeill (1966). In their study, Brown and McNeill produced instances of TOT in their subjects by giving them definitions of rare words and asking them to supply the word defined. When subjects reported being in a TOT state, Brown and McNeill asked them to give the number of syllables in the missing word, the first letter of the missing word and so on. It was found that subjects could recall the number of syllables in words although they could not recall the words. They also found that the initial letter was correctly recalled 57 per cent of the time, a percentage obviously well above chance level. They also found that when recall was imminent, subjects could distinguish between words which came to mind that resembled the missing word and those that did not. Yarmey (1973) has extended the findings of Brown and McNeill by using famous faces as the stimulus material.

What do these findings tell us about memory storage? Words are not stored in memory as whole units, little parcels each stored in a separate location. A word consists of a number of dimensions. Take the word 'dog' for example. It has a variety of dimensions: it is an animal, it has four legs, it looks hairy, it is something which is usually friendly, it makes a peculiar noise, it chews up the carpet when young, it gives feelings of pleasure, it has a short name, the name begins with a particular letter – D, and so on. These various aspects are tied together to define the thing which is a dog. When one is searching in memory for a word, one is searching for the representation of all these dimensions. It is likely that the representation sought is primarily acoustic. Hence if one is aware of all the aspects of the word, except for the actual sound pattern, it is perhaps not surprising that 'one knows one knows' the missing sound pattern even though one cannot get it back. Furthermore, as the experiment of Brown and McNeill shows, certain aspects of the sound pattern may be accessible yet the whole word may not be, indicating that even the sound pattern is not stored as one unit.

Yet exactly what causes a TOT state is not actually clear. As Brown (1991) notes, it could be that a TOT state represents the breakdown of retrieval because of inadequate target activation or it could represent a retrieval that is side-tracked because of inaccurate information. Neither possibility has been tested adequately, mainly because of the difficulty of experimental control with TOT experiments. Again as Brown points out, it is not clear whether similar words to the target word, which come to mind, help to overcome the TOT or actually cause the TOT in the first place.

Nevertheless, in spite of the lack of understanding of what causes a TOT, a number of studies do suggest ways of overcoming them when they arise. Gruneberg, Smith and Winfrow (1973) set out to examine this question using an experimental design which was as naturalistic as possible. Subjects were required to produce their own memory blocks in their own way, then to try to overcome them. Almost all the subjects could do this by searching through categories, such as old school friends, picturing their faces then trying to recall the name. In all, twenty subjects reported 206 such memory blocks in 30-minute sessions. Of these blocks, 66 per cent were recovered during the experimental session following a memory search. Whilst the greatest number of items, forty-eight, were recalled within 10 seconds of reporting a memory block, some fifteen were recalled after subjects persisted with their memory search for more than 90 seconds after reporting the block. These results, therefore, suggest that for practical purposes it is well worth-while persisting with one's memory search for what is, subjectively, a considerable period of time. The second part of the experiment involved contacting subjects some 2 to 9 hours after the experimental session, and asking them again to try to recall unretrieved items. Following this second retrieval attempt thirteen items were recalled and two further items were recalled very rapidly following the discontinuation of the second retrieval attempt. Only four items were recalled in the intervening period between the first and second retrieval attempts. For these four items, however, subjects admitted actively searching for the missing word. In the whole experiment, therefore, not one item was recalled 'spontaneously' during other activity, without a conscious attempt on the part of the subject to search for the missing word. Since this experiment, however, a number of investigations, such as Burke *et al.* (1991) have found a considerable number of 'pop-ups'. Brown (1991) suggests that the incidence of such 'pop-ups' is higher in experiments involving naturally occurring TOTs, so that experiments such as Gruneberg *et al.* may be underestimating the possibility of spontaneous recovery. On the other hand, as Brown points out, it is difficult to be sure that 'pop-ups' are really spontaneous recoveries, rather than individuals rapidly retrieving a blocked item following a further retrieval attempt and simply not remembering what triggered a second retrieval attempt.

Obviously, however, waiting for 'pop-ups' is no strategy to adopt in, say, examinations or when faced with someone whose name you cannot recall! A number of strategies have been suggested, and some do appear to be successful. Gruneberg and Monks (1976), for example, instructed subjects who were blocking to search through the alphabet in order to try to find the first letter of the missing item. Following a second retrieval attempt, without any instruction, subjects were instructed on a third retrieval attempt to recall items still unrecalled by going through the alphabet in order to find what the first letter of the missing item might be. Recall on the third trial was significantly greater than on the previous trial, indicating that the instruction to use a first-letter search strategy had increased the probability of recall. A control group given no instruction on the third trial showed a decrease on this trial, indicating that the probability of recall did not normally rise with each succeeding retrieval attempt. Unfortunately, it cannot be concluded that it is the first-letter strategy *per se* which increases recall as there was a significant increase in search time under the first-letter search strategy instruction. It might be, therefore, that instruction to use a first-letter search strategy induces subjects to spend more time than they otherwise would in searching for a missing item and this is what improves recall. At the very least, however, there is a practical value to adopting a strategy which spontaneously involves the subject in searching for longer than he or she normally would, and which can be shown to be superior in producing recall of blocked items to the normal strategies which the subject spontaneously employs and terminates following a retrieval failure.

Other strategies which have been shown to be successful include leaving the blocked item for a period of time, then actively trying again to retrieve it (Gruneberg *et al.* 1973) and switching from one form of search strategy to another, e.g. seeing a particular event from another perspective as in the cognitive interview (Fisher and Geiselman 1988).

In social situations, of course, a common strategy adopted is to keep talking to a person whose name you cannot recall until hopefully some triggering association comes to mind. In such social situations errors of omission are almost always less embarrassing than actually getting the name wrong, so in the event of uncertainty it is usually best to say nothing and certainly to avoid introducing someone whose name you have forgotten!

GENERAL DISCUSSION

It seems clear that a failure to find any long-term effects of the use of mnemonic strategies from memory improvement instruction cannot be taken to indicate that such instructions are of no practical value or that laboratory findings are not generalizable to the real world. A detailed knowledge of the quality of the 'knowing how', 'knowing when' and the 'knowing when not' instruction is essential before such a conclusion can be drawn. Furthermore, statistical analysis may be misleading in that such strategies may be useful in few, but nevertheless critical situations. An analogy might be with teaching someone to swim. If an individual, 5 years after learning to swim, entered the water for the first time and it saved him or her from drowning, it would be of great value, even if an evaluation 6 months after being taught found that the individual never went swimming. What memory improvement course evaluations cannot do is assess the value to the individual of the potential for using such techniques when he or she feels the need to use them.

The same argument can be used to question the conclusion of Park *et al.* (1990) that, to quote Bacon, a mnemonic aid 'is a barren thing for human uses'. Infrequency of usage cannot be taken as indicating that they are of limited use if they are of critical use in infrequently occurring but important situations.

To further their argument on the limited utility of mnemonic aids, Park *et al.* argue that even memory experts rarely use such techniques. However, the 'experts' he questioned were not necessarily experts on, or interested in, mnemonic strategies. Again, the argument is not that such strategies are necessarily frequently used, but that a knowledge of their use might sometimes be critical. A good example of this is given by Morris (personal communication) who, as can be seen, was initially sceptical about the use of such techniques.

He writes:

> As you know, I have tended, in the past, to be sceptical about
> the frequency with which even those of us who know about the
> effectiveness of mnemonic aids will actually use them in our
> everyday life. I use them myself mainly in memory experi-
> ments, although I do find it very useful to retain password
> numbers by the phonetic mnemonic.
>
> What I have realized recently is that, even if one does not had
> a frequent need to use the mnemonics they are a very valuable
> emergency resource to have stowed away ready for use! The
> particular incident that brought this home to me vividly was
> when, as President of the British Psychological Society, I had to
> take charge of the Official Launch of the Register of Chartered
> Psychologists during the summer. All sorts of representatives
> attended: representatives of all the branches of the Civil Service
> where psychologists work, the local Member of Parliament, the
> Chair of the County Council, the Mayor and the Vice Chancellor
> of the local University and so on, more than a dozen dignitaries.
> The problem was that each had to be presented with a copy of
> the new Register and a short speech made by me relating to their
> special connection with psychology. It was very important that
> they were addressed in the correct order of seniority, elected
> representatives first, names and titles exactly correct (The First
> Commissioner of the Civil Service; Assistant Secretary Special
> Needs at the Department of Education and Science, etc.) and
> so on. I realized that there would be no opportunity for looking
> up any details between each presentation – and I was right! I
> used a mixture of various mnemonics to learn the details on the
> train travelling to the meeting – I had been too busy earlier.
> Basically, I looked for meaningful concrete translations of the
> names, occupations and central points of the speeches and strung
> them together with imagery or story connections. I was surprised
> myself that I survived with no insults or mishaps. Each recipient
> felt obliged to make a speech back in response, and I stood smiling
> and nodding and desperately reviewing my mnemonic aids! I was
> really relieved to get it over, but most of all I was thankful that I
> had the mnemonics to get me through!

Park *et al.* argue that whilst mnemonic aids might be of use in
limited situations, they require such a substantial investment in
cognitive effort and training time that their use in everyday life is

impracticable. But, as has been argued above, it is not possible to substantiate general statements of this kind. Using the Peg System to remember points to be raised at a meeting involves little cognitive effort, and the cognitive effort in remembering names at a workshop might well be worth the effort in terms of smoothing interactions during the day. On the other hand, considerable cognitive effort and training time might well be worth the effort in the case of brain-injured patients if the end result is more social control over the environment. Furthermore, as noted earlier, the role of individual differences in the ability to use visual imagery strategies has not been systematically examined, and for some individuals, at least, there may be little cognitive effort in utilizing such strategies relative to the difficulties they have in remembering, using other strategies. In fact, it can be argued that many skills require extended training before they become effective, and that the value of mnemonic strategies in real-life situations has hardly been tested because few training programmes extend beyond an introduction on how to use the various techniques plus a limited practice. It might well be, however, that extended practice with the various techniques in socially useful situations would lead to their greater application in everyday life. The question of when it is and when it is not appropriate to use such techniques, and how potentially useful they might be, in other words, cannot be argued on *a priori* grounds.

In fact, whilst the study of the effectiveness of 'knowing how' has been amply demonstrated over the last twenty years, the study of 'knowing when' and 'when not' has hardly begun. The argument of this chapter is not that psychologists such as Herrmann *et al.* (1988), Park *et al.* (1990) and Cornoldi (1988) are wrong in drawing attention to the limitations of mnemonic strategies, but that the conclusion that many mnemonic techniques have limited practical utility is premature and might discourage a proper investigation of 'knowing when' to apply them. It certainly does seem clear from the papers of Herrmann *et al.* (1988), Cornoldi (1988) and Park *et al.* (1990) that merely teaching mnemonic strategies *per se*, i.e. 'knowing how' is of little practical significance. On the other hand, it seems equally clear from the research reported here that, when appropriately applied, mnemonic strategies can have an important part to play in areas as diverse as examinations, business meetings, help for the elderly and brain damaged in new social situations, and in foreign language learning. Nor is it being suggested that the real-life applications outlined in this chapter are anything approaching an exhaustive list. Higbee (1988), for example, suggests a number of other practical applications including maths, science and basic language skills. It is, however, argued that their use, restricted to clearly useful and appropriate situations, is likely to be more effective than over-using such strategies in situations where the ratio of effort to reward is not clearly positive.

Finally, it should be emphasized that this chapter is not intended to show the superiority of mnemonic strategies over other strategies. It is now quite clear (see chapter 6) that many factors are involved in memory improvement and facilitation, other than the use of mnemonic strategies. What this chapter aims to show is that in coming to appreciate the value of a 'multi-modal' approach to memory improvement or facilitation those in need of memory skills should not abandon the old for the new, but rather use them together.

REFERENCES

Atkinson, R.C. and Raugh, M.R. (1975) 'An application of the mnemonic keyword method to the acquisition of Russian vocabulary,' *Journal of Experimental Psychology: Human Learning and Memory* 1: 126–33.

Bacon, J.H. (1862) *The Science of Memory*, London: Simpkin.

Bellezza, F.A. (1981) 'Mnemonic devices: Classification, characteristics, and criteria,' *Review of Educational Research* 51: 247–75.

Bower, G.H. (1967) 'Mental imagery and memory (1967),' Cited in P.E. Morris, 'Practical strategies for human learning and remembering,' in M.J.A. Howe (ed.) *Adult Learning* (1977), New York: Wiley.

Bower, G.H. (1972) 'Mental imagery and associative learning,'in Gregg, L.W. (ed.) *Cognition in Learning and Memory*, New York: John Wiley.

Brown, A.S. (1991) 'A review of the tip of the tongue experience,' *Psychological Bulletin* 109: 204–23.

Brown, R. and McNeill, D. (1966) 'The "tip of the tongue" phenomenon', *Journal of Verbal Learning and Verbal Behavior* 5: 325–37.

Bugelski, B.R. (1968) 'Images as a mediator in one trial paired associate learning,' *Journal of Experimental Psychology* 77: 328–34.

Burke, D.M., MacKay, D.G., Worthley, J.S. and Wade, E. (1991) 'On the tip of the tongue: What causes word finding failures in young and older adults,' *Journal of Memory and Language* 30: 542–79.

Cook, N.M. (1989) 'The applicability of verbal mnemonics for different populations: A review,' *Applied Cognitive Psychology* 3: 3–22.

Cornoldi, C. (1988) 'Why study mnemonics?,' in M.M. Gruneberg, P.E. Morris and R.N. Sykes (eds) *Practical Aspects of Memory*, vol. 2., pp. 397–402, Chichester: Wiley.

DeBeni, R. (1988) 'The aid given by the "loci" memory technique in the memorization of passages,' in: M.M. Gruneberg, P.E. Morris and R.N. Sykes (eds) *Practical Aspects of Memory*, vol. 2., pp. 421–4, Chichester: Wiley.

DeBeni, R. and Cornoldi, C. (1985) 'Effects of the mnemotechnique of loci in the memorization of concrete words,' *Acta Psychologica* 60: 11–24.

Desroches, A., Gelinas, C. and Wieland, L.D. (1989) 'An application of the mnemonic keyword to the acquisition of German nouns and their grammatical gender', *Journal of Educational Psychology* 81: 25–32.

Dyer, J.C. and Meyer, P.A. (1976) 'Facilitation of sample concept identification through mnemonic instruction', *Journal of Experimental Psychology: Human Learning and Memory* 2:767–73.

Elliot, J.L. and Gentile, J.R. (1986) 'The efficacy of a mnemonic technique for learning disabled and nondisabled adolescents,' *Journal of Learning Disabilities* 19: 237–41.

Fisher, R.P. and Geiselman, R.E. (1988) 'Enhancing eyewitness memory with the cognitive interview,'in: M.M. Gruneberg, P.E. Morris and R.N. Sykes (eds) *Practical Aspects of Memory*, vol. 1, pp. 34–9, Chichester: Wiley

Fuentes, D.J. (1976) 'An investigation into the use of imagery and generativity in learning a foreign language vocabulary,' Doctoral Dissertation, Stanford University.

Furst, B. (1949) *Stop Forgetting*, Psychology Publishing, UK.

Groninger, K.D. (1971) 'Mnemonic imagery and forgetting,' *Psychonomic Science* 23: 161–3

Gruneberg, M.M. (1973) 'The role of memorisation techniques in finals examination preparation – a study of psychology students,' *Educational Research* 15: 134–9.

Gruneberg, M.M. (1978) 'The feeling of knowing, memory blocks and memory aids,'in M.M. Gruneberg and P.E. Morris (eds) *Aspects of Memory* 1st edn, London: Methuen

Gruneberg, M.M. (1985) *Computer Linkword: French, German, Spanish, Italian, Greek, Russian, Dutch, Portuguese, Hebrew*, Penfield, New York: USA Artworx Inc.

Gruneberg, M.M. (1987) *Linkword French, German, Spanish, Italian, Greek, Portuguese*, London: Corgi Books

Gruneberg, M.M. and Monks, J. (1974) 'Feeling of knowing and cued recall', *Acta Psychologica* 38: 257–65.

Gruneberg, M.M. and Monks, J. (1976) 'The first letter search strategy,' *I.R.C.S. Medical Science: Psychology and Psychiatry* 4: 307.

Gruneberg, M.M. and Jacobs, G.C. (1991) 'In defence of Linkword,' *Language Learning Journal* 3: 25–9.

Gruneberg, M.M. and Sykes, R.N. (1991) 'Individual differences and attitudes to the keyword method of foreign language learning,' *Language Learning Journal* 4: 60–2.

Gruneberg, M.M., Smith, R. and Winfrow, P. (1973) 'An investigation into memory blocking,' *Acta Psychologica* 37: 187–96.

Gruneberg, M.M., Sykes, R.N. and Hammond, V. (1991) 'Name–face association in learning disabled adults: The use of a visual associative strategy', *Neuropsychological Rehabilitation* 1, 2: 113–16.

Hall, J.W. (1991) 'More on the utility of the keyword method', *Journal of Educational Psychology* 83: 171–2.

Hall, J.W., Wilson, K.P. and Patterson, R.J. (1981) 'Mnemotechnics: Some limitations of the mnemonic keyword method for the study of foreign language vocabulary,' *Journal of Educational Psychology*, 345–57.

Herrmann, D. and Searleman, A. (1990) 'The new multi-modal approach to memory improvement', in G. Bower (ed.) *Advances in Learning and Motivation*, New York: Academic Press

Herrmann, D., Rea, A. and Andrzejewski, S. (1988) 'The need for a new approach to memory training,' in M.M. Gruneberg, P.E. Morris and R.N. Sykes (eds) *Practical Aspects of Memory* vol. 1, pp. 415–20, Chichester: Wiley.

Higbee, K.L. (1988) *Your Memory*, 2nd edn, New York: Prentice-Hall

Higbee, K.L. (1990) 'Some motivational aspects of imagery mnemonics,' *Perceptual and Motor Skills* 70: 871–9.

Higbee, K.L. and Millard, R.J. (1981) 'Effects of an imagery mnemonic and imagery value on memory for sayings,' *Bulletin of the Psychonomic Society* 17: 215–16.

James, W. (1890) *Principles of Psychology*, New York: Harry Holt

Katz, A.N. (1987) 'Individual differences in the control of imagery processes,' in M.A McDaniel and M. Pressley (eds) *Imagery and Related Mnemonic Processes* pp. 177–203, New York: Springer.

Levin, J.R. Pressley, M., McCormick, C.B., Miller, G.E. and Shriberg, L.K. (1979) 'Assessing the classroom potential of the keyword method,' *Journal of Educational Psychology* 71: 583–94.

Loisette, A. (1896) *Assimilative Memory*, New York: Funk and Wagnalls.

McCarty, D.L. (1980) 'Investigation of a visual imagery mnemonic device for acquiring name-face association', *Journal of Experimental Psychology: Human Learning and Memory* 6: 145–55.

McDaniel, M.A. and Pressley, M. (1984) 'Putting the keyword method in context,' *Journal of Educational Psychology* 76: 598–609.

McDaniel, M.A., and Pressley, M. (1989) 'Keyword and context instruction of new vocabulary meanings: Effect of text comprehension and memory,' *Journal of Educational Psychology* 81: 204–13.

McDaniel, M.A., Pressley, M. and Dunay, P.K. (1987) 'Long term retention of vocabulary after keyword and context learning,' *Journal of Educational Psychology* 79: 87–9.

Merry, R. (1980) 'The keyword method and childrens vocabulary learning in the classroom,' *British Journal of Educational Psychology* 50: 123–36.

Miller, G.E., Levin, J.R. and Pressley, M. (1980) 'An adaptation of the keyword method to children's learning of foreign verbs', *Journal of Mental Imagery* 4: 57–61.

Morris, P.E. and Greer, P.J. (1984) 'The effectiveness of the phonetic mnemonic system', *Human Learning* 3: 137–42.

Morris, P.E. and Reid, L.R. (1970) 'Repeated use of mnemonic imagery', *Psychonomic Science* 20: 337–8.

Morris, P.E. and Stevens, R.S. (1974) 'Linking images and free recall', *Journal of Verbal Learning and Verbal Behavior* 13: 310–15.

Morris, P.E., Jones, S. and Hampson, P.J. (1978) 'An imagery mnemonic for the learning of peoples' names', *British Journal of Psychology* 69: 335–6.

Ott, R.E., Butler, D.C., Blake, R.S. and Ball, J.R. (1973) 'The effect of interactive imagery elaboration on the acquisition of a foreign language vocabulary,' *Language Learning* 23: 197–206.

Park, D.C., Smith, A.D. and Cavenaugh, J.C. (1990) 'Metamemories of memory researchers', *Memory and Cognition* 18: 321–7.

Pressley, M. (1977) 'Children's use of the keyword method to learn simple Spanish vocabulary words', *Journal of Educational Psychology* 69: 465–72.

Pressley, M., Levin, J.R. and McCormick, C.B. (1980) 'Young children's learning of foreign language vocabulary: A sentence variation of the keyword method,' *Contemporary Educational Psychology* 5: 22–9.

Raugh, M.R. and Atkinson, R.C. (1975) 'A mnemonic method for learning a second language vocabulary', *Journal of Educational Psychology* 67: 1–16.

Rosenbeck, M.B., Levin, M.E. and Levin, J.R. (1989) 'Learning botany concepts mnemonically: Seeing the forest and the trees', *Journal of Educational Psychology* 81: 196–203.

Ross, J. and Lawrence, K.A. (1968) 'Some observations on memory artifice,' *Psychonomic Science* 13: 107–8.

Sheikh, J.I., Hill, R.D. and Yesavage, J.A. (1986) 'Long-term efficacy of cognitive training for age associated memory impairment: A six month follow-up study,' *Developmental Neuropsychology* 2: 413–21.

Which Report (1990) *Language Learning Report*, September.

Wilson, B.A. (1987) *Rehabilitation of Memory* New York: Guilford.

Yarmey, A.D. (1973) 'I recognize your face but I cannot remember your name: Further evidence on the tip of the tongue phenomenon', *Memory and Cognition* 1: 287–90.

Yates, F. (1966) *The Art Of Memory* London: Routledge and Kegan Paul.

8

PROSPECTIVE MEMORY
Remembering to do things

Peter E. Morris

When most people are asked what type of memory error they would like to avoid, forgetting to carry out some action that had been planned comes high on the list (e.g. Reason and Mysielska 1982). Gene Winograd (1988) remarks that the failure of memory that caused him most pain was the time that he forgot to pick up his 3-year-old son and friends from nursery school and take them to their play group. He describes it as 'an embarrassing lapse' and as being 'not easily forgiven'. That captures much of the reason for the importance of remembering to do things. Forgetting often causes consequences not only for ourselves but also for others to whom we are attached or with whom we need to retain a mutual respect. It is an interesting characteristic of forgetting to carry out such actions that it is the person him or herself who is blamed, whereas a failure to describe, for example, a scene from our past is blamed upon the individual's memory rather than so directly on the individual themselves (Munsat 1966). The fallibility of retrospective memory provides an excuse that deflects the criticism from the person in a way that rarely happens for failures to keep appointments.

Meacham (1988) sees in these social consequences the main difference between what are known as prospective and retrospective remembering. Prospective memory is memory for intentions, for actions that we wish to carry out in the future, while retrospective memory is recall of information from the past. Meacham argues that we form intentions to carry out actions in social contexts and it is the public nature of the success and failure to carry out the actions that defines prospective memory. He argues that isolated individuals could escape the responsibility for their decisions by neglecting or denying them. However, individual rememberers are enmeshed in a network of interpersonal relationships that give the checks and frequently the meaning to any intentional decision.

Perhaps Meacham's position is too extreme. Even a Robinson Crusoe would need to plan his future actions in order to survive, and many intentions are formed for personal reasons. Nevertheless, it is the enmeshing of prospective memory with the needs and wishes of other people that gives it much of its primary importance and which makes instances of forgetting embarrassing and memorable. However, it is not just the social consequences of prospective memory failure that give such failure its central importance. It is also their inherent involvement in our plans and goal-directed behaviour. One of the characteristics of humans in comparison with other animals is the extent to which we live for the future. Many of our actions are best understood as goal directed, and the goals are often far in the future. Students study for degrees that require 3 or 4 years of full time commitment. Much of our lives are less directed to the distant future, or at least we are working towards sub-goals as part of a greater aim. It might be revision for a test, or preparing an essay, or, as in the author's case, writing for the completion of the chapter. Most behaviour is directed to some goal, and it is the flexibility of such planning that both distinguishes human behaviour and creates the need for prospective memory. Without memories of our goals and sub-goals, and of the steps we must take to reach even a sub-goal, this complex human behaviour would collapse as its guiding principles were lost. Prospective memory thus plays a central part in a central aspect of our lives.

It is no coincidence that we analyse the actions of others in terms of the goals that they are seeking and fulfilling, we remember the goal-directed activities far more easily than those that are less relevant, and we recall the actual achievement of the goals best of all. Lichtenstein and Brewer (1980), for example, found that when a video film of the stages of writing a letter was recalled, the goals and goal-directed actions were far better remembered than the actions that were not steps towards the goal or the achievement of the goal itself. Furthermore, it is the goals of the actions of others that we have observed that are best remembered, when, over time, the steps that led to those goals are forgotten (Brewer and Dupree 1983). The lives of ourselves and of others are organized around seeking and reaching goals. In this, prospective memory plays an integral part.

REFINING THE DEFINITION OF PROSPECTIVE MEMORY

So far we have defined prospective memory as the memory for intentions, for actions that we wish to carry out in the future. Such a definition brings with it all of the problems associated with the term *intention*. Some philosophers (e.g. Ryle 1949) have wished to analyse the concept in terms of the behaviour of the individual and to exclude any reference to internal acts. However, I believe that it is important to distinguish between the decision to act in a certain way at some time in the future and the action itself, which may or may not occur. Failure to act is a necessary condition of a prospective memory error. It is not, however, a sufficient condition, since intentions may be unfulfilled for other reasons than memory failure. The person may remember that they wished to act in a particular way, but fail to do so. Embarrassment, fear, or changes in circumstances in the intervening period can all lead us to think better of fulfilling our intentions. For example, we may decide to continue an argument with an aquaintance the next time we meet them. However, when the time comes, we may have calmed down and think better of re-opening old disputes. Thus, it is not the occurrence of the intended action, but the recalling that it had been planned to act in that way at that time that is important in identifying the success of prospective memory.

Considered in this way, it becomes clear that the decision to act in a specific way in the future is the central feature of prospective memory. Meacham (1988) elaborates this through Searle's (1979) notion of direction of fit in categories of speech acts. One direction of fit is word to world. The object, for example, of a description is to make the words match the world. That is also the object of most retrospective memory – it is the matching of the memory to the way the world was. However, another type of speech act identified by Searle is world to word, where the point of the speech act is to make the world eventually match the words. Such speech acts include making requests, and giving promises and directions. Meacham sees prospective memory as involving a world to word direction of fit. He defines prospective memory as having a memory of one's own speech act of world to word direction of fit in which one has made a public commitment to do something. As discussed above, the necessity of the social and public commitment is debatable, but the memory of the act seems central to the concept of prospective memory.

What about the memory errors such as forgetting to put sugar in one's coffee, or to feed the cat before leaving for work? These are not actions that any longer have a specific preceding intention. No doubt, long ago when sugaring coffee or feeding the cat was a novel event, it was necessary to plan to do so. Now, however, they are habitual actions, part of one's daily routine. Where there is no conscious decision preceding an action, the underlying memory processes will be different to those where a specific intention has to be formed before the action can be carried out. Thus, the failure to carry out many habitual actions, such as forgetting to brush one's teeth before going to bed, is a different type of failure to that of forgetting that today was the day you were to pick up your mother after work. For actions that have become habitual parts of our regular routines there are no longer points at which we make conscious decisions to carry them out. We will call these action slips rather than prospective memory failures.

There is, of course, a close relationship between action slips and prospective memory failures. This is clarified when we consider that our normal day is made up of a framework of routine activities: getting up, washing, dressing, going to work, having coffee, lunch, etc. The framework is flexible; we probably follow different routines at the weekend to weekdays, for example. Nevertheless, we possess a collection of habitual routines that require little thought to initiate and maintain. One very important area of psychological inquiry is to understand the mechanisms that develop and maintain these habitual routines (see e.g. Reason 1984, Reason and Mysielska 1982). However, the main concern for this chapter is for prospective memory and its failures. Prospective memory involves a modification of the background pattern of habitual routines. So, instead of driving home as usual you have, for example, to remember to go home a different way to collect something from a shop. Prospective memory involves the interrupting of habitual routines. That seems to require conscious decisions that we call intentions.

Conscious intentions and The BOSS model

The need for a conscious decision to modify an habitual routine, but not for the running of the routine itself, is one of the issues considered by Morris and Hampson (1983) in the development of their model of the place of consciousness in cognition: The BOSS model (see also Hampson and Morris 1990). This model was developed initially to account for the place of mental imagery in the cognitive system. However, the model has proved valuable in helping to account for which other cognitive processes are associated with conscious awareness and which are not.

Morris and Hampson reviewed the situations in which consciousness seemed to be implicated. They proposed that it is useful to think of the processes controlling our behaviour as being hierarchically organized. The lower level stages in the hierarchy control routine actions, and are called EMPLOYEE systems in the model. However, to handle the highest level of planning and to analyse and control novel situations, it was hypothesized that a top-level control system has been evolved. Morris and Hampson argue that consciousness is associated with the information that is being made available to the BOSS system to make possible the high-level planning and control. This includes the information supplied in a form suitable for such decision-making by the EMPLOYEE systems to this BOSS system, as well as the feedback from the BOSS system itself that it uses to monitor and plan further actions. Within this model, the intentions that are the basis of prospective memory will be formed by the BOSS system, and the information that this has occurred will be fed back to aid the future decisions of the BOSS system. We are, therefore, conscious of the existence of these intentions.

The BOSS model is very specific about the place of consciousness within the system. We are aware of the information being made available to BOSS for its planning. We are not, however, aware of the processes that go on in the BOSS system itself, nor of how the BOSS system interacts with the EMPLOYEE systems to modify their functioning. We, therefore, have conscious access to the result of the BOSS system's decision to modify future habitual routines through the feedback from BOSS. This is experienced as awareness of having formed an intention to act at some point in the future. However, we are not consciously aware of what has gone on inside the BOSS system to initiate this intention. Neither are we aware of how the BOSS system's activities have interacted with

EMPLOYEE systems to seek to put the intention into action at the appropriate time. As in so many areas of psychology, inspecting our own conscious processes takes us almost no way towards trying to understand what underlies prospective memory. For that we must turn to psychological research.

INVESTIGATING PROSPECTIVE MEMORY

A classic study of prospective memory by Wilkins and Baddeley (1978) will provide an introduction to the research issues and problems in the area. Wilkins and Baddeley chose to simulate one important memory task that is dependent upon prospective memory, namely pill taking. Most people, at some time in their lives, need to take regular medication. For much of this medication, it is important that the doses are maintained. Failure to do so may undermine the effectiveness of the treatment and may even lead to death.

Wilkins and Baddeley simulated a pill-taking routine by requiring their thirty-one subjects to press a button on a small box at 8.30 a.m., 1.00 p.m., 5.30 p.m. and 10.00 p.m. each day for 1 week. If they were late for any reason, the subjects were still requested to press the button. The device recorded the time of the button press.

The vast majority of the responses were within 5 minutes of the target time. The later in the week, the greater the instances of lateness, and late responses were more likely at 1.00 p.m. and 5.30 p.m. than at 8.30 a.m. However, the actual day of the week and the diary kept of the activities of the subjects did not relate to any differences in late responses. There were, however, two intriguing findings. One was that the subjects who scored poorly on the free recall of a list of words were significantly *less* late in their responses than those good at free recall. Furthermore, on no occasion did any subject press the button twice within a response period, as they would have done if they had forgotten that they had made a response.

This study by Wilkins and Baddeley illustrates several of the features of prospective memory research. The first is the need to find a simulation of a real-world situation combined with a way of monitoring the responses of the subjects. Both of these problems were successfully tackled by the experimenters. However, despite the activity diaries kept by the subjects, there was uncertainty surrounding what was happening in the subject's life when she was late in making a response, or, just as interestingly, when she remembered correctly to press the button. The lack of experimental control over the surrounding conditions, the lack even of a description of what the conditions are when recall occurs, severely inhibits the developing and testing of hypotheses about the factors influencing prospective memory. On the other hand, if the conditions are too artificial it is unlikely that the normal processes that control prospective memory will be brought into play. Rather, the subjects are likely to construct a specific technique for dealing with the novel task while at the same time not being subject to the distractions and competing goals of everyday life. One difficulty in trying to bring prospective memory under tight experimental control is the length of time that needs to elapse between the encoding of the intention and the recall if the task is to simulate many real-world situations. There are, however, real-world conditions under which recall must take place after only short time intervals. They have proved easier to simulate and this research will be discussed shortly.

Despite the problems faced by Wilkins and Baddeley in carrying out their study they identified several interesting effects. In the first place, there is the success of the subjects in recalling on most occasions. This is hardly surprising, but it defines one of the challenges to explanations of prospective memory: what happens to allow recall to take place? The problem of understanding how the memory system so frequently successfully ensures recall despite the variability of the conditions under which encoding and recall have taken place is a key issue for prospective memory research.

More surprising than the successful recall was the failure of any of the subjects to commit the error of responding twice. While such errors do occur in everyday life, it is clear from this study that they are relatively rare. What happens to cancel the intention and prevent it being retrieved again? This is as interesting a question as is how is recall accomplished in the first place. The cancelling of memories is not a feature of retrospective memory, although there are conditions under which memory seems to be updated (Loftus and Loftus 1980, Bjork 1978).

The final point for comment here is the negative relationship between the ability of the subjects in the laboratory task of free recall and their performance on the prospective memory task. While this negative relationship has not been replicated in other prospective memory experiments, what has often been reported is a lack of correlation between performance on prospective and retrospective tasks (e.g. Maylor 1990). A lack of correlation between different memory tasks is a common finding (see e.g. Morris 1984). It suggests that there is not a general memory ability, so that some people have good and others bad memories. Rather, our memories are skills, specifically developed for particular aspects of cognition. Someone who is good at recognizing faces may be poor at remembering stories, and vice versa. In the present instance, it suggests that prospective and retrospective memories are sufficiently different in their underlying processes to lead to unrelated performance by the same individual in the two types of tasks.

Short-term prospective memory and monitoring

It is easier to gain experimental control over short-term prospective memory tasks than those involving recall after days or weeks.. The distinction between short- and long-term prospective memory tasks has been discussed by Baddeley and Wilkins (1984). They refer to the major divisions of retrospective memory into short-term/long-term and episodic/semantic; the episodic/semantic distinction being between episodic memories for events that have been encoded in memory in terms of a definite time and/or place of occurrence in our personal lives, while semantic memories are for facts, concepts or meanings that are remembered independently of the place and time in which they were acquired. Baddeley and Wilkins suggest that a similar set of distinctions would be useful when considering prospective memory. They describe the Wilkins and Baddeley (1978) study as long-term episodic prospective memory. This they contrast with studies of action slips in habitual routines which they describe as long-term semantic prospective memory. A similar distinction between episodic and habitual prospective memories had previously been drawn by Meacham and Leiman (1975). While studies of short-term retrospective memory have helped in clarifying the components of working memory (see Baddeley 1990), Wilkins and Baddeley comment on the relatively few studies of short-term prospective memory. However, they do refer to another classic study by Harris and Wilkins (1982), and this experiment provides a good example of an attempt to control short-term prospective memory.

In the Harris and Wilkins study the subjects watched a 2 hour film about a hijack. While doing so, they sat with a pile of cards on their knees. On each card was a time; the spacing between successive times was 3 or 9 minutes. The subjects' task was to hold up the card at the given time. To monitor the time they had to look at a clock behind them, so the movement was easily noted from the video that was taken of each experimental session.

Harris and Wilkins found that the subjects were accurate to within 15 seconds on the vast majority of trials, but were later than 15 seconds on about 12 per cent of the trials. They found no effect of the length of the interval between the cards. Neither did they find a relationship between the more engrossing parts of the film, as rated by other subjects, and the frequency of omissions of holding up the cards. Here, as often in studies of prospective memory, the variables that anecdotal evidence would suggest should be related to performance failed to have a major effect. What Harris and Wilkins did note, however, was that looking at the clock increased dramatically as the time for a card to be displayed approached. Where a correct response was made, the average rate of checking the clock in the last few seconds had reached a rate of nine observations per minute. However, where errors occurred the rate at the time that the response was due was only two observations per minute. Harris and Wilkins found that those who looked more frequently were more accurate. However, on over a quarter of the late responses the subject had looked at the clock in the last 10 seconds. This Harris and Wilkins interpret as evidence for very rapid forgetting.

The subjects in the Harris and Wilkins study were clearly monitoring the passing of time using some internal mechanism, and would then use the clock to check whether the correct time had arrived. Harris and Wilkins proposed what they termed a Test-Wait-Test-Exit (TWTE) mechanism for such monitoring. This they derived from the Test-Operate-Test-Exit loops of Miller, Galanter and Pribram (1960). In the TWTE loop, the individual tests whether the time has arrived for the action, and, if not, sets a Wait period that is to elapse before the next test. If that turns out to be too soon (and it will often be sensible to err on the side of testing early rather than too late – when the cake is burned or the train has gone etc.) then a new, shorter Wait period is set and a new loop run.

The TWTE model applies most easily to the monitoring of an ongoing processes such as cooking or waiting for a train. It seems more appropriate to short-term tasks that are happening concurrently with the TWTE process. While it is conceivable that TWTEs could be set up for long-term prospective memory – one could imagine setting a Wait period of a couple of years before asking one's boss about the prospects for promotion – it is hard to believe that the mechanisms will be similar. It is easier to imagine an internal cognitive clock measuring minutes than one measuring years. A short-term TWTE task will normally occupy the central place in one's current planning. However, a long-term TWTE would need to break in upon the then current dominating activity.

Harris (1984) tried to elaborate these differences in prospective memory tasks. He distinguished between single and dual activity and between simple and compound tasks. A single activity is one in which there is a single goal (e.g. remembering to put tea leaves in the pot while making the tea). A dual activity is one in which there are competing goals, such as driving home and buying some bread on the way. The single activity is, perhaps, best conceptualized as a sub-routine of a more general habitual routine, while the dual activity is one in which one activity, usually a habitual one, must be interrupted. This is the basic feature of prospective memory, as we discussed earlier.

Harris' distinction between simple and compound tasks applies to dual activity memory tasks. Some of these tasks involve monitoring the activity that is to be interrupted itself – Harris' example is monitoring progress on the way home to reach the bread shop. These tasks Harris calls simple. However, it is often necessary to monitor something other than the ongoing task itself. So, for example, any task that depends on time as measured by a clock has to be interrupted so that the clock can be monitored. Harris called these tasks compound, and argued that the TWTE description was appropriate only to these tasks.

Ceci and Bronfenbrenner (1985) extended the Harris and Wilkins research to study the monitoring of cooking by children. While waiting for cupcakes to cook the necessary 30 minutes the child's checking of the clock was monitored. Ten-year-olds in their own homes showed a similar pattern of checks of the clock to that of the subjects in the Harris and Wilkins study. That is, they made several checks in the first 5 minutes, as if calibrating their internal time monitoring system, then made few checks in the next 15 minutes, and checked frequently over the last 5 minutes. The resulting graphs have a J shape.

Ceci and Bronfenbrenner found several factors that modified this behaviour in the children. For example, when tested in the laboratory the unusual setting removed the dip in the middle of the curve (see Figure 8.1). It appeared that where the children were concerned about the seriousness of errors they abandoned the J-shape strategy.

Ceci, Baker and Bronfenbrenner (1988) tested the theory that the children were first calibrating a psychological clock and then applying a TWTE strategy, by the ingenious strategy of providing the 10-year-old children with a wall clock that ran faster or slower than it should. They manipulated the rates to be 10, 33, or 50 per cent too fast or too slow. Where the rates were 10 or 33 per cent too fast or too slow the children showed the J-shape response, adjusting to the new rate and looking frequently in the first 5 minutes as shown by the clock, but little during the next 20 minutes (see Figure 8.2). In the case of the 50 per cent fast or slow clocks, however, the children did not adopt the J-shape strategy, but looked frequently throughout the time. Ceci *et al.* concluded that the children were able to recalibrate a psychological clock to speeds within a third of normal rates, but that for the 50 per cent fast or slow clocks the discrepancies with the children's expectations were so great that they became suspicious and/or anxious and began to check regularly. The studies by Ceci and his collaborators illustrate the value of research that both uses as realistic designs as possible while incorporating strong experimental controls. This is discussed further in Chapter 1.

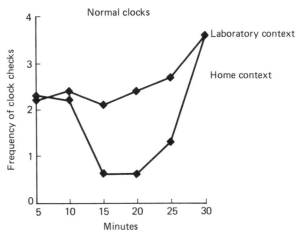

Figure 8.1 Children's frequency of monitoring a clock during cooking in a laboratory and home context (from Ceci, Baker and Bronfenbrenner 1988).

Long-term prospective memory

The study of long-term prospective memory requires ingenuity in devising a task that will receive due regard from the subjects and at the same time allow for both experimental manipulation and an interpretation of the factors leading to differences in performance. These are major challenges and a few experimenters may have been so pleased that they have overcome the problems in creating a prospective memory simulation that the aims of the experiment have not been fully thought through in advance. Certainly, considerable ingenuity has often been shown in the designs but with relatively little conclusive evidence resulting.

One commonly used technique has been the postcard study.

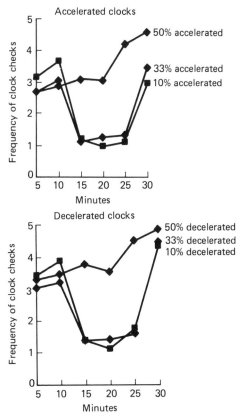

Figure 8.2 Children's frequency of monitoring accelerated or decelerated clocks (from Ceci, Baker and Bronfenbrenner 1988).

Subjects are given a collection of postcards to be returned to the experimenters at specified times. The postmark on the cards gives an indication of the date when the card was posted, and the numbers returned provide an objective measure of the accuracy of recall.

The postcard method was used by Wilkins (1976) to investigate the influence of the delay before recall. His subjects had to recall just one postcard from between 2 to 36 days later. He found no effect of time, but the test may have been too insensitive, since only twelve cards were not returned on time. This study illustrates another problem for researchers in this area; that of the small amount of information that can usually be extracted from the testing of a large number of subjects. For the research to be sampling relatively natural conditions the same subjects cannot be tested too frequently. Furthermore, the data from any one subject is often the minimum that can be extracted in any research: just one bit of information, the success or failure of one opportunity to recall. Against a background of uncontrolled variability in the subjects' environment, commitment and ability there is always the danger that even a well-designed experiment that has taken a considerable investment of time and subjects will produce no significant differences because of the low reliability when single measures are taken from each subject and the high error variance inherent in studies of this kind.

Using the postcard technique, Meacham and Leiman (1975) found some evidence for the cuing of the posting of cards by providing subjects with a coloured tag on their key rings. In their follow-up questionnaire, Meacham and Leiman asked the subjects how they had tried to cue their memories. Fifty-two per cent had put the cards in a conspicuous place; 32 per cent had used calendars as reminders; most of the remaining subjects reporting no special ways of trying to remember. These responses indicate the open-ended nature of such studies, and the difficulty of unpacking the specific details of reminding that may underlie the individual instances of recall. For example, the value of using calendars will interact with the subjects' normal use of calendars and diaries. A busy business person may regularly look in a diary; someone with few appointments may write them on a calendar, but rarely consult it.

The postcard technique has been used by Orne (1970) and Meacham and Singer (1977) to explore the influence of monetary incentives on prospective memory. Orne required subjects to return one card a day for 56 days. He obtained the best response by prepaying the subjects, with an amount specified (10c) for each card, the subjects being told that they were being paid in advance because the experimenters were confident that they would send the cards. Meacham and Singer required one card to be returned per week for 8 weeks. In one condition the cards were to be posted on the Wednesday, in another the day was randomized within the week. In the 'high-incentive' condition the subjects were told that four of the cards posted on time would be drawn and their senders given a maximum of $5. This condition led to better responding.

One problem in postcard studies is to separate differences resulting from actual variations in recall from those due to differences in compliance. The subjects in the Meacham and Singer study, for example, may have recalled the need to post the cards equally often, but the next step of actually getting around to doing it may have differed because of the possible reward. Another factor in this study is that the offer of incentives may alter the use of memory aids rather than the underlying efficiency of prospective memory. This possibility was supported in the Meacham and Singer study when they found a significantly higher reported use of external memory aids in the high-incentive condition.

Compliance in real-world situations has been a research topic in its own right (e.g. Levy and Loftus 1984). Failures to keep appointments with professionals such as at doctors or dentists can be costly to the institution and to the private practitioner. Such failures to keep appointments will sometimes be a result of memory failure, sometimes for other reasons such as cost, fear, the problem having eased, or an emergency. Studies of compliance have often taken the form of manipulations in the reminders. Gates and Colborn (1976) for example, compared letter reminders (84 per cent compliance) with telephone reminders (80 per cent) and a group with no reminder (55 per cent kept the appointment). Reminders have a bigger effect where the interval before the appointment is lengthy. Levy and Claravall (1977) found that reminders almost doubled compliance for patients with appointments made longer than 15 days away.

Memory aids

Given the combination of the importance of prospective memory and our awareness of the fallibility of our recall, it is not surprising that it is for prospective memory that the majority of us adopt memory aids. Traditionally, these have been diaries, notes, and disturbances to our normal situations were some cue is placed in a prominent position so that it reminds us that we have something to remember (the proverbial knot in the handkerchief). Nowadays, watches and pocket computers can be programmed to give schedule reminders. Harris (1980) and Intons-Peterson and Fournier (1986) have surveyed the use of memory aids. Harris questioned students and housewives on their use of a wide variety of memory aids. The commonly used memory aids were those for improving prospective memory. Almost everyone used diaries, shopping lists and notes to themselves at some time. Harris (1984) noted that the middle-aged women that he interviewed regarded it as their role to remember the birthdays of friends and relatives and family social events. To help them, they used at least one diary, calendar or wall chart.

Intons-Peterson and Fournier asked a hundred subjects how often they used a range of memory aids in hypothetical memory situations. As in Harris' survey, there was a preference for external memory aids – that is, for those like diaries that do not themselves depend on memory. Intons-Peterson and Fournier reviewed the situations in which these external aids were likely to be used. These included(a) situations where the memory must override the potentially interfer-ing events that separate the intention and recall,(b) where there is a long interval to wait,(c) where a high premium is placed on accuracy or where internal aids cannot be trusted,(d) where memory load was to be avoided. Intons-Peterson and Fournier believed that the preference for external aids occurred because they were seen as easier, more dependable and accurate. In surveying the effectiveness of external memory aids, Harris (1980) emphasizes the need for an active cue (e.g. a buzzer) that is given as close as possible to the time when the action is required, with a specific reminder, rather than the general buzzer or knotted hanky. It should be very easy to use and portable. Even so, the individual must develop the habit of using the device. I have found that a watch that can be scheduled to give an alarm and a short message combined with a small diary carried at all times provides the better system of reminders than larger personal organizers or pocket computers that tend to be left behind for convenience when it turns out they are needed.

A problem facing researchers studying prospective memory is the correct incorporation of external memory aids. In the exploration of unaided prospective memory, such aids may be a confounding variable. However, in the search for practical advice on how to improve prospective memory, or in any assessment of the naturally occurring instances of prospective errors, it would be unwise to eliminate external aids. Rather, one aim of research should be to devise the best integration of external aids with any effective internal mnemonic aids and with the procedures that will lead to the optimal accuracy with the least outlay in effort. Memory improvement techniques that require a considerable investment of effort during encoding are rarely applied, even by those who are aware of their effectiveness (see e.g. Morris 1979 and Chapter 7 of this volume).

Age and prospective memory

Most of the studies discussed so far have involved young or middle-aged adults. Two questions that have received some attention are (a) how does prospective memory develop in children and (b) does it decline with old age? Beal (1988) has reviewed studies of the development of prospective memory in children. She found that preschool children do not recognize prospective memory situations and do not appear to realize that they need to take action to facilitate recall. For example, Beal gave children extended practice with a shell game in which a sweet was hidden under one of a set of cups. Despite repeated failures to find the sweet, the children needed much encouragement to adopt a strategy of marking the cup. Even when children discover a strategy they often need prompting to continue it.

An understanding of what will make effective reminders develops with age. Four-year-olds do not know that a reminder needs to be placed where it will be encountered at the time of retrieval. In the shell game, they are happy for reminders to be placed inside the cups, out of sight. By 8 years of age they know that reminders need to be visible to be effective. The younger children, if given cards to remind them, tended to place them in safe places, but ones that were often out of their sight. Beal also found that the preschool children have particular difficulty in realizing that the reminder needs to be distinctive. For example, in the shell game they often thought a marker would be effective, even though another cup had an identical marker. Beal concluded that younger children assume that they will automatically remember, and they have to develop a metamemory knowledge of their own limitations.

While age-related effects, with the elderly performing more poorly, have often been found for retrospective memory some studies have suggested that older subjects may perform as well or better than young adults in prospective memory tasks. Moscovitch and Minde (1982), for example, required their subjects to telephone an answering machine once a day for 2 weeks. The older group (65–75-year-olds) were more reliable than the younger group (22–37-year-olds). Questionnaire studies of memory failures have often found the elderly reporting fewer problems. Harris and Sunderland (1981), for example, in two studies compared subjects in their twenties with groups in their fifties or seventies. The younger subjects complained far more frequently of completely forgetting what they said they would do, forgetting to take things with them and forgetting to tell someone something important.

Various explanations have been offered for the apparent superiority of older subjects on these tasks. Jackson, Bogers and Kerstholt (1988) explored the possibility that older subjects may use more memory aids. When questioned on how they would attempt to remember in a number of hypothetical retrospective and prospective memory tasks, the older subjects were more likely to say that they would use external memory aids for prospective tasks.

Poon and Shaffer (1982) found that older adults remembered to make more of twenty-five prearranged calls over a 3 week period. Across the 3 weeks the performance of the young group deteriorated but that of the older group did not. Poon and Shaffer accounted for their findings in terms of a more structured and orderly lifestyle being led by the older group.

There is nothing inconsistent about both explanations being true. Older people probably do lead more organized lives and they may have learned how to use memory aids to help them cope with the demands of life.

Einstein and McDaniel (1991) distinguished between time-based and event-based tasks. They found that while the elderly were as good as younger subjects in the event-based task of indicating when a particular word was presented, they were poorer at performing an action every 10 minutes, and this was reflected in less frequent monitoring of the clock near the critical time. It appears, therefore, that the type of task will influence any changes with age.

ELABORATING OUR UNDERSTANDING OF PROSPECTIVE MEMORY

So far in this chapter there has been little consideration of the nature of prospective memory. In this section some of the theoretical issues relating to prospective memory will be considered. These include whether there is any fundamental difference between prospective and retrospective memory, and the important questions to be answered by research on prospective memory.

There is no doubt that prospective and retrospective remembering are different tasks. This was highlighted at the beginning of the chapter. However, it is possible for the same basic mechanisms to fulfil quite different functions, just as a painter may use the same canvas and oils to produce an abstract or a landscape painting. Are the underlying processes that support prospective memory different from those used in retrospective remembering?

Loftus (1971) argued that prospective and retrospective memories used the same memory mechanisms. She showed that a prospective and a retrospective memory task were both influenced beneficially by the provision of retrieval cues and negatively by increasing the number of interpolated items in the period between encoding and recall. The problem with her conclusion is that these two fundamental findings are likely to be true of any memory systems, even if their basic mechanisms are different. The same results would be found, for example if the two storage systems were a card index and books on a library shelf, but it would obviously be wrong to conclude that because cues helped find cards and books and more cards and books delayed retrieval that a card index and a shelf of books were the same storage system. On the other hand, the approach taken by Loftus is sensible. If no conditions can be identified under which the two types of memory behave differently then it becomes very dubious to maintain that different processes are involved.

There is, however, evidence that the two processes are different. Where researchers have compared the recall of the same subject in prospective and retrospective memory tasks performance has rarely been significantly correlated. For example, Maylor (1990) compared the accuracy of several hundred late middle-aged and elderly subjects in remembering to telephone with their abilities at digit span, learning lists of words and free recall, finding no sign of a relationship.

Kvavilashvili (1987) asked her subjects to remind her to pass on a message that the subject had been asked to convey. Subsequent testing showed that subjects who remembered to remind the experimenter were not better at remembering the content of the message.

Special aspects of prospective memory

In what ways will prospective remembering be different from retrospective tasks? One way is that the prospective recall, at least in some prospective tasks, is less open to reliance on external cues. Much of our retrospective remembering depends on the match of the current activities in our cognitive system with that when encoding took place. As such, it is appropriate to many of the uses of retrospective recall, since one of our main uses of our past experience is to make sense of what is happening to us and to predict what will happen next. To do so we need to draw quickly on stored knowledge related to our current concerns. This account of memory has been elaborated especially by Tulving (1983). On the other hand, the central feature of prospective memory is that it is involved in the modification of habitual routines to allow the intention to be carried out. As such, it is likely that there will be fewer relevant cues at the time that recall is required. So, when leaving work, intending to collect some friends on the way, we have to remember to set off by a different route to normal. At that time there is unlikely to be much similarity in our current cognitive processing either to the circumstances when we formed the intention or to our friends, their house, etc.

Of course, this divorcing of the encoding and retrieval contexts from the act to be carried out does not mean that if there are similarities in these contexts that performance will not be enhanced. There is little doubt that the lack of possible cues from the current environment is one reason for failure in prospective memory, and that the provision of such cues often leads to recall. When, for example, James (1990) investigated the putting forwards or backwards of clocks by 1 hour at the start and end of British Summer Time he found many reports of, for example, seeing a clock, acting as cues to recall. Similarly, most external memory aids for prospective memory depend on the provision of a cue to recall. Nevertheless, the challenge faced by the memory system in providing redirection to ongoing activities so that intentions can be fulfilled depends on the retrieval of the intentions with what may be little direct cuing from the current cognitive activities.

To compensate for the lack of specific cues the prospective memory system may have developed to exploit whatever cues that are available. Accounts of prospective recall (e.g. James 1990) are rich in reports of intentions being cued by objects and scenes that are only marginally related to the task itself. Examples given by James (1990)

214

from a study in which the subjects had to telephone the experimenter are: 'cued by using the phone on a separate call', 'saw a poster for another psychology experiment on campus'. These were actions that the subjects do every day, but they provided access to their intentions. A rich set of concepts loosely related to that to be recalled must be primed so that they trigger recall.

A related aspect of this priming is the occurrence of perseveration, the remembering that one has to carry out the action perhaps days or hours prior to the planned time. These memories are sometimes described as popping up with no obvious cues, while on other occasions there may be an obvious reminder. Kvavilashvili (1987) found a small but significant correlation between the number of such pop-ups her subjects reported and the likelihood of correct recall. The number of such perseverations was higher during an uninteresting rather than an interesting intervening task. James (1990) showed that perseveration increases as the time for the completion of the intention approaches.

Kvavilashvili concluded that these perseverations were a significant feature of remembering to do things. They certainly tell us something about the underlying processes. However, one would predict that better-encoded intentions would lead to more perseveration, so it is not clear that the perseverations are more than a symptom of the prospective memory mechanism, rather than part of the recall mechanism itself.

One question that underlies understanding prospective memory is what happens when an intention is formed that makes retrieval possible? What modifications to the cognitive system take place so that later you will remember your plan? A complication is that the level of planning in which intentions are formed will vary as the level of cognitive control of the actions itself varies. Vallachner and Wegner (1985) have illustrated how the level of specification in planning changes with differing demands from the task. So, for example, planning a holiday is initially done at a high level, and we consider the details of packing and cancelling deliveries to the house only near our time of departure. The point that is relevant for prospective memory is that the way in which the planned action is conceptualized at the time must influence what is encoded and therefore available to cue recall. This may account for some prospective memory errors, but it adds another challenge to those attempting to understand the underlying processes.

Types of prospective memory

So far, much of the discussion may have implied that prospective memory is a single type of task. However, there are many different types of demands for prospective remembering, and these will require different types of cuing to make recall possible. Ellis (1988) has distinguished between what she calls 'pulses' and 'steps'. Pulses have a short 'window of opportunity'. Ellis gives the example of a dental appointment. Steps are more flexible; one of Ellis' examples is 'phone to book a holiday at some time today'. In a diary study, Ellis found that pulses tended to be rated as higher in personal importance, to involve more use of memory aids and that subjects reported either recalling the pulse action once or 'being aware of it all day'. This may reflect the greater personal importance of pulses or their tighter time window.

James (1990), with the help of a cluster analysis of prospective memory errors recorded in a diary study developed a classification of the errors (see Figure 8.3). The classification is based around what James calls the 'Wh' dimensions: namely, Who, What and Where. The Who aspect has as its highest level whether the decision is made by the person themselves or by another person. These four themselves break down into who is to benefit, and that, in turn, needs to be analysed in terms of the reasons for the decision. Questions arising from the Who aspect include how personal choice and the object of the intention may influence recall. The What aspect depends on the analysis of the action to be carried out and suggests categories of prospective tasks that may differ in their memorability. The Where aspect may be the most important. It recognizes an important distinction between intentions that depend upon completion at a particular time and those that are dependent on being in the correct place. So, for example, a dental appointment is time dependent. However, my asking a friend advice on car insurance may depend on when I meet her. In the latter case a time is not specified when the intention is formed. Questions that arise from this Where aspect include whether event-based tasks are easier to recall than time-based ones, and whether the degree of specification of the intention is important. Other factors identified by James include the importance of the action for the individual, and problems that may arise when the intention is modified before recall.

CONCLUSIONS

Prospective memory is a complex challenge to the researcher. Its importance in making possible our complex life, devoted as it is to trying to reach future goals, is undeniable. However, the incorporation of prospective memory in such a role also makes it hard to study in realistic conditions. Many empirical studies have produced uncertain findings. Despite our concern over possible failure of prospective memory, errors are rare enough to make research frustrating. For example, in James' (1990) studies of changing the clock, only nine out of 140 subjects forgot, making any interpretation of the factors influencing the forgetting virtually impossible. Furthermore, no study of prospective memory has yet demonstrated a major variable that accounts for a large variation in forgetting. Even such apparently good candidates for such variables as personal importance and time before recall have yet to be shown to play a major part.

One of the more successful research areas has been on individual differences. James (1990), using questionnaires to obtain reports not only from the subjects but also independently from close friends, found consistent patterns where individuals saw themselves as being well organized and good at remembering, and vice versa, and this was supported by their friends, and, on occasions, in objective measures.

Prospective memory research will benefit from richer theories on the way our actions are planned and controlled. New research techniques are required that allow for a better specification of the circumstances in which errors occur and which allow for the manipulation of potentially important variables. The vast investment in subjects and experimental time in seeking ecologically valid explorations of real-world prospective memory tasks is admirable. James (1990), for example, studied the handing in of essays, changes in teaching rooms, and taking the contraceptive pill in addition to the more traditional telephone and postcard studies. However, it may be necessary to seek ways of simulating prospective memory tasks under closer control if we are to generate enough errors and specify the conditions under which they occur.

There is, as yet, little practical advice on improving prospective memory that has the support of empirical data. It is clear that the use of external retrieval cues through diaries, alarms, etc. can effectively support those who have a very heavy load on their

The Who aspect:

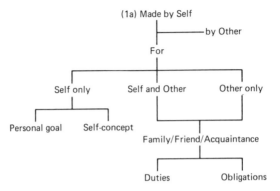

The What aspect:

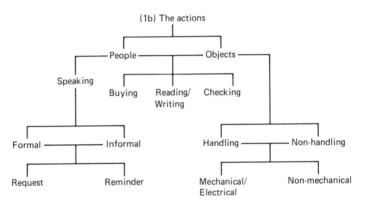

The Where aspect:

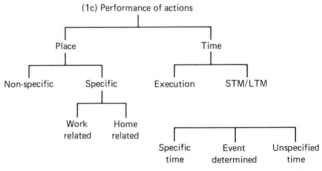

Figure 8.3 Classification of prospective memory errors using the Who, What and Where dimensions (from James 1990).

prospective remembering. The use of such aids requires their incorporation into a regular routine and the initial inconvenience of entering the reminders. As with most activities this becomes less tedious with practice. There are possible mnemonic strategies that have, on occasions, been suggested as aids to prospective remembering. Lorayne (1958), for example, recommends using an imagery mnemonic to help to remember what you must do when leaving the house. If you should remember to post a letter you will need to image a letter on the handle of the door that you will use when leaving the house. Seeing the door should cue recall of the letter. This mnemonic has the characteristics of other successful imagery mnemonics (see Chapter 7), but has not, to my knowledge, been tested experimentally. Lorayne goes on to recommend replacing diaries with peg-word-based mnemonics that one rehearses regularly. This is also likely to be successful, given the appropriate investment of effort. In general, however, a technology for improving prospective memory based on the findings of psychological research is likely to have to wait upon the development of a fuller theoretical understanding of the nature of prospective memory.

Much remains to be done. However, enough has been done to demonstrate that the investigation of prospective memory is an essential and potentially very important area of memory research.

REFERENCES

Baddeley, A. (1990) *Human Memory: Theory and Practice*, Hove: Erlbaum.

Baddeley, A.D. and Wilkins, A. (1984) 'Taking memory out of the laboratory', in J. Harris and P.E. Morris (eds) *Everyday Memory, Actions and Absentmindedness*, London: Academic Press.

Beal, C.R. (1988) 'The development of prospective memory skills', in M.M. Gruneberg, P.E. Morris and R.N. Sykes (eds) *Practical Aspects of Memory: Current Research and Issues*, vol. 1, Chichester: Wiley.

Bjork, R.A. (1978) 'The updating of human memory', in G.H. Bower (ed.) *The Psychology of Learning and Motivation*, vol. 12, New York: Academic Press.

Brewer, W.F. and Dupree, D.A. (1983) 'Use of plan schemata in the recall and recognition of goal-directed actions', *Journal of Experimental Psychology: Learning, Memory and Cognition* 9: 117–29.

Ceci, S.J. and Bronfenbrenner, U. (1985) '"Don't forget to take the cupcakes out of the oven": Prospective memory strategic time-monitoring and context', *Child Development* 56: 152–64.

Ceci, S.J., Baker, J.G. and Bronfenbrenner, U. (1988) 'Prospective remembering and temporal calibration', in M.M. Gruneberg, P.E. Morris and

R.N. Sykes (eds) *Practical Aspects of Memory: Current Research and Issues*, vol. 1, Chichester: Wiley.

Eistein, G.O. and McDaniel, M.A. (1991) 'Aging and time – versus event-based prospective memory', paper to the 32nd annual meeting of the Psychonomic Society, San Franscisco.

Ellis, J.A. (1988) 'Memory for future intentions: Investigating pulses and steps', in M.M. Gruneberg, P.E. Morris and R.N. Sykes (eds) *Practical Aspects of Memory: Current Research and Issues*, vol. 1, Chichester: Wiley.

Gates, S.J. and Colborn, D.K. (1976) 'Lowering appointment failures in a neighbourhood health center', *Medical Care* 14: 263–7.

Hampson, P.J. and Morris, P.E. (1990) 'Imagery, consciousness and cognitive control: the BOSS model reviewed', in P.J. Hampson, D.E. Marks, and J.T.E. Richardson (eds) *Imagery: Current Developments*, London: Routledge.

Harris J.E. (1980) 'Memory aids people use: Two interview studies', *Memory and Cognition* 8: 31–8.

Harris, J.E. (1984) 'Remembering to do things: A forgotten topic', in J.E. Harris and P.E. Morris (eds) *Everyday Memory, Actions and Absentmindedness*, London: Academic Press.

Harris, J.E. and Sunderland, A. (1981) 'Effects of age and instructions on an everyday memory questionnaire', Paper presented to the British Psychological Society Cognitive Psychology Section Conference on Memory, Plymouth.

Harris, J.E. and Wilkins, A.J. (1982) 'Remembering to do things: A theoretical framework and illustrative experiment', *Human Learning* 1: 123–36.

Intons-Peterson, M.J. and Fournier, J. (1986) 'External and internal memory aids: When and how do we use them?', *Journal of Experimental Psychology* 115: 276–80.

Jackson, J.L., Bogers, H. and Kerstholt, J. (1988) 'Do memory aids aid the elderly in their day to day remembering?', in M.M. Gruneberg, P.E. Morris and R.N. Sykes (eds) *Practical Aspects of Memory: Current Research and Issues*, vol. 1, Chichester: Wiley.

James, I. (1990) 'Prospective memory in the real world: Practical considerations for effective recall of future intentions', unpublished PhD Thesis, Lancaster University.

Lorayne, H. (1958) *How to Develop a Super Power Memory*, Preston: A. Thomas.

Kvavilashvili, L. (1987) 'Remembering intention as a distinct form of memory', *British Journal of Psychology* 78: 507–18.

Levy, R.L. and Claravall, V. (1977) 'Differential effects of a phone reminder on patients with long and short between-visit intervals', *Medical Care* 15: 435–8.

Levy, R.L. and Loftus, G.R. (1984) 'Compliance and memory', in J.E. Harris and P.E. Morris (eds) *Everyday Memory, Actions and Absentmindedness*, London: Academic Press.

Lichtenstein, E.H. and Brewer, W.F. (1980) 'Memory for goal directed events', *Cognitive Psychology* 12: 412–45.

Loftus, E.F. (1971) 'Memory for intentions', *Psychonomic Science* 23:

315–16.

Loftus, E.F. and Loftus, G.R. (1980) 'On the permanence of stored information in the human brain', *American Psychologist* 35: 421–34.

Maylor, E.A. (1990) 'Age and prospective memory', *The Quarterly Journal of Experimental Psychology* 42A: 471–93.

Meacham, J.A. (1988) 'Interpersonal relationships and prospective remembering', in M.M. Gruneberg, P.E. Morris and R.N. Sykes (eds) *Practical Aspects of Memory: Current Research and Issues*, vol. 1, Chichester: Wiley.

Meacham, J.A. and Leiman, B. (1975) 'Remembering to perform future actions', paper presented at the meeting of the American Psychological Association, Chicago, in U. Neisser (ed.) *Memory Observed: Remembering in Natural Contexts*, San Francisco: W.H. Freeman.

Meacham, J.A. and Singer, J. (1977) 'Incentive effects in prospective remembering', *Journal of Psychology* 97: 191–7.

Miller, G.A., Galanter, E. and Pribram, K.H. (1960) *Plans and the Structure of Behavior*, New York: Holt, Reinhart and Winston.

Morris, P.E. (1979) 'Strategies for learning and recall', in M.M. Gruneberg and P.E. Morris (eds) *Applied Problems in Memory*, London: Academic Press.

Morris, P.E. (1984) 'The validity of subjective reports of memory', in J.E. Harris and P.E. Morris (eds) *Everyday Memory, Actions and Absentmindedness*, London: Academic Press.

Morris, P.E. and Hampson, P.J. (1983) *Imagery and Consciousness*, London: Academic Press.

Moscovitch, M. (1982) 'A neuropsychological approach to memory and perception in normal and pathological aging', in F.I.M. Craik and S. Trehub (eds) *Aging and Cognitive Processes*, New York: Plenum.

Munsat, S. (1966) *The Concept of Memory*, New York: Random House.

Orne, M.T. (1970) 'Hypnosis, motivation and the ecological validity of the psychology experiment', in W.J Arnold and M.M. Page (eds) *Nebraska Symposium on Motivation*, vol. 18, Lincoln, Nebraska: University of Nebraska Press

Poon, L.W. and Shaffer, G. (1982) '*Prospective memory in young and elderly adults*', Paper presented to the American Psychological Association, Washington DC.

Reason, J.T. (1984) 'Absentmindedness and cognitive control', in J.E. Harris and P.E. Morris (eds) *Everyday Memory, Actions and Absentmindedness*, London: Academic Press.

Reason, J.T. and Mysielska, K. (1982) *Absent-Minded? The Psychology of Mental Lapses and Everyday Errors*, Englewood Cliffs, New Jersey: Prentice-Hall.

Ryle, G. (1949) *The Concept of Mind*, London: Hutchinson.

Searle, J.R. (1979) *Expression and Meaning*, Cambridge: Cambridge University Press.

Tulving, E. (1983) *Elements of Episodic Memory*, Oxford: Oxford University Press

Vallachner, R. and Wegner, D. (1985) *A Theory of Action Identification*, Hillsdale, New Jersey: Erlbaum.

Wilkins, A.J. (1976) 'A failure to demonstrate effects of the "retention interval" in prospective memory', unpublished manuscript reported by J.E. Harris (1984) in J.E. Harris and P.E. Morris (eds) *Everyday Memory, Actions and Absentmindedness*, London: Academic Press.

Wilkins, A.J. and Baddeley, A.D. (1978) 'Remembering to recall in everyday life – an approach to absentmindedness', in M.M. Gruneberg, P.E. Morris and R.N. Sykes (eds) *Practical Aspects of Memory*, London: Academic Press.

Winograd, E. (1988). 'Some observations on prospective memory', in M.M. Gruneberg, P.E. Morris and R.N. Sykes (eds) *Practical Aspects of Memory: Current Research and Issues*, vol. 1, Chichester: Wiley.

9

AUTOBIOGRAPHICAL
MEMORY

John A. Robinson

Autobiographical memory is memory for biographical information and life experiences. It can be distinguished from knowledge of other people's experiences or public events (see Larsen 1988), and from general knowledge and skills. It has been of interest from the beginnings of scientific psychology, but has recently become a very active topic of discussion and research. The historical context has been summarized by Robinson (1986) and discussed in detail by Conway (1990b). The subject has been referred to by other labels, e.g. personal memory, and has been discussed analytically as well as descriptively in philosophy and literature for centuries. Warnock (1987) and Glover (1988) provide accessible discussions of recent philosophical thinking on personal memory. The interest of writers in memory is recounted in two works by Salaman (1971, 1973). One of these, *A Collection of Moments*, is a unique and fascinating combination of literary history and psychological inquiry which offers many provocative hypotheses for psychologists. In spite of its obvious appeal, sustained empirical study of autobiographical memory languished until the 1970s. The principal reason for this was methodological: recollections of life experiences were treated as anecdotal information because they were hard to verify and did not lend themselves to experimental control. Consequently, this domain of memory study could not satisfy the criteria of objective science. Theorists argued that the experimental study of memory would yield reliable and generalizable principles applicable to memory in any form. Whether that promise has been or will be fulfilled is still actively debated. However, the present heterodoxy in memory theory has encouraged renewed attention to problems of diverse

223

kinds, and autobiographical memory is one of them. There is still energetic debate about what is proper and potentially meaningful research (see the polemical essay of Banaji and Crowder (1989) and replies to it in the January 1991 issue of the *American Psychologist*), but little chance that psychologists will again abandon a subject so richly interesting.

KINDS OF MEMORIES

Autobiographical memory comprises several qualitatively different kinds of information, or memoria. Brewer (1986), Linton (1986) and Barsalou (1988) have each attempted to identify and distinguish them. One dimension of contrast is general versus specific. Activities or events which recur frequently may be represented in memory by a generic schema. These generalized event memories embody the cumulative skill and experience of the individual. Memories of specific occasions are numerous, but seem to decline in proportion to the frequency of similar episodes. Specific memories of recurrent activities are usually significant in some distinctive way. Event memories are also organized into temporal sequences of heterogeneous but thematically related experiences. Linton (1986) refers to them as extendures, Barsalou (1988) as extended events and time lines. These structures exemplify the general versus specific dimension extended in time and to several hierarchical levels.

Another contrast is between autobiographical knowledge and autobiographical episode memories. One kind of biographical information (e.g. the places you've worked, resided, visited; the cars you have owned; illnesses or injuries; military service) provides a summary description of a life history. This information may be associated with a rich set of personal episode memories, but can be abstracted from those memories and is meaningful in its own right. Self-descriptions are another kind of autobiographical knowledge. Each person can provide a description of his or her personal characteristics, interests, and beliefs. Self-descriptions are generalizations about oneself. They are presumed to be abstracted from specific experience, but may also be ascriptions based on motive patterns as much as actual experience. The functional validity of the distinction of fact and event components of autobiographical memory is supported by two kinds of research. Klein, Loftus and Burton (1989) have shown that the advantages of self-referenced encoding of material can occur in two different ways: by accessing autobiographical episodes, or by accessing self-descriptions. Their studies also indicated that the two systems of self-referenced information could be independently accessed. Though obviously related, neither system is subordinate to the other. Clinical case studies of memory disorders provide another kind of support for the distinction. Tulving, Schacter, McLachlan, and Moscovitch (1988) describe a patient who knows his life history but cannot remember any specific experiences. For example, he correctly answers questions about his occupation, but does not recall any specific incidents from work.

Are there other kinds of memoria than these in the domain of autobiographical memory? It is hard to know which of the many distinctions we can detect among memories have taxonomic significance. Event memories vary in vividness, completeness, ease of recall, emotionality, and many other attributes. But, fundamentally, they are still memories of the same kind – specific episodes. Memory types might be distinguished by functions as well as by attributes or content. For example, vivid memories and first experience memories could have a special place in the organization of a life history (see Fitzgerald 1988; Pillemer, Rhinehart and White 1986; Robinson 1992). Some memories seem to be emblematic of entire patterns of experience. Neisser (1981; 1985) terms them repisodes. They may be blends of several overlapping events, or prototypes of recurrent concerns. For example, a student told me that when she is having difficulty with academic work, she frequently thinks of a grade school incident where she successfully overcame a problem. This memory seems to exemplify a recurrent predicament. Its function is motivational: 'I succeeded before (though in a different circumstance), so I can succeed again'. As we learn more about autobiographical memory these taxonomic questions should get clarified.

THE AVAILABILITY OF THE PAST

One way to assess autobiographical memory is to explore what people remember about different life periods. A strategy which has proved productive has been to sample personal memory in an unconstrained manner. This is done by providing words as cues and requesting memories as responses. What incident in your life are you reminded of by 'car', or 'hand', or 'dog'? When did each of these incidents occur? The distribution of reports in relation to date (elapsed time) provides an estimate of the accessible memories at each temporal interval. When the reports of many subjects are aggregated the data display a consistent pattern. Figures 9.1 (a) and (b) show the results from three independent studies of 50- and 70-year-old subjects, respectively. The top curve in each panel integrates the three data sets and displays the pattern most clearly. Rubin, Wetzler, and Nebes (1986) propose that the horizontal s-shaped function represents the contribution of three factors: a retention function, a reminiscence factor, and a childhood amnesia factor. The general picture they present is that from adolescence into old age there is a moving 20-year memory window which exhibits a generic forgetting rate independent of the person's current age. However, that rate cannot be extrapolated back to infancy. First, people aged 40 and older exhibit a reversal of the trend for those years corresponding to late childhood through adolescence and into early adulthood. Rubin *et al.* attribute this to a reminiscence factor. Second, adults of any age report disproportionately fewer memories from the preschool years than would be projected by a uniform forgetting rate. That is a manifestation of childhood amnesia.

The pattern emerging from these studies is robust and sensible, and provides a lifespan perspective of autobiographical recall. Two points need further discussion. First, the sampling method described here may underestimate the proportion of memories which could be retrieved from any life period. Second, identifying a pattern does not explain why it occurs. The analytical synthesis of Rubin *et al.* needs to be followed by research into the causes of forgetting, childhood amnesia, and reminiscence. Research pertaining to these issues will be surveyed in the following sections.

Forgetting

It is well known that hints or cues can assist people in recalling events which they could not recall by their own efforts. Moreover, the most effective cues are those which directly specify some part of the to-be-remembered episode, or which distinguish the target occasion from others which resemble it in various details (see Baddeley (1990) for a review of these issues and relevant research). Diary-based studies of retention and forgetting of autobiographical episodes (Linton 1975, 1986; Wagenaar 1986) have yielded considerably higher estimates of retention than Rubin has extracted from research with the cue-word method (Rubin 1982; Rubin, Wetzler and Nebes 1986). One plausible reason for this discrepancy is

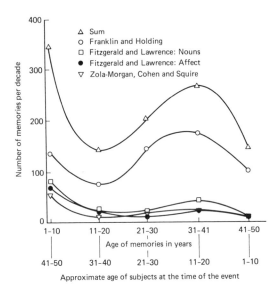

Figure 9.1(a) Distributions of memories obtained from 50-year-old respondents (from Rubin, Wetzler and Nebes 1986).

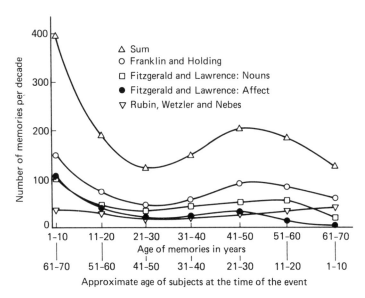

Figures 9.1(b) Distributions of memories obtained from 70-year-old respondents (from Rubin, Wetzler and Nebes 1986).

227

that the diary studies provided more cues for recall. In Linton's early studies the entire event record was used as a basis for recalling the event date. In subsequent variations she examined the effect of various retrieval strategies on recall. She observed that different strategies were necessary for older memories than for recent memories. Wagenaar's self-study is particularly significant because he systematically assessed the effect of varying the number and kind of retrieval cues on recall of autobiographical episodes. Information specifying who, what, where, or when served as cues. As shown in Figure 9.2, as the number of such cues increased, the extent of recall for remaining details also increased. Recall did decline with elapsed time, but the effect of adding cues was proportionally the same at all intervals. These studies indicate that at least within a span of 1 to 10 years many more autobiographical episodes are recallable than would be deduced using the Galton–Crovitz cue technique. It is also clear that forgetting does occur: the number of details which can be correctly recalled, even when amply cued, decreases markedly within 2 years and continues to decline at a slower rate thereafter.

Childhood

In her autobiographical memoir 'A sketch of the past' Virginia Woolf describes two of her earliest memories. Both are isolated moments, and both are primarily sensory and affective in their contents. One memory is of the colours and pattern of her mother's dress; another is of a garden. She remarks 'the peculiarity of these two strong memories is that each was very simple. I am hardly aware of myself, but only of the sensation' (1976: 67). Woolf's observations echo those of many other writers who have described their memories of early childhood, and the reports of psychologists who have studied the topic. Sensory and affective elements predominate in early memories. They are isolated from a temporal sequence of related events, and lack a clear sense of self. From one perspective this trio of qualities can be seen as mirroring the psychological immaturity of the preschool-age child. From another, Freud's, they are seen as masks – screen memories, conscious substitutes for repressed memories of emotionally conflicted experiences. Another well-attested fact about early childhood memories is that they are few in number. Statistical studies of autobiographical memory have confirmed the informal impressions of earlier investigators that disproportionately fewer memories can be voluntarily recalled from early childhood than from any other life period. The terms 'childhood amnesia' and 'infantile amnesia' have been in use since Freud to both describe and explain this fact.

Numerous hypotheses have been advanced as explanations of childhood amnesia. Schactel (1947) proposed that cognitive and linguistic development were the key factors. He argued that conscious experience is organized in perceptual rather than conceptual schemes before the development of language. Thereafter, experience is organized and represented increasingly according to the categories communicated through language. Thus, experience is encoded in qualitatively different ways before and after the acquisition of language. Schactel concluded that preverbal experience could not be effectively revived with the verbal–conceptual system and strategies which dominate adult memory and thought.

Several observations are consistent with this account. Early memories frequently have the immediacy of direct perception, with sensory and affective qualities predominant. People who score high

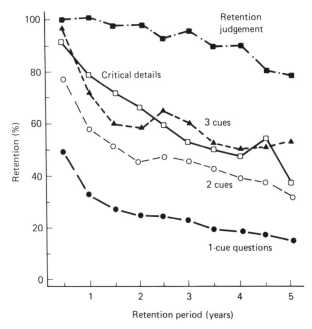

Figures 9.2 Percentages of memories recalled to different numbers of cues (from Wagenaar 1986).

229

on mental imagery tests report more early memories than those who score low (Karis 1979). If we assume that imagery is less conceptually-driven than language (a controversial premise), then this result might be taken as support for Schactel's hypothesis. Two facts present difficulties for his views. First, imagery appears to be a pervasive feature of autobiographical memories irrespective of age (Brewer 1986, 1988). This suggests that differences in memory codes cannot be the primary basis of childhood amnesia. Second, extensive research has found little evidence that long-term event memory is organized differently in young children than in older individuals (Nelson 1988; Fivush and Hudson 1990). Preschool-age children can remember novel or salient events for months, perhaps indefinitely. However, like adults, they construct general memories from repeated experiences and confuse separate occasions in recall. The impact of repetition on memory development is central to Katherine Nelson's perspective of childhood amnesia. She proposes that a general event memory system develops prior to the development of autobiographical memory *per se*. Since the bulk of daily experience in childhood is repetitious, it is not surprising that few specific episodes can be recalled then or later. Reading Woolf's memoir before and after reading Nelson is a revealing experience. Many of Woolf's observations describe routines, not specific episodes, and scenes or locales which were a recurrent context of activities in her daily life. The latter resemble what Salaman (1971) calls memories of the background. Nelson's research is a forceful reminder of the importance of distinguishing general and specific memories.

Although Freud's repression theory is no longer given much credence as an explanation of childhood amnesia, his attention to the impact of affect on children's memory should not be ignored. As adults, people differ quite noticeably in the number and variety of childhood memories. This interindividual variation is not easily explained by any normative theory of cognitive development or memory development. However, differences in personality dynamics have been shown to be linked with differences in the number and qualities of such memories. This literature spans many decades, but two recent studies have demonstrated that it is still a viable issue. Kihlstrom and Harackiewicz (1982) found that the earliest recollections from students who scored high on Harmavoidance were more recent or exhibited more signs of screen memories than reports from other students. Thus, young adults who differ in their tendency to perceive threats to the self also differ in the extent and quality of their childhood memories. Davis (1987) has shown that individuals who as adults rely on a repressive coping style recall fewer childhood experiences which made them feel either happy, sad, angry, or fearful than students displaying other coping styles. Moreover, this pattern of diminished recall held true when there was no constraint on the life periods sampled in memory. These studies indicate that a defensive stance towards experience is associated with an impoverished autobiography for childhood experience, as well as subsequent life periods. This could be due to encoding deficits, inhibited retrieval, or both. Such persons may simply not form memories of experiences which trigger their defences. However, Salaman's (1970) discussion of her own 'involuntary memories' and her success at reconstructing many childhood episodes indicates that retrieval problems do contribute to the paucity of childhood memories.

Persistent memories: reminiscence or personal history?

As noted above, there is a reversal of trend in the distribution of prompted autobiographical recall which brackets the years from late childhood to early adulthood. Rubin *et al.* (1986) attributed this to a preference for selective sampling from those years and regarded it as a kind of reminiscing. Subsequent research has replicated the phenomenon but suggests other explanations of it. Fitzgerald (1988) obtained reports of vivid memories from adults 60 to 75 years of age. When arranged according to decades the highest proportion occurred for the period under discussion. Fromholt and Larsen (1991) asked elderly subjects to tell about the important events in their lives. They found that proportionally more events came from the 'reminiscence' period than any other. Events which are conventional landmarks in lives, such as births, deaths, marriages, starting a career or school, accounted for 20 to 30 per cent of the reports in the two studies. The remainder were diverse, for the most part deriving their importance from individual circumstances and values. Fitzgerald (1988) asks why vivid as well as ordinary memories should cluster in one life period and proposes that it is due to the central place those events have in the person's life story or self-narrative. For him it is not nostalgia but salience which accounts for the discontinuity in memory distributions. Fromholt and Larsen (1991) concur, but argue that salience is determined by both social and personal values and probably affects such memory maintenance processes as rehearsal. Thus, Fitzgerald has initially stressed a structural perspective where Fromholt and Larsen favour a multifactor perspective. In either approach preferential recall is attributed to factors which increase retention and availability of certain life events rather than to retrieval biases guided by current attitudes or concerns. Reminiscing is a genuine phenomenon, but is probably not the basis of the distributional discontinuity identified in autobiographical memory research.

It would help to have detailed information on autobiographical memory for major life events. Surprisingly little is available beyond the descriptive summaries found in studies of life stages, or adaptation to life changes. Two topics which have been studied are memories of college life, and memory for the onset of menstruation. Alumnae of Wellesley College were asked to report four memories of their freshman year, to date them by month, and to rate them on several dimensions (Pillemer, Goldsmith, Panter and White 1988). The temporal distribution of memories, shown in Figure 9.3, was noteworthy in two respects: first, nearly half of the reports were attributed to the first month at college (September), and 37 per cent of those were of events which occurred on the first day; second, the distributions of recent and older graduates were virtually identical. Furthermore, one-third of these persistent memories were rarely recounted in the interim, and most were given only moderate ratings for surprise and life impact. Thus memories of events clustered at the beginning of a novel and significant life period are maintained indefinitely in personal memory. Pillemer et al. (1986) attribute such persistence to both cognitive and social variables. Novel experiences cannot be assimilated to pre-existing schemas. Instead they initiate the development of new ordering structures in memory, and provide examples to guide behaviour in subsequent circumstances. This account is compatible with Fitzgerald's narrative hypothesis, but is more specific about the cognitive processes entailed.

A study of women's memories for the onset of menstruation offers additional support for the hypothesized relationship between novelty, schematization, and memory (Pillemer, Koff, Rhinehart and Rierdan 1987). Menarche is a physiological and psychological benchmark in development; it is not surprising that the first occasion of menstruating is memorable. However, some women remember it more fully than others. In the Pillemer et al. (1987) study a small but meaningful negative correlation was obtained between number of details reported about the event and self-ratings of preparation for the experience. Those who felt more adequately prepared recalled fewer details than those who felt less well-prepared. Preparation introduces new information into memory which can affect the perception and encoding of a relevant event in the same way that other knowledge structures such as scripts (Abelson 1981) influence the processing of routine experiences. Effectively, a prepared event is prescripted. It should be less surprising and would not need to be as completely registered in memory as one which has unexpected aspects.

ORGANIZATION OF AUTOBIOGRAPHICAL EVENT MEMORY

A person's autobiography is more than a collection of discrete events or a simple chronological series of experiences. Temporal patterning is only one dimension of organization in experience, and though important is not the only dimension organizing experience in memory. Metaphors such as 'life is a story' or 'life is a journey'

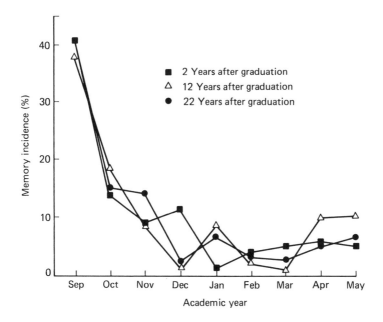

Figure 9.3 Distribution of memories of the freshman year for three alumnae classes (from Pillemer, Goldsmith, Panter and White 1988).

233

(see Lakoff 1986; Lakoff and Johnson 1980) emphasize the global patterning of lives, the integration of experiences, and the significance of goal-directed activity and change. These themes are echoed in much of the recent work on organization in autobiographical event memory. The notion of life story or self-narrative mentioned in the preceding section directly incorporates these cultural models into memory theory. Other proposals are less literal in this regard, but use structuring principles which are compatible with narrative forms. The central premise is that autobiographical event memory is hierarchically organized though the definition of units and levels is quite varied (Barsalou 1988; Conway and Berkerian 1987; Linton 1986; Neisser 1986; Reiser, Black and Abelson 1985). The basic unit is an event. It can be decomposed into its defining qualities (such as time, place, activity). It can be related to superordinate structures (contexts) of similar events. It can also be embedded in other more inclusive superordinate structures which are temporally extended but thematically integrated such as 'attending school', 'working at the bank', 'my summer vacation in Colorado'. Finally, these extendures (Linton 1986) may coincide with or overlap other sustained enterprises such as 'being married' or 'the years I lived in Boston'.

Considering this array we might concur with the narrator of a recent novel that 'all lives are messy aggregates' (Powers 1985). But from another perspective we get a hint of underlying simplicity. Barsalou (1988) proposes that goals may be a central organizing feature of autobiographical memory. Figure 9.4 illustrates his thesis. Any event can be seen as action directed toward a goal. The proximate goal, however, may be related to other more long-term goals. So, completing high school is an essential step toward attending university. Completing one enables the person to attempt the other. In this way goals can be scaffolded and link quite diverse events over extended periods of time. Several recent studies have examined the validity of a goal-based system of organization in autobiographical memory. Conway (1990a) had subjects report the images which came to mind for words designating taxonomic categories (e.g. furniture), goal-derived categories (e.g. camping equipment) and emotions. Autobiographical episodes were the basis of the majority of images reported for both emotions and goal-based categories, but not for the taxonomic category words. In a subsequent set of experiments Conway (1990c) found that retrieval of autobiographical memories was faster when the memory prompt was primed with a goal-based category than with a taxonomic term. Thus, memories were retrieved more quickly for a prime–prompt pair such as BIRTHDAY PRESENT/Jewelry than a pair such as FURNITURE/Chair. Many goals derive from personal dispositions and needs (e.g. be successful, be a person liked by others). Events which were associated with attainment of such dispositional goals tend to evoke stronger emotions when recalled than those which were not (Singer 1990). Thus preliminary investigations are encouraging of the proposition that goals may be a generic structuring principle of autobiographical memory.

An interesting problem is how the structures of memory originate. Organization is a byproduct of perceptual and cognitive processing. Some of the dimensions by which experience is organized are determined by innate structures of the perceptual systems and the brain. Others are necessary accommodations to the ways society interprets and uses experience. The manner in which personal experience is represented and organized in memory must be responsive to the ways we are called upon to use it in our society. For example, the kinds of memory questions that arise in conversation can specify a class of events ('How many movies have you seen this year?'), a time period ('What did you do last night?'), activities ('How was your trip?'), and relationships ('Why did you breakup with Bob?'). In order to provide relevant and socially acceptable replies we need to have memory organized in ways which permit retrieval of appropriate information – that is, a 'socially addressable memory system' (Pillemer et al. 1986: 109). Much of this task is accomplished in childhood through daily interactions with adults (Edwards and Middleton 1988). However, we should not assume that events are registered in memory in some exhaustive classification which anticipates any possible query. There is often an element of improvisation and problem solving involved in remembering. What is required are inference strategies which can operate on the information in memory to construct a satisfactory response.

Memory organization is not a static structure. Many chunks of one's autobiography are emergent and aggregate experiences retroactively (Linton 1986; Neisser 1986). For example, a temporary job will acquire additional meaning if it develops into a career, and a casual date will acquire more meaning as 'the first time we went out' if a relationship develops. The career and relationship will become defined units of your autobiographical memory. However, since they emerged over time they can only assume organizational control retroactively over prior experiences. This process may help explain some of the gaps in autobiographical memory. By the time that events assume a stable pattern and it is represented in memory, some earlier activities could have been forgotten, or have merged with other similar occasions. Hence, they are not available to be integrated retroactively with the emergent theme. Since organization retards forgetting, the point at which a superordinate unit is defined should be a major determinant of how detailed memory will be in

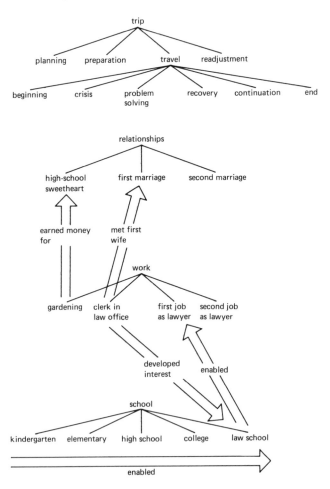

Figure 9.4 Examples of goal structures and their interrelations (from Barsalou 1988).

that domain of experience. However, even this principle may under-estimate the degree of instability in memory organization. Barclay and Hodges (1988) argue that memories are regularly reconfigured as we revise our self-perceptions and personal histories.

RECOLLECTIVE EXPERIENCE

Suppose you are telling friends about a dining experience you had on a recent vacation trip. As you recount the experience you may be aware of visual images, taste sensations, feelings of pleasure. You may also 'see' yourself in memory images, as if you were observing the incident you are recalling. Phenomenal elements are characteristic of the distinctive state of awareness we associate with remembering the past, a state Tulving (1985) refers to as autonetic consciousness. Sometimes our phenomenal experience is so vivid and complete – as with Proust's madeleine, or Penfield's patients – that we seem to relive or reinstate the past. In the usual case the imagery, sensory or affective qualities experienced while remembering are quite variable, ranging from fragmentary and hazy to connected and clear. The phenomenal qualities of consciousness have been studied for clues about the processes which enable us to distinguish perception and imagination (Johnson and Raye 1981). Many of the same dimensions of subjective awareness are relevant to questions about memory (Johnson, Foley, Suengas and Raye 1988). Indeed, one view of memory is that it preserves the contents of consciousness, and that remembering is a matter of re-entry of those contents into current awareness. In what follows the term 'recollective experience' will be used to distinguish our memory focus from other concerns with phenomenal data.

A prototype experiment

The study of the subjective experiences associated with remembering raises fascinating questions and unique challenges. A first problem is to develop methods for obtaining quantitative descriptions of rec-ollective experience. Brewer's (1988) exploratory research provides a useful model of such procedures. He adapted thought-sampling techniques to the study of autobiographical memory. Student vol-unteers were provided with radio paging devices. When these were activated, subjects recorded their current activity and answered questions about their thoughts and feelings. These records were used in later tests of subjects' memory for the events they reported. In addition to standard recall and recognition tests, participants rated the extent to which they re-experienced in their mind qualities of the recalled event as they were tested. Seven different modalities of re-experienced qualities were assessed. These included sensory and perceptual aspects as well as feelings and thoughts. Two results are especially interesting. First, some degree of re-experiencing was reported for the majority of events assessed. Visual imagery tended to predominate, but other modalities of imagery and feelings were often reported. Second, accuracy of recall, confidence in recall, and degree of re-experiencing were highly intercorrelated. Thus, this study not only documented the frequency and richness of recollective experience, it also provided information about the correspondences between overt (i.e. the performance data which could be objectively evaluated) and covert aspects of remembering.

What is the source of the imagery which accompanies recall? In referring to it as re-experiencing, Brewer implies that it is information encoded in a memory record which is activated by retrieving the memory. There are reasons to question that interpretation. First, it seems possible to recall an event and not experience any accompanying imagery. Conway (1990b) proposes that memory imagery is the result of the way retrieval is accomplished rather than an inevitable occurrence. Retrieval conditions also seem to affect the extent of phenomenal re-experiencing. Reminiscing, daydreaming, and reflection seem to induce more imagery and feeling than occurs with recall in less solitary contexts. This may be a matter of the focus of attention rather than of differences in memory processes. When we are reminiscing we pay more attention to our internal experiences, whereas, in interpersonal contexts we may divide our attention between recollections, our reports, and our audience and be less aware of internal experiences. Second, we know from anecdotal report that memory imagery can be erroneous. Salaman (1971) describes a strong visual memory from childhood which blended parts of two different homes into a single scene. I have a strong visual memory of a particular birthday, which I discovered was flawed in a similar way. These errors escape notice unless we analyse our memories; I never doubted my birthday memory until a few years ago and was surprised by the confabulatory aspect of it. Both of these observations suggest that at least some memory imagery is due to constructive processes rather than simple retrieval and reactivation of memory traces. Neisser (1967) expressed similar doubts in his critique of the reappearance hypothesis and Penfield's brain stimulation protocols.

The fact that in Brewer's study recall accuracy and degree of re-experiencing were positively correlated is intriguing. Does this mean that vivid or extensive imagery is a reliable index of memory authenticity and accuracy? McCauley (1988) suggested another interpretation. He agrees that memory imagery can be constructed instead of retrieved, and adds that ratings of recollective experience may be affected by other kinds of memory inferences. One source of such inferences are implicit theories of memory, i.e. a person's informal generalizations about the nature and operation of memory processes. For example, most people believe that recent events are remembered better than older events. If you are aware that an event is recent, you may tend to give your recollective experience of it a higher score. That is, your rating may not be an absolute magnitude judgment, but a decision based on what you experience and your beliefs about memory. Robinson (1990) has shown that memory age is a robust element in implicit theories, and that recollective experience is assumed to vary with memory age. He also compared ratings of recollective experience for an event with estimates from people who had vicarious knowledge but no direct experience of the event, and found that they were indistinguishable. This shows that implicit theories are powerful enough to generate consistent and plausible patterns of reported recollective experience. The result gives weight to McCauley's argument and indicates the need to interpret such data with caution.

Memory perspective

We can imagine how a scene would look from different perspectives, and that observers might have different attitudes toward an event than participants. This generic capacity to experience different points of view is manifested in dreams, fantasies, deliberate thought, and in remembering. Nigro and Neisser (1983) distinguished two perspectives in recollection: field and observer. We may visualize an event as if we were experiencing it again – a field memory; or we may visualize ourself in the scene – an observer memory. Nigro and Neisser (1983) propose that the way an event is framed in awareness may signify what memory processes have shaped the recollection. Field memories seem to reproduce the original context and perspective of events. Observer memories seem to portray events from a different point of view than the original experience. Thus, more reconstruction may have occurred with observer than with field memories. Consistent with this view, Nigro and Neisser (1983) found that observer memories tended to be older and less well-recalled than field memories. Other research indicates that the relationship of memory age to perspective is inconsistent (Robinson and Swanson 1990b). By definition, 'seeing' oneself in a recollection is a constructive act, but time (memory age) may not be the most salient determinant of this phenomenal feature of remembering.

Most people can change their initial memory perspective. This indicates that perspective is an aspect of the remembering process, not a fixed property of recollections. What functions are served by this ability to switch between contrasting memory perspectives? Two have been identified thus far. The way events are interpreted in retrospect may be associated with memory perspective. Frank and Gilovich (1989) showed that field and observer perspectives produced somewhat different patterns of causal attribution in recall of a previous interaction. With an observer perspective people attributed greater responsibility to themselves than their partners for the conduct of the interaction. The attributional pattern was reversed with a field perspective. Qualities of an experience may be differentially accessible or salient depending upon the perspective adopted. Nigro and Neisser (1983, Study 4) found that when feelings were emphasized the field perspective was reported more often than an observer perspective. Similarly, in our current research (Robinson and Swanson 1991), we have found that switching from a field to an observer perspective reduces the awareness of feelings in recall.

Remembering is more than the reactivation of a trace. We cannot be simultaneously aware of all the elements or aspects of an event in recall, but we can choose which to focus on. Memory perspective may be a structuring process which mediates that selectivity. Remembering also entails reaction and (re)interpretation. If we could observe consciousness, we might see a sequence of alternating points of view as remembering progresses, a sequence which is co-ordinated with shifting concerns, and reactions. The analogue of this in fantasizing is described by one informant in Caughey's ethnographic studies (1984: 123) of the stream of consciousness. Jaynes (1986) argued that spatial metaphors play a prominent role in the processes we designate as conscious mental acts. Memory perspective may be a case in point. It could be interpreted as a metaphoric mapping of spatial relations onto various mnemonic qualities and objectives. In the case of memory age, temporally distant events may be represented as spatially distant by adopting the spectator (observer) frame of reference. In this way the acts of a former self may be recalled as if being viewed by a present self. In the case of feelings, the field perspective places the self in a participant role which encourages re-experiencing. Where self-attributions are entailed the observer mode may be a literal rather than a metaphoric representation since the self is the focus of attention in such cases. Presumably, 'seeing' oneself facilitates thinking about oneself. The common ground of these representations is consciousness itself. The only way we can experience the past is through our representations of it, and for some properties we may rely on metaphoric correspondences.

USES OF AUTOBIOGRAPHICAL MEMORY

Autobiographical memory is not just an archive, it is a resource which we use in a variety of ways every day. Research into the functions of autobiographical memory is just beginning, but several functions have already been identified. Barclay and Smith (in press) suggest that two categories of functions can be defined: intrapersonal and interpersonal. This is a convenient dichotomy so long as we bear in mind that individual dynamics can affect social relations and vice-versa. Four functions will be discussed: two intrapersonal and two interpersonal.

Interpersonal functions

Neisser (1988) proposed that memory talk ('remember when . . .') is a way of using the past to maintain and extend relationships with others. He believes that this function is 'the most fundamental one in an evolutionary sense' (p. 555), and claims it is the developmentally earliest use of autobiographical memory by children. Evoking a shared past can sustain interest in a current interaction and promote bonding. It is an intuitively understood practice of people of all ages. Two observations reinforce Neisser's argument. First, self-disclosure is a typical precursor of friendship and intimacy, whereas withholding oneself is usually perceived as a distancing tactic or as a rebuff. A common form of self-disclosure is to recount a personal experience or to remind another of common experiences. Second, relationships are affected when a person's ability to engage in memory talk is impaired. Meltzer (1983) incurred some brain damage from anoxia following a heart attack. He had to relearn his autobiography, and found conversations with friends and colleagues strained because he couldn't remember doing anything with them. He was keenly aware of what was happening, grew depressed and became progressively isolated. Family and friends of Alzheimer's patients may find that they grow distant from the patient for similar reasons.

Autobiographical memory may contribute in important ways to our ability to empathize with others and interpret their behaviour (Robinson and Swanson 1990a). We are faced continuously with a need to interpret and predict the behaviour of others, and to adjust our own actions accordingly. Our ability to symbolize experience, retrieve it, and use it for this purpose has been augmented by consciousness and self-awareness. These capacities enable us to generate analogue models of the inner life of other persons (Humphrey 1986). That is, we can use our own experience to generate reasons for the actions of others and test appropriate reactions. Two interesting predictions follow from this analysis of social functions for autobiographical memory: First, there should be strong connections in development between autobiographical memory, social skills, and inferential thought about others. Second, these skills may exhibit significant individual differences which should be correlated with differences in various features of autobiographical memory. Individual differences are important for testing an ecological and evolutionary perspective of memory (Bruce 1985), so autobiographical memory research may make valuable contributions to general memory theory.

Intrapersonal functions

Remembering is important in mood regulation. Personal memories can be used to sustain a desirable mood, or to alter an undesirable one. Since mood can affect motivation and behaviour, the ability to regulate it internally through memory retrieval is a very adaptive process. From this perspective the recent emphasis on mood-congruent recall is one-sided. We should observe recall of contrasting experiences when mood change is desired. This has been confirmed in recent research by Parrott and Sabini (1990). It would also be expected that any impairment of the capacity to retrieve mood-contrasting memories would be a factor in the development or maintenance of mood disorders. Much research on cognitive factors in depression supports this claim. In a wide-ranging essay Smith and

Barclay (1990) conjoin the intrapersonal and interpersonal functions of autobiographical memory. They examine the links between autobiographical memory, the management of emotion, and regulation of relationships in the larger context of a theory of attachments. In their view autobiographical memory has instrumental functions, but is also transformed by its uses. A different perspective on memory, mood, and relationships emerges from Caughey's (1984) ethnographic studies of the stream of consciousness. His protocols demonstrate that real and imagined relationships and their predicaments are a frequent focus of daydreaming. Moreover, his data strongly imply that negative emotions and experiences are more common than studies of memory *per se* indicate. People replay and repair their experience in these episodes of fantasy. It is likely that memories are also revised in the process. Thus, autobiographical memory is a vital resource in managing moods and motives, but its contents may also be modified when recruited for those purposes.

One of the most important and extensive uses of autobiographical memory is to construct self-concepts and self-histories. The relationship of self to memory has been a concern since Locke's analysis of personal identity in the seventeenth century, and is presently a topic of intense investigation by psychologists. Although there are many theories of self and personal identity, one postulate is widely shared among them: the self is a knowledge structure encoding self-descriptive information abstracted from experience. In some theories the self stands in a class-instance relationship to autobiographical memory. That is, personal memories exemplify the traits or interests a person attributes to himself. Some theorists emphasize the provisional character of self-concepts, nothing that people routinely explore alternative or possible selves (Markus and Nurius 1986), and that there are inconsistencies among a person's set of self-perceptions (e.g. Gergen 1967). According to this view memories provide an inductive database for constructing preferred self-perceptions (see Sanitioso, Kunda and Fong 1990). The point made above about mood and memory also applies to self and memory: each revision of the self revises memory, and selves are revised by rewriting or reconfiguring memory (Barclay and Hodges 1988; Greenwald 1980).

Self-histories are narrative constructions. They are informal autobiographies. As we have seen some theorists believe that autobiographical event memory is organized as a self-narrative. At present, one could with equal justice claim that memory is narratively organized, or that we are misled by the narrative forms of discourse into supposing that it is (Rubin 1988). Perhaps, self-narratives stand in relation to memory in the same ways that self does. At any given time a person can relate a coherent life history and illustrate it with recollections. However, the narrative can be elaborated, updated, edited, or revised many times during a life. Thus, self-narratives may be an additional structure rather than the formal organization of memory itself.

IS AUTOBIOGRAPHICAL MEMORY A DISTINCTIVE TYPE OF MEMORY?

Now that we have surveyed several topics in autobiographical memory, its relationship to other types of memory can be examined. It is clearly a form of long-term memory, but is it a different kind of long-term memory? One way to attempt an answer is to ask where autobiographical memory fits in the classification system proposed by Tulving (1983). He distinguishes episodic from semantic memory (as well as other kinds unrelated to this discussion). The former is memory for events, the latter is remembered knowledge. Nelson (1989) proposes that autobiographical memory is a functionally distinct subsystem of episodic memory. A limitation of this view is that autobiographical memory has elements which correspond to semantic as well as episodic memory. Biographical knowledge, and the structures comprising the self appear to be conceptually nearer to semantic than episodic memory. Nelson's proposal could be extended to include an autobiographical component in both semantic and episodic memory. The fact that these forms of memory are in place before autobiographical memory appears (see Nelson 1989) is consistent with the hypothesis. Functional dissociations provide another test. If one form of memory remains intact when another is impaired they are assumed to be separable, hence distinct. Is there any evidence that non-autobiographical memory can be impaired without comparable impairment to autobiographical memory? DeRenzi, Liotti and Nichelli (1987) describe a case which comes close to demonstrating this. Their patient had severe losses of memory for general knowledge, linguistic knowledge, and for most public events and personalities. Her memory for her own life history, however, seemed to be much better preserved including both autobiographical facts and specific events. Thus an autobiographical system comprising analogues of semantic and episodic memory appeared to be intact, whereas both the semantic and episodic components of a non-autobiographical system were compromised. However, this case should not be given undue weight. As Conway (1990b) describes, assessments of autobiographical memory in brain-damaged patients have produced inconsistent results.

Tulving's taxonomy is only one model of human memory and it may not provide the most appropriate framework for understanding autobiographical memory. There are pragmatic grounds for treating autobiographical memory as distinct: it forms a coherent system of self-referring information (Brewer 1986; Fivush 1988). How it relates to other components of memory and the general cognitive system (e.g. Holland and Rabbitt 1990) are matters for further investigation.

AREAS OF APPLICATION

As we learn more about autobiographical memory we will be able to contribute helpful guidance to those studying specific practical issues. The distinction between specific and general memories or memory structures has already proven useful. A clinical context of application has been examined by Williams and Dritschel (1988). Adults who attempt suicide show a loss of specificity in prompted autobiographical recall which persists for a year or longer. Williams and Dritschel speculate that this retrieval deficit may support a cognitive style often associated with severe depression: global attributions about oneself and others. Perhaps, if ways can be found to moderate the retrieval deficit and promote recall of specific events, patients can learn to moderate their generalizations and begin to construct more specific and appropriate coping responses.

The global versus specific contrast has also been examined in an area of health psychology. Means et al. (1989) questioned people about their visits to a health-care organization during the past year. Initially, fewer visits for a chronic problem were recalled than those for non-recurrent problems. However, an intervention technique almost doubled the recall of recurrent visits. Using a personal timeline and prompting the person to reconstruct visits one at a time brought the level of recall up to par with that for non-recurrent events. The success of the intervention indicates that subjects' motivation and metacognitive assumptions may have contributed to their initially poorer recall of recurrent episodes. This study has interesting implications for ways of improving the taking of medical histories and techniques to use in surveys of health care practices.

Autobiographical memory may also provide useful insights into aesthetic experience. Literary theorists may descry the biographical fallacy, but the fact remains that art not only examines experience but frequently is shaped by specific events in the artists' lives (see Warnock 1987). The ways we respond to art are also influenced by personal experience. Larsen and Laszlo (1990) have examined the patterns of remindings which occur as people read literature. The meaning of a story cannot be reduced to a cognitive schema or form. It also has a personal meaning which develops from interactions among story features and the personal experiences which are evoked in the reader.

A last area of application is education. Many critics of modern schooling argue that instruction has become one-sided, focusing on conceptual and abstract matters and excluding personal experience. Some believe that chronic underachievement of minorities and lower socioeconomic groups has roots in this kind of alienation from experience (e.g. Barnes, Britton and Rosen 1971; Cazden and Hymes 1978). Contemporary research in cognitive science and autobiographical memory can contribute to this debate. For example, current work in cognition is re-examining the relationship between specific episodic experience and conceptual representations in memory. We may find that knowledge and meaning are different though connected domains. Research in autobiographical memory has clarified how people organize personal experience, remember it, and recount it narratively for themselves or others. Both programmes may provide valuable clues about how to make education a more meaningful and successful activity.

CONCLUSION

Autobiographical memory is a recent topic of inquiry but already a substantial amount has been learned about it. It is as central to human life as language, consciousness, and self-awareness. It certainly would not develop without the latter two, and may be significantly compromised without some form of language. To be a person one must have an identity and a personal history. Autobiographical memory is instrumental in the construction and maintenance of these psychological structures. Our memories also link us to others: they are a resource for establishing and sustaining relationships. Thus impairment of autobiographical memory can undermine both individual and social functioning. As Katherine Nelson has written:

> autobiographical memory is as representative of human functioning as language itself . . . it is reflected in and forms the basis for song, story, epic, and myth in all human cultures. Any complete account of human memory, and the development of human memory, must include it as a specific and distinct type of memory.
>
> (Nelson 1989: 147)

REFERENCES

Abelson, R.P. (1981) 'Psychological status of the script concept', *American Psychologist* 36: 715–29.

Baddeley, A. (1990) *Human Memory: Theory and Practice*, Boston: Allyn & Bacon.

Banaji, M.R. and Crowder, R. (1989) 'The bankruptcy of everyday memory', *American Psychologist* 44: 1185–93.

Barclay, C.R. and Hodges, R.M. (1988) 'Content and structure in autobiographical memory: an essay on composing and recomposing the self', in *Actes du Colloque Européen: Construction et Functionement de l'Identité*, pp. 205–12, Aix-en-Provence: University of Provence.

Barclay, C.R. and Smith T.S. (in press) 'Autobiographical remembering and self-composing', *International Journal of Personal Construct Psychology*.

Barnes, D., Britton, J. and Rosen, H. (1971) *Language, the Learner and the School*, revised edn, New York: Penguin.

Barsalou, L.W. (1988) 'The content and organization of autobiographical memories', in U. Neisser and E. Winograd (eds) *Remembering Reconsidered: Ecological and Traditional Approaches to Memory*, pp. 193–242, Cambridge: Cambridge University Press.

Brewer, W.F. (1986) 'What is autobiographical memory?', in D.C. Rubin (ed.) *Autobiographical Memory*, pp. 25–49, Cambridge: Cambridge University Press.

Brewer, W.F. (1988) 'Memory for randomly sampled autobiographical events' in U. Neisser and E. Winograd (eds) *Remembering Reconsidered: Ecological and Traditional Approaches to Memory*, pp. 21–90, Cambridge: Cambridge University Press.

Bruce, D. (1985) 'The how and why of ecological memory', *Journal of Experimental Psychology: General* 114: 78–90.

Caughey, J.L. (1984) *Imaginary Social Worlds* Lincoln, Nebraska: University of Nebraska Press.

Cazden, C. and Hymes, G. (1978) 'Narrative thinking and storytelling rights: A folklorist's clue to a critique of education' *Keystone Folklore Quarterly* 22: 21–36.

Conway, M.A. (1990a) 'Conceptual representation of emotions: The role of autobiographical memories', in K.J. Gilhooly, M.T.G. Keane, R.H. Logie and G. Erdos (eds) *Lines of Thinking*, vol. 2, pp. 133–43 London: Wiley.

Conway, M.A. (1990b) *Autobiographical Memory: an Introduction*; Milton Keynes: Open University Press.

Conway, M.A. (1990c) 'Associations between autobiographical memories and concepts', *Journal of Experimental Psychology: Learning, Memory and Cognition* 16(5): 799–812.

Conway, M.A. and Berkerian, D.A. (1987) 'Organization in autobiographical memory', *Memory and Cognition* 15: 119–32.

Davis, P.J. (1987) 'Repression and the inaccessibility of affective memories', *Journal of Personality and Social Psychology* 53: 585–93.

DeRenzi, E., Liotti, M. and Nichelli, P. (1987) 'Semantic amnesia with preservation of autobiographic memory: a case report', *Cortex* 23: 575–97.

Edwards, D. and Middleton, D. (1988) 'Conversational remembering and family relationships: how children learn to remember', *Journal of Social and Personal Relationships* 5: 3–25.

Fitzgerald, J.M. (1988) 'Vivid memories and the reminiscence phenomenon: the role of a self narrative', *Human Development* 31: 261–73.

Fivush, R. (1988) 'The functions of event memory: some comments on Nelson and Barsalou', in U. Neisser and E. Winograd (eds) *Remembering Reconsidered: Ecological and Traditional Approaches to Memory*, pp. 227–32; Cambridge: Cambridge University Press.

Fivush, R. and Hudson, J.A. (1990) *Knowing and Remembering in Young Children*; New York: Cambridge University Press.

Frank, M.G. and Gilovich, T. (1989) 'Effect of memory perspective on retrospective causal attributions', *Journal of Personality and Social Psychology* 57: 399–403.

Fromholt, F. and Larsen, S.F. (1991) 'Autobiographical memory in normal aging and primary degenerative dementia (dementia of Alzheimer type)', *Journal of Gerontology* 46, 3: 85–91

Gergen, K.J. (1967) *To Be or not To Be a Single Self: Existential Perspectives on the Self*; Gainsville, Florida: University of Florida Press.

Glover, J. (1988) *I: The Philosophy and Psychology of Personal Identity*; London: Allen Lane.

Greenwald, A.G. (1980) 'The totalitarian ego: fabrication and revision of personal history', *American Psychologist* 35: 603–18.

Holland, C.A. and Rabbitt, P.M.A. (1990) 'Autobiographical and text recall in the elderly: an investigation of a processing resource deficit', *Quarterly Journal of Experimental Psychology* 42A: 441–70.

Humphrey, N. (1986) *The Inner Eye*; London: Faber & Faber.

Jaynes, J. (1986) 'Consciousness and the voices of the mind', *Canadian Psychology* 27: 128–39.

Johnson, M.K., and Raye, C.L. (1981) 'Reality monitoring', *Psychological Review* 88: 67–85.

Johnson, M.K., Foley, M.A., Suengas, A.G. and Raye, C.L. (1988) 'Phenomenal characteristics of memories for perceived and imagined autobiographical events', *Journal of Experimental Psychology: General* 117: 371–6.

Karis, D. (1979) 'Individual differences in autobiographical memory', Paper presented at a meeting of the American Psychological Association, New York.

Kihlstrom, J.F. and Harackiewicz, J.M. (1982) 'The earliest recollection: a new survey', *Journal of Personality* 50: 134–48.

Klein, S.B., Loftus, J. and Burton, H.A. (1989) 'Two self-reference effects: The importance of distinguishing between self-descriptiveness judgments and autobiographical retrieval in self-referent encoding', *Journal of Personality and Social Psychology* 56: 853–65.

Lakoff, G. (1986) 'A figure of thought', *Metaphor and Symbolic Activity* 1: 215–25.

Lakoff, G. and Johnson, M. (1980) *Metaphors We Live By*, Chicago: University of Chicago Press.

Larsen, S.F. (1988) 'Remembering without experiencing: memory for reported events', in U. Neisser and E. Winograd (eds) *Remembering Reconsidered: Ecological and Traditional Approaches to Memory*, pp. 326–55, Cambridge: Cambridge University Press.

Larsen, S.F. and Laszlo, J. (1990) 'Cultural-historical knowledge and personal experience in appreciation of literature', *European Journal of Social Psychology* 20: 425–40.

Linton, M. (1975) 'Memory for real-world events', in D.A Norman and D.E. Rumelhart (eds) *Explorations in Cognition*, San Francisco: Freeman, pp. 376–404.

Linton, M. (1982) 'Transformations of memory in everyday life', in U. Neisser (ed.) *Memory Observed: Remembering in Natural Contexts*, pp. 77–81, San Francisco: Freeman.

Linton, M. (1986) 'Ways of searching and the contents of memory', in D.C. Rubin (ed.) *Autobiographical Memory*, pp. 50–67, Cambridge: Cambridge University Press.

McCauley, R.N. (1988) 'Walking in our own footsteps: Autobiographical memory and reconstruction', in U. Neisser and E. Winograd (eds) *Remembering Reconsidered: Ecological and Traditional Approaches to Memory*, pp. 126–44, Cambridge: Cambridge University press.

Markus, H. and Nurius, P. (1986) 'Possible selves', *American Psychologist* 41: 954–69.

Means, B., Nigam, A., Zarrow, M., Loftus, E. and Donaldson, M.S. (1989) 'Autobiographical memory for health-related events', Series 6: Cognition and Survey Measurement, No. 2, Hyattsville, Maryland: National Center for Health Statistics.

Meltzer, M.L. (1983) 'Poor memory: A case report', *Journal of Clinical Psychology* 39: 3–10.

Neisser, U. (1967) *Cognitive Psychology*, Englewood Cliffs, New Jersey: Prentice-Hall.

Neisser, U. (1981) 'John Dean's memory', *Cognition* 9: 1–22.

Neisser, U. (1985) 'Toward an ecologically oriented cognitive science', in T.M. Schlecter and M.P. Toglia (eds) *New Directions in Cognitive Science*, pp. 17–32, Norwood, New Jersey: Ablex.

Neisser, U. (1986) 'Nested structure in autobiographical memory', in D.C. Rubin (ed.) *Autobiographical Memory*, pp. 71–81, Cambridge: Cambridge University Press.

Neisser U. (1988) 'Time present and time past', in M.M. Gruneberg, P.E. Morris and R.N. Sykes (eds) *Practical Aspects of Memory: Current Research and Issues*, vol. 2, pp. 545–60, New York: Wiley.

Nelson, K. (1988) 'The ontogeny of memory for real events', in U. Neisser and E. Winograd (eds) *Remembering Reconsidered: Ecological and Traditional Approaches to Memory*, pp. 244–76, Cambridge: Cambridge University Press.

Nelson, K. (1989) 'Remembering: A functional developmental perspective', in P.R. Solomon, G.R. Goethals, C.M. Kelley and B.R. Stephens (eds) *Memory: Interdisciplinary Approaches*, pp. 127–50, New York: Springer.

Nigro, G. and Neisser, U. (1983) 'Point of view in personal memories', *Cognitive Psychology* 15: 467–82.

Parrott, W.G. and Sabini, J. (1990) 'Mood and memory under natural conditions: Evidence for mood incongruent recall', *Journal of Personality and Social Psychology* 59: 321–36.

Pillemer, D.B., Rhinehart, E.D. and White, S.H. (1986) 'Memories of life transitions: the first year in college', *Human Learning* 5: 109–23.

Pillemer, D.B., Goldsmith, L.R., Panter, A.T. and White, S.H. (1988) 'Very long-term memories of the first year in college', *Journal of Experimental Psychology: Learning, Memory and Cognition* 14: 709–15.

Pillemer, D.B., Koff, E., Rhinehart, E.D. and Rierdan, J. (1987) 'Flashbulb memories of menarche and adult menstrual distress', *Journal of Adolescence* 10: 187–99.

Powers, R. (1985) *Three Farmers on Their Way to a Dance*, New York: William Morrow.

Reiser, B.J., Black, J.B. and Abelson, R.P. (1985) 'Knowledge structures in the organization and retrieval of autobiographical memories', *Cognitive Psychology* 17: 89–137.

Robinson, J.A. (1986) 'Autobiographical memory: a historical prologue', in D.C. Rubin (ed.) *Autobiographical Memory*, pp. 19–24, Cambridge: Cambridge University Press.

Robinson, J.A. (1990) 'Metacognitive influences on reports of recollective experience', paper presented at the meeting of the Psychonomic Society, New Orleans.

Robinson, J.A. (1992) 'First experience memories: contexts and functions in personal histories', in M.A. Conway, D.C. Rubin, H. Spinnler and W.A. Wagenaar (eds) *Theoretical Perspectives on Autobiographical Memory*, Netherlands: Kluwer.

Robinson, J.A. and Swanson, K.L. (1990) 'Autobiographical memory: The next phase', *Applied Cognitive Psychology* 4: 321–35.

Robinson, J.A. and Swanson, K. (1991) 'Testing the reconstruction hypoth esis of memory perspective in autobiographical recall', paper presented at the meeting of the Psychonomic Society, San Francisco.

Rubin, D.C. (1982) 'On the retention function for autobiographical memory', *Journal of Verbal Learning and Verbal Behavior* 21: 21–38.

Rubin, D.C. (1988) 'Go for the skill', in U. Neisser and E. Winograd (eds) *Remembering Reconsidered: Ecological and Traditional Approaches to Memory*, pp. 374–82, Cambridge: Cambridge University Press.

Rubin, D.C., Wetzler, S.E., and Nebes, R.D. (1986) 'Autobiographical memory across the lifespan', in D.C. Rubin (ed.) *Autobiographical Memory*, pp. 202–21, Cambridge: Cambridge University Press.

Salaman, E. (1971) *A Collection of Moments: A Study of Involuntary Memories*, London: Allen Lane.

Salaman, E. (1973) *The Great Confession: From Aksakov and DeQuincey to Tolstoy and Proust*, London: Allen Lane.

Sanitioso, R., Kunda, Z. and Fong, G.T. (1990) 'Motivated recruitment of autobiographical memories', *Journal of Personality and Social Psychology* 59: 229–41.

Schactel, E. (1947) 'On memory and childhood amnesia', *Psychiatry* 10: 1–26.

Singer, J.A. (1990) 'Affective responses to autobiographical memories and their relationship to long-term goals', *Journal of Personality* 58: 535–63.

Smith, T. and Barclay, C.R. (1990) 'Memory and interaction: emotional regulation through joint reconstruction of autobiographical knowledge', unpublished manuscript.

Tulving, E. (1983) *Elements of Episodic Memory*, New York: Oxford University Press.

Tulving, E. (1985) 'Memory and consciousness', *Canadian Psychology* 26: 1–12.

Tulving, E., Schacter, D.L., McLachlan, D.R. and Moscovitch, M. (1988) 'Priming of semantic autobiographical knowledge: a case study of retrograde amnesia', *Brain and Cognition* 8: 3–20.

Wagenaar, W.A. (1986) 'My memory: a study of autobiographical memory over six years', *Cognitive Psychology* 18: 225–52.

Warnock, M. (1987) *Memory*, London: Faber & Faber.

Williams, J.M.G. and Dritschel, B.H. (1988) 'Emotional disturbance and the specificity of autobiographical memory', *Cognition and Emotion* 2: 221–34.

Woolf, V. (1976) *Moments of Being*, edited by Jeanne Schulkind, New York: Harcourt Brace Jovanovich.

NAME INDEX

252

SUBJECT INDEX

OLD MOORE'S

HOROSCOPE
AND ASTRAL
DIARY

VIRGO